# Liberating Mission in Mozambique

# Liberating Mission in Mozambique

*Faith and Revolution in the Life of Eduardo Mondlane*

ROBERT FARIS

*With a Foreword by John W. de Gruchy*

PICKWICK *Publications* · Eugene, Oregon

LIBERATING MISSION IN MOZAMBIQUE
Faith and Revolution in the Life of Eduardo Mondlane

Copyright © 2014 Robert Faris. All rights reserved. Except for brief quotations in critical publications or reviews, no part of this book may be reproduced in any manner without prior written permission from the publisher. Write: Permissions, Wipf and Stock Publishers, 199 W. 8th Ave., Suite 3, Eugene, OR 97401.

Pickwick Publications
An Imprint of Wipf and Stock Publishers
199 W. 8th Av.e, Suite 3
Eugene, OR 97401

www.wipfandstock.com

ISBN 13: 978-1-61097-207-9

*Cataloging-in-Publication data:*

Faris, Robert N.

Liberating mission in Mozambique : faith and revolution in the life of Eduardo Mondlane / Robert Faris ; with a foreword by John W. de Gruchy.

xviii + 218 p. ; 23 cm. Includes bibliographical references.

ISBN 13: 978-1-61097-207-9

1. Mondlane, Eduardo, 1920–1969. 2. FRELIMO—History. 3. Protestant churches—Missions—Mozambique—History—20th century. 4. Mozambique—Church history—20th century. 5. Religion and state.

I. De Gruchy, John W. II. Title.

BR1443.M6 F185 2014

Manufactured in the U.S.A.

*This work is dedicated to two men who have been mentors
in my understanding of God's mission in the world, the late
Dr. Simão Chamango, former Rector of the Seminário Unido de Ricatla,
and my late father, Neil Faris. Their generosity of spirit and deep
commitment to the church have greatly inspired me.*

# Contents

*Foreword by John W. de Gruchy*   ix

*Acknowledgments*   xiii

*List of Abbreviations*   xvii

1. The Protestant Churches in Mozambique in Context   1
2. A Grounding in Faith: Mondlane's Early Life in Mozambique and Integration into the Swiss Mission   14
3. Reformed and Reforming: Living Faith in South Africa   29
4. Into the Heart of Empire   46
5. Study in the United States—Oberlin College   62
6. Study in the United States—Northwestern University, Chicago   89
7. Discerning the Future   110
8. Return to Mozambique   130
9. Faith in FRELIMO   151
10. Mondlane's Legacy of Faith   181

*Bibliography*   211

*Archives Consulted*   217

# Foreword

I AM DELIGHTED TO write this foreword to Robert Faris's fine book for several reasons. Not the most important, but certainly personally satisfying is the fact that I was privileged to supervise his PhD thesis upon which the book is based. Bob was not only a mature and highly capable graduate student and researcher, but he brought to his task all the ingredients necessary to ensure that his work would be well done and that the outcome would make a significant contribution to his field of enquiry. As a former theological educator in Mozambique he had the hands on experience of his subject, an insider's knowledge with an outsider's critical distance, and an ability to work in the several languages needed to achieve his goals. But equally, he had the necessary passion and commitment to both undertake the task and to pursue it to its conclusion. To say that I supervised his work is to give me far more credit than I deserve. The truth is, I learnt an enormous amount from Bob's careful research and the many informative and lively conversations that we had together over the years during which he wrote his thesis.

But to simply commend the book for these personal reasons, which I do so warmly, would be totally inadequate. What Bob has produced makes a significant contribution to the narrative of Christianity in southern Africa within the framework of the struggle for liberation from colonial rule. And Bob does so by focusing on the story of a Protestant political and ecumenical leader, Eduardo Mondlane, of note within a dominantly Roman Catholic country. Mondlane's story is Faris' entrée into exploring the role of the churches and missions, especially the Swiss Mission, in the struggle for African Independence.

Mondlane's name needs to be as well known as that of Nelson Mandela, both of whom were products of Christian mission education, but also spoken of alongside the likes of Dietrich Bonhoeffer. A layman, Mondlane was theologically well-informed, ecumenically engaged, and, in the end was assassinated in the struggle for justice. Reared in evangelical piety, he became more radical in his Christianity, anticipating the emergence of liberation theology in Latin America and in the end finding himself on the boundaries of both Christianity and the church. It is noteworthy that Mondlane was invited, together with Martin Luther King Jr., to address the Fourth Assembly of the World Council of Churches in Uppsala, though in the end neither could attend.

Mondlane's name and story are well-known within some circles, but certainly not as much as they should be beyond them. The reasons are obvious. The story of the liberation struggle in Mozambique, which is so well told by Faris, was in many ways over shadowed by what was occurring in the former Rhodesia and in South Africa at the time. This was so largely because Mozambique was a Portuguese colony which, for language reasons did not get the media coverage it deserved within the Anglo-Saxon world. Those outside the Lusophone sphere could not easily access the story except through ecumenical and mission board reports which, in any case, were not widely circulated. But Mondlane was also a Protestant in a predominantly Catholic country where the official Church worked hand in glove with the colonial authorities. It was not in their interests to give him publicity except as a terrorist.

Of course, Mondlane was well-known to the liberation movements in southern Africa, especially South Africa, as he was also to the Portuguese authorities and the security forces in Rhodesia and South Africa who helped bring about his death. The latter rightly feared his charismatic leadership for, in the end, Mondlane and his movement FRELIMO changed the face not only of Mozambique, but also of southern Africa as a whole. It was only after the liberation of Mozambique that the struggle against Ian Smith's regime could achieve success, and only after both countries were free that pressure could be exerted on the apartheid government in the way that it was. The withdrawal of the Portuguese from Mozambique and Angola created a domino effect which suddenly meant that South Africa was isolated, surrounded by post-colonial countries hostile to its policies and incapable of indefinitely protecting its borders. No wonder blacks in South Africa celebrated the liberation of Mozambique in anticipation of their own.

Faris' discussion goes well beyond simply telling the story of Mondlane—it is not, after all, a biography—or providing a history and analysis of what happened in the political struggle in Mozambique. He digs deeper in relating this to the role of the Protestant churches and to

Mondlane's own theological journey away from mission based piety and growing skepticism about the ability of the church to take a stronger political stand. And yet Mondlane was a product of both. The fact that he grew beyond them should not obfuscate the fact that missionary education made his journey possible in the first place or the fact that much of his thinking and action was influenced by ecumenical thinkers and activists well beyond Mozambique. This indicates again the important role which the World Council of Churches and other ecumenical agencies played in bringing about political liberation in southern Africa.

These few words cannot possibly do justice to the well-honed book that Faris has produced. My hope is that it will be widely read and discussed. It certainly deserves to become required reading amongst those who are interested in the twentieth-century history of Christianity in Africa, the ecumenical movement, and the political struggles of southern Africa. But it also invites a much wider readership both within the worldwide church and in those concerned about justice and peace. I was not surprised that one of Bob's distinguished examiners commented that his thesis was "a fine piece of work, beautifully written and well structured," and that it constituted "a real contribution to knowledge." This says it all. I, too, commend it highly.

John W. de Gruchy
Hermanus, South Africa,
September 2013

# Acknowledgments

THIS WORK IS BASED largely on my doctoral dissertation at the University of Cape Town which I worked on over six years from 2000 to 2006. I am deeply grateful to my supervisor, Professor John de Gruchy who guided me through this study. Both his patience and wisdom were needed to help me finish the work. I am grateful to colleagues and friends at UCT for their support. I very much appreciated the comments of the three external examiners, Professor T. Balcomb from the University of KwaZulu-Natal, Professor Paul Gifford from the University of London and Professor Patrick Harries from the University of Basel and have tried to incorporate their suggestions into the present work.

I have used extensive quotations from sources in Portuguese, French and Shangaan and provided an English translation in the text. For quotations from Portuguese and French I have provided the text in the original language in a note. Although responsibility for the translation is mine, Redha Belhachemi assisted in translating the French text and Samuel Ngale, assisted in translating the text in Shangaan. I am deeply grateful to them both.

The origin of the doctoral work was in classes and informal conversations with faculty and students at the Seminário Unido de Ricatla and with ministers and members of the Igreja Presbiteriana de Moçambique when I lived in Mozambique from 1989 to 1994. Although I did not conduct formal interviews, the information I gained from them was invaluable. Those who assisted me in beginning my journey with Eduardo Mondlane include but are certainly not limited to (at the risk of offending all instead of some, I will not use titles): Simão Chamango, Adelaide Chamango, Amosse Zitha, Casimiro Mathié, Ruth Minter, Jamisse Taimo, Oriente Sibane, Obede Baloi, Felix Khosa, Valente Matsinhe, Marta Sitoe, Lina Magaia, Glenn and Darla Rowley, Dinis Sengulane, Osias Mucache, Gabriela Mucavele, Bento Sitoe, João Machado, Isaias Funzamo, Arão Litsure, Claude Morier-Genoud, Francisca Libombo, Teresa Cruz e Silva,

Lucas Tivane, Paulo Matsinhe, Jonas Ngomane, Azarias Cossa and Fiel Ruco.

The research and writing for this project was done on three continents. It began on a three month study leave from my position as Director at the Canadian Churches' Forum for Global Ministries in Toronto in 2001 when I was first able to spend an extended period of time in Cape Town. The wealth of experiences and conversations with people involved in global mission and with members of the Board and staff in my time at the Forum contributed a great deal to this work. I also benefited from generous study time provided to me when I was Executive Director of the Churches' Council on Theological Education in Canada. I am grateful for the financial assistance I received from the Cameron Bursary Fund of the Presbyterian Church in Canada to assist with my expenses.

When in Switzerland in 2003, I was greatly assisted by the hospitality and generosity of the staff of the Département Missionaire in Lausanne, especially Irénée Haniss Pierrehumbert who opened the rich archives of the DM to me. In Lausanne, I also met with Eric Morier-Genoud who opened many doors for me. I had more extensive conversations with several former missionaries to Mozambique, especially Georges Andrié and Michele and Juliette Morier-Genoud whose memories and perspectives on Mozambique and the Swiss Mission were invaluable. In Basel, I was welcomed and hosted by Benedict Schubert and other staff at Mission 2000. They were able to assist me in visiting the archives at the Basler Afrika Bibliographien. I was also able to meet briefly with Patrick Harries and Didier Peclard and with Patrick Chabal who was visiting the university at the time. In Geneva I was grateful to the staff at the archives of the World Council of Churches who helped immensely in finding material. It was a joy to share the archives with Philip Potter who was also doing research at the time.

In Lisbon, the PIDE/DGS archives at the Instituto dos Arquivos Nacionais/Torre do Tombo opened a whole new world to me. The staff was extremely helpful in facilitating my use of the collection and in retrieving, photocopying and mailing material for me. The staff at the Centro de Documentação of CIDAC was also helpful and I wish that I had had more time to investigate their important collection. In Lisbon, I was also able to meet with Andreas Ding, the General Secretary of the Igreja Evangélica Presbiteriana de Portugal and have some conversation with him about the role of Protestant churches in Portugal in relation to the liberation struggle in Mozambique.

Back in South Africa in 2005, I was grateful for the support and friendship of former colleagues and now doctors Lyn Holness and Robert Steiner and also the friendship and fellowship of Rondebosch United Presbyterian Congregational Church. Two beautiful locations in Hermanus and Stellenbosch helped in really beginning the task of writing. The graduate study area in the Faculty of Humanities also provided a good space for working and I was once again grateful for the assistance of the UCT library staff and the help of the administrative staff in the Graduate Humanities Faculty, especially Anne Wegerhoff. Redha Belhachemi's care, companionship and cooking also assisted in keeping me happy and writing. In 2006, the warmth of the reception of the community at Volmoed was very moving when I returned to South Africa and once again the beauty of the place assisted in writing.

In Canada, it was a joy to have access to the marvellous library resources of my alma mater the University of Toronto. I benefited from conversation with Jim Kirkwood, Garth Legge and Omega Bula, all former Africa Secretaries with the United Church, Rick Fee and Rodger Talbot, former Africa Secretaries with the Presbyterian Church and also colleagues from the Board of Cooperation Canada Mozambique (COCAMO), especially Charlotte Maxwell and Zaida Bastos from the Anglican Church, Steven Allen with Oxfam, Judith Marshall with the Humanity Fund of the Steelworkers, Frank Luce with CAW and Michael O'Connor, the former Executive Director. The support of family, especially my mother, Alma and my sister, Mary as well as friends and colleagues has been very important. Once again, Redha's patience and encouragement to "write a few more pages on Eduardo" and his deep care was essential to finishing this task and getting the manuscript to publication. I cannot say how much it has meant to me.

To all these people and communities I am grateful. Of course the responsibility for what follows in these pages is my own and especially for any errors or inadequacies. I have been inspired in this work by the life and witness of Eduardo Mondlane and I trust that this project might help in some way to let others know of his important contribution to the people of Mozambique and to the world.

# Abbreviations

| | |
|---|---|
| AAI | African American Institute |
| ANC | African National Congress |
| CCM | Conselho Cristão de Moçambique |
| CIA | Central Intelligence Agency |
| CICARWS | Commission on Inter-Church Aid, Refugees and World Service |
| CONCP | Conferência das Organizações Nacionalistas das Colónias Portuguesas |
| COREMO | Comité Revolucionário de Moçambique |
| DGS | Direcção Geral de Segurança |
| DM | Département Missionaire des Églises Protestantes de la Suisse Romande |
| FF | Ford Foundation |
| FRELIMO | Frente de Libertação de Moçambique |
| IPM | Igreja Presbiteriana de Moçambique |
| MANU | Mozambique African National Union |
| MI | Mozambique Institute |
| MPLA | Movimento Popular para a Libertação de Angola |
| MSAS | Mission Suisse en Afrique du Sud |
| NATO | North Atlantic Treaty Organization |
| PCR | Programme to Combat Racism |
| PSF | Phelps Stokes Fund |
| PIDE | Polícia Internacional e de Defesa do Estado |
| UDENAMO | União Democrática Nacional de Moçambique |
| UN | United Nations |
| UNAMI | União Africana de Moçambique Independente |
| UNEMO | União Nacional dos Estudantes Moçambicanos |
| UNITA | União Nacional para a Independência Total de Angola |
| UPA | União dos Povos Angolanos |
| WCC | World Council of Churches |

# 1

# The Protestant Churches in Mozambique in Context

## A Minority Church

THROUGHOUT THEIR HISTORY, THE Protestant churches of Mozambique have existed on the margins. They were founded and grew within the context of the Portuguese Empire of the late nineteenth and twentieth centuries, a minor player in relation to the other European colonial powers in Africa despite the exaggerated and romantic pretensions of António Salazar and the *Estado Novo*.[1] Although it was true that the Portuguese had been in the region longer than any other European power, the colony was grossly underdeveloped in economic terms in relation to its neighbors in British territory and in South Africa. It remained dependent on various forms of *chibalo* or forced labor including income received from contracted labor in the mines of South Africa and elsewhere[2] and on income derived from large foreign controlled concession companies operating over vast swaths of the colony's territo-

---

1. In 1926, a military coup overthrew the Republican government in Portugal. António Salazar, a professor from Coimbra University gradually consolidated his power and developed what was called the *Estado Novo* or the New State, modelled to a large degree on fascist lines and emphasizing the need for national autonomy both in Portugal itself and in the overseas territories. Salazar remained in power until his death in 1968.

2. See Newitt, "Labor Migration," 482–516. Newitt estimates that in 1967 there were 300,000 Mozambican migrants working in South Africa and another 150,000 in Rhodesia.

ry.[3] Railways and ports were developed to service South Africa and the British colonies and even by the time of independence in 1975 there was no direct overland transportation link between north and south.

Within this very particular context of Portuguese colonialism, the Protestant churches themselves developed as marginalized minorities. Charles Biber's history of the Igreja Presbiteriana de Moçambique (IPM), the Presbyterian Church of Mozambique, written at the time of its centenary in the 1980s, is aptly titled, *Cent ans au Mozambique: Le parcours d'une minorité* (*One Hundred Years in Mozambique: The Journey of a Minority*). The Swiss missionaries defined it as the church of the Tsonga and Ronga, an ethno-linguistic minority of the African population contained within the two southern most districts of Portuguese East Africa and divided by the border with South Africa from those of common language, culture, and mission history in the Transvaal.[4] It had its origins, as several Protestant churches in Mozambique did, in the evangelistic work of Mozambican migrants who were in contact with missionaries in South Africa and who returned home with the message of Christian faith to their families and communities. Although Reformed Swiss missionaries Paul Berthoud and Arthur Grandjean followed soon after from their station in Spelonken, the work of Josefa Mhalamhala and his sister Lois Xintomane together with Jim Ximungana established the first churches at Antioca, Ricatla and Catembe in the early 1880s and led the religious revival known as the "Awakening."[5] Although the mission grew substantially over the decades and was known and respected among the population for its educational and medical work, it remained a minority and found itself as one of several Protestant missions developing in the region, including the American Board for Foreign Mission, the Methodist Episcopal Church, Wesleyan Methodists, and Free Methodists as well as the Anglican Church. Although these missions began while the territory was still largely under the control of the Nguni king Ngungunyane, they

---

3. Notably, the Niassa Company north of the Lurio River, the Sena Sugar Company along the Zambezi River and the Mozambique Company from the coast to the Rhodesian border. Despite the nationalizing policies of the *Estado Novo* and the termination of the major concession companies under Salazar, foreign investment remained crucial to the colonial economy.

4. For a discussion of the construction of Tsonga identity as a creation of Swiss missionaries see Harries, "The Roots of Ethnicity," 25–52.

5. See Butselaar, *Africanos, Missionarios e colonialistas* for a thorough discussion of the origins of the IPM. See also Chamango, "A Chegada do Evangelho em Moçambique".

developed under Portuguese colonial rule after Ngungunyane's defeat in 1895. Despite the fact that missions, regardless of their denomination or national origin, were to be allowed to work in any colonial territory according to the international Conferences of Berlin and Brussels[6] the Portuguese were able to restrict Protestant activity almost exclusively to the south of their East African territory.

## The Roman Catholic Church

Although the relationship between the Portuguese state and the Roman Catholic Church varied greatly throughout the long colonial period, it was generally given a privileged position in the overseas territories, especially in the period of the Estado Novo, in relation to the Protestant missions and churches. Roman Catholicism arrived in Mozambique with the Portuguese explorer Vasco da Gama in 1498. However, the first mission was not initiated until 1560 with Gonçalo da Silveira and four other Jesuits at the court of the Monomotapa; da Silveira was murdered in 1561, probably under the orders of the Monomotapa. A later mission succeeded in opening up the court of the Monomotapa to Christian influence and to conversion in 1629.[7] Mission work continued under the Jesuits and the Dominicans in the *prazos* of the Zambezi region with limited success until the expulsion of the Jesuits in 1759 and of the Dominicans in 1834 with the intent of establishing a secular clergy. Although the Jesuits and other missionary orders returned after 1875 their work was again limited, especially in the face of expanding Protestant missions in the region. In 1910, with the proclamation of the Republic in Portugal and the strict separation of church and state, the Jesuits and other religious orders were again expelled from Mozambique. The position and role of the Roman Catholic Church in Mozambique changed dramatically with the advent of the *Estado Novo* in 1926 and particularly with the signing of the *Concordat* between Portugal and the Vatican in 1940 with its attendant *Accordo Missionário* and the *Estatuto Missionário* of April 1941. The *Concordat* established the Roman Catholic Church as the state church, in many ways subordinate to the authority of the state with the Portuguese government able to veto the appointment of bishops and other church officials. In return, the *Accordo Missionário* gave the

---

6. Morier-Genoud, *Of God and Caesar*, 6.
7. See Mudenge, *Christian Education at the Mutapa Court*.

Portuguese Roman Catholic Church an exclusive missionary role in the overseas territories with responsibility for providing rudimentary education for the *indígina* and state funding to support it. Mission activity was enhanced but also became nationalized and was seen to be a tool of "portugalization" of the subject people in the colonies. As Alf Helgesson notes, these agreements also distanced the Vatican's *Propaganda Fide* from its oversight of mission activity and its policy of freeing mission work from nationalism and political interference.[8]

### The Protestant Churches and the Portuguese Empire

It was within this context and from this minority position, that the IPM together with other Protestant churches, played a significant role in the unfolding of events that led to the independence of Mozambique under the *Frente de libertação de Moçambique* (FRELIMO) in 1975. From their earliest days, the Protestant churches had been held suspect by the Portuguese colonial authorities as a front for British and South African political and commercial interests and possible territorial expansion. Portugal's weak claims to its African territory, even after the Berlin Conference of 1885 fixed the colonial boundaries in Africa, made it especially concerned about this possibility. In particular, the Calvinist theology of the Swiss missionaries and their anti-Roman Catholic bias made them automatically suspect by the Portuguese. They were seen as a first wave of Protestant infiltration which foreshadowed a much larger onslaught from the growing Protestant missions throughout the region.

Not only were the Protestant churches seen as a front for the expansion of other imperial and regional powers and Protestant missionary ambitions, but also for the aspirations for independence of the African population of the colony. The early connections between the Swiss Mission and the local chiefs and Ngungunhana at the time of the wars of subjugation of the late nineteenth century were never forgotten. In particular, the role of the medical missionary, Dr. Georges Liengme, who established a mission in the court of Ngungunhana in 1893 and was seen to side with him in negotiations with the Portuguese, brought into question the loyalty of the Swiss.[9] Perhaps even more significant in this regard

---

8. Helgesson, *Church, State and People*, 266–67. Cf. Adrian Hastings, "The Clash of Nationalism and Universalism within Twentieth-Century Missionary Christianity" in Stanley, ed., *Missions, Nationalism, and the End of Empire*.

9. See Ennes, *A Guerra de África em 1895*, 217–19. A first-hand account of the war

was the insistence on the part of the Swiss missionaries that the life of the church, including its worship, should be carried out in the language of the people and beyond this that the mission enterprise should be carried out with a knowledge of and a respect for the indigenous culture[10] and that eventually the church should become completely autonomous. This ran completely counter to the policy of integration and assimilation of African people into Portuguese culture and the de-valuation of local African cultures advocated within the Portuguese colonial project and within the mission approach of the Roman Catholic Church. Although this was often portrayed in a positive way in relation to the policies of British colonialism in the region which emphasized the distinction of races, the so-called *lusotropicalismo* of the Portuguese was largely a myth and did little to dignify or improve the life of the vast majority of the African population.[11]

Throughout the colonial period, the Protestant churches and in particular the Swiss Mission and the IPM, had to defend their existence before the colonial authorities and to demonstrate their loyalty to the Portuguese nation. They came under even more exacting scrutiny when it came to programs of education and work with youth. In fact, the recent work of Teresa Cruz e Silva concerning the role of the Protestant churches in the formation of political consciousness in Mozambique[12] demonstrates that this suspicion was not without warrant. Within the context of Portuguese colonialism in the twentieth century, upholding even the possibility that a person or community might be enriched or enlightened in some way outside the narrow boundaries of the official colonial system or outside the accepted norms of Portuguese culture and

---

with Ngunghunhana by the commander of the Portuguese forces. Also, cf. Butselaar, *Africanos, Missionarios e colonialistas*, 194–206 for an account of the role of Liengme.

10. Perhaps most noteworthy and one of the earliest examples of this is Henri Junod's, *The Life of a South African Tribe* published in 1927. However, this does not mean that the Swiss Mission nor Junod's work was free of the paternalism and racialism which characterized the mission enterprise of this period. Cf. Harries "The Theory and Practice of Race," 41–54. Indeed, Harries argues that Junod's work was used as a basis for the understanding of race as a social category which could be used to justify the various forms of racial separation, including *apartheid*, as developed in South Africa.

11. For a critical assessment, see Helgesson, *Church, State and People*, 317–22. Lusotropicalism asserted that Portuguese colonialism had developed a unique new society that brought together people of different cultures without any reference to race unlike other forms of European colonialism.

12. See especially Cruz e Silva, *Protestant Churches*.

Roman Catholic religion was enough to bring a charge of "denationalization" or treason. It is really not surprising that the Protestant churches came under such close scrutiny nor that they were seen as subversive to the Portuguese colonial project.

Indeed, it can be argued that it was this suspicion and this antipathy to the Portuguese colonial ideology that led to the Protestant churches being seen to play a much larger role within the political and social life of colonial Mozambique than might be warranted by the size of their membership.[13] From within the colonial system, they presented an alternative identity for the African population to the official categorizations of *indígena* or *assimilado*.[14] Within the Protestant churches, albeit within a highly paternalistic structure, Africans could be educated, hold positions of responsibility and be part of decision making processes, functioning primarily in their own language and to a certain extent at least, with appreciation and respect for their own culture. Although as in most western Protestant churches of the time, only men could be ordained to the ministry, education, work in a variety of professions, and participation in the church women's societies were open to women.[15] It could be said that this modeled an alternative society to that of the Portuguese colonial project, certainly still racialized and not equal on the basis of gender but presenting a different vision of what the future might hold in a more egalitarian and democratic society.

Behind the official pledges of loyalty to the Portuguese state, what did the members and those involved in the leadership of the Protestant churches understand the role of their churches to be within the colonial

---

13. Estimated at 4 percent of the population in 1964. Newitt, *History of Mozambique*, 479.

14. See Newitt, *History of Mozambique*, 440–42. In the late Monarchy and early Republican periods of Portuguese colonialism, the population was divided between *indígena* (native) and *não-indígena* (non-native). However, the latter category included not only Europeans and Asians but also mixed race people and Africans who practiced a profession or who held a position in government. During the later Republican period and under the *Estado Novo* the procedure for an African to acquire *não-indígena* status or to be considered an *assimilado* was tightened and in fact very few Africans achieved this status.

15. Although I do not have any hard evidence, anecdotally it was believed that the leadership role of women in the Protestant churches and especially the IPM was enhanced because of the large numbers of men who worked as migrant labour in the gold mines of the South African rand and were absent from their communities for most of the year.

society and in particular the role of their churches, if any, in the struggle for an independent Mozambique? If, indeed, they did envision an independent Mozambique, what would be the role of their churches in that context? It is difficult to know what these Mozambican Christians may have been thinking. Any discussion of independence was immediately curtailed and one risked one's life to even raise the possibility of independence. This fear was increased with the establishment of the Portuguese secret police, the Polícia Internacional e de Defesa do Estado (PIDE), later the Direcção Geral da Segurança (DGS), in the colonies after 1956 and even more so after the beginning of the armed insurrection under FRELIMO in 1964. Another significant factor which increased pressure on the Protestant churches to demonstrate their loyalty to Portugal was the growing activism of the global ecumenical movement and its criticism of white minority rule in southern Africa, especially the World Council of Churches (WCC) and its Programme to Combat Racism (PCR).

## A Changing Paradigm of Mission

The present study will argue that within the Protestant churches of Mozambique, particularly in the IPM-Swiss Mission, in the period between 1940 and independence, there was a fundamental shift in the understanding of the role of the church in relation to Portuguese colonialism and the struggle for political independence. Although this was not universal, it did impact upon a significant proportion of the membership and perhaps more significantly, of the leadership of the churches. The focus of this study will not be primarily on the raising of political consciousness in the Protestant churches, although this of course is not unrelated, but rather on the changing theological understanding of the nature and role of the church within the particular context in which these faith communities found themselves. This change will be understood broadly within the paradigms identified by the South African theologian, David Bosch in his *Transforming Mission: Paradigm Shifts in Theology of Mission*. It will be argued that in this period, the churches were made to assess critically their understanding of mission in the light of their lived reality and to reject the compromise they had made with the Portuguese colonial project in order to more adequately live out the *missio Dei*, that is where and how they were called to witness to God's mission in the world. In Bosch's framework, this could be understood as a movement from the paradigm he identifies as the Protestant "Mission in the Wake of the Enlightenment" to what he identifies as an "Emerging Ecumenical Missionary Paradigm." Of particular interest are three elements he explores in this emerging paradigm namely, "Mission as the Church-With-Others," "Mission as the Quest for Justice," and "Mission as Liberation." It will also seek to assess whether this changed understanding of the nature and role of the church was adequate for the post colonial context under a FRELIMO government.

Within this dynamic, it can be argued that another of Bosch's paradigms of mission can be identified, the "Medieval Roman Catholic Paradigm." Alf Helgesson argues that in the *Concordat* signed between the Vatican and the Portuguese state, and the understanding of the missionary role of the church in this agreement, the church had "renewed official apostolic recognition and guarantee of the 500 year old *Padroado*."[16] Bosch comments on the nature of the *padroado*:

> The ruling by which the kings of Spain and Portugal were made "patrons" of missionary expansion in their colonies was not without its difficulties. The propagation of the faith and colonial policies became so intertwined that it was often hard to distinguish the one from the other. The dioceses founded in the colonies were given bishops approved by the civil authorities. These bishops were not allowed to communicate directly with the pope; in addition, papal decrees had to be endorsed by the king before they could be made public and acted upon in the colonies. The rulers of Spain and Portugal soon regarded themselves not merely as representatives of the pope, but as immediate deputies of God.[17]

Faced with this renewed identification of the Portuguese Roman Catholic Church with the colonial state and being aware of the inadequacy of their own compromised position within the colonial project, yet drawing on their own history of resistance and their own theological tradition, how could the Protestant churches respond to *missio Dei* in their context?

---

16. Helgesson, *Church, State and People*, 267.
17. Bosch, *Transforming Mission*, 228.

## Eduardo Mondlane

This dilemma will be explored primarily through an historical critical study of the life and thought of Eduardo Mondlane. From an early age, he became integrated into the Swiss Mission, was supported by the church to study in South Africa, Portugal and the United States and was to have returned to Lourenço Marques, now Maputo, to coordinate the work of a YMCA in the city. He received a PhD from Northwestern University in Chicago, worked with the Trusteeship Department of the United Nations and became the leader of FRELIMO at its founding in Tanzania in 1962. He was assassinated in Dar-es-Salaam in 1969 by a letter bomb, usually attributed to the PIDE in collaboration with disaffected members of the FRELIMO leadership.

Mondlane came to believe that his involvement in the struggle for independence had to be broader than his participation in the life and work of the church. He used his experience to forge alliances with many other groups in order to create a movement which would be able to confront the power of the Portuguese state and its many allies. By the end of his life, Mondlane found himself alienated from many in the church, principally because of his decision to be engaged in an armed struggle. In many accounts of his life, his participation in the life of the church is minimized. Yet clearly in reading his correspondence and in discussion with those who were engaged with him in the church, he understood himself to be a person of faith. Perhaps more importantly, over his life Mondlane developed a very clear critique of the mission work of the Protestant churches and particularly the IPM and the Swiss missionaries working with it. Mondlane not only remained within the church, he constantly pushed the churches to engage with the world around them and to respond prophetically to the call to justice in the face of colonial oppression. He challenged the Protestant churches to recognize and to break their compromise with colonialism and with racism no matter what the cost, not because of any political allegiance or ideology but because this was the clear call of the gospel and consistent with his own Reformed theology. He posed this challenge to his colleagues and friends in the IPM, to the leadership of the Swiss Mission and to the global church through the WCC. Indeed, it will be demonstrated that Mondlane was one of the key voices that led the WCC to establish the PCR.

Clearly this changed understanding of mission and the role of the church would have significant implications for those in the local churches. The increasing repression by the PIDE/DGS was felt by all members of the Protestant churches and in almost every aspect of their life and witness. However, because of his close connection with Mondlane and his position as leader of the IPM, Zedequias Manganhela became the focus of Portuguese accusations. Manganhela did his theological studies at Ricatla, was ordained in 1948, served as a local pastor and did further studies at the Seminário Teológico Evangélico de Carcavelos in Portugal. He became General Secretary of the IPM (*Presidente do Conselho Sinodal*) after a convention was signed granting its autonomy from the Swiss Mission in 1963 and made frequent trips in the north of the country as well as internationally. He was killed by the PIDE in prison in 1972 after being accused of having provided funding to FRELIMO. Manganhela chose to remain within the country and to seek to advance the cause of the church as a means to develop an alternative model to the colonial project but he found himself and the other Protestant leadership criticized for their timid response to continuing Portuguese repression by Mondlane and many in the global ecumenical movement. However, Manganhela provided a helpful complement to Mondlane in understanding the role of the church. While not denying the danger it posed to him, Mondlane's call to the prophetic witness of the church came from outside; Manganhela lived out his life within the colonial context where his every word and action was monitored and had immediate consequences for himself and all those in the churches.

## The Protestant Churches and FRELIMO

In the final section of this work, it will be argued that it is within the interplay of these broad models of the role of the church, and its relation with the state and with the international ecumenical community, that the Protestant churches, and particularly the IPM, came to understand their role as church within the newly independent country under a FRELIMO government. Although the constitution approved in 1975 guaranteed the freedom to "practice or not practice" a religion (Article 33), the churches and other religious institutions were discredited and marginalized as being obscurantist and counter-revolutionary within the dominant ideological framework of scientific socialism. No church member could be a member of the party. Although primarily directed toward the Roman Catholic Church, which in fact had been deeply compromised with the colonial regime, the Protestant churches also found themselves having to defend their existence and role in the new state. This was unexpected, particularly in the IPM, given its support for FRELIMO in the liberation struggle and the fact that many of the leaders and militants of FRELIMO, including both Mondlane and Samora Machel, had come from Protestant families and schools. Many Protestant Christians found themselves in a dilemma of loyalties between their church and the party while others felt a strong sense of betrayal. This situation began to change after 1982, with a key meeting between Machel and the religious leaders of the country which brought a more open attitude to the place of religious institutions on the part of the government. Although the paradigm of mission of the Protestant churches had changed through the years of the liberation struggle, its close identification with FRELIMO led them into a further dilemma after independence.

## Significant Sources

This study is dependent on the research of other authors who have done significant work on the relation of the Protestant churches to the liberation struggle and the post-independence context in Mozambique. Alf Helgesson's, *Church, State and People in Mozambique: An Historical Study with Special Emphasis on Methodist Developments in the Inhambane Region* is an historical study of the Methodist Church during the colonial period and in his introduction he looks at the tension between FRELIMO and the churches in the early period following independence. Much of Teresa Cruz e Silva's recent work, including her *Protestant Churches and the Formation of Political Consciousness in Southern Mozambique (1930–1974)*, has been looking at the importance of the Presbyterian Church/Swiss Mission in the raising of political consciousness in its members prior to independence. Eric Morier Genoud and others associated with *Le Fait Missionnaire* in Lausanne have also written extensively in this area. Several historical works concerning the Presbyterian Church/Swiss Mission, including Charles Biber's, *Cent Ans au Mozambique: Le parcours d'une minorité* and Jan van Butselaar's, *Africanos, Missionarios e Colonialistas: As origins da Igreja Presbiteriana de Moçambique (Missão Suiça), 1890–1896* chronicling the early years of the Swiss mission in Mozambique and the intersection of cultures in this period have also contributed significantly to this study. Finally, Nadja Manghezi's biography of Janet Mondlane, *O meu coração está nas mãos de um negro* has been invaluable in documenting many of the details of both her and Eduardo's lives. Although there is little focus on the role of the Protestant churches, Malyn Newitt's major volume, *A History of Mozambique*, has provided significant information concerning the historical background for this study. Three other volumes, Norrie MacQueen's, *The Decolonization of Portuguese Africa: Metropolitan Revolution and the Dissolution of Empire*, Patrick Chabal's, *A History of Postcolonial Lusophone Africa*, and António Costa Pinto's, *O Fim do Império Português*, have also provided important background material.

In addition to these published works, this study is highly dependent on archival material from several sources. Of primary importance were the archives of the *Département missionnaire des Eglises Protestantes de Suisse romande* in Lausanne. These archives contain a wealth of correspondence and reports related to the IPM/Swiss Mission during this period and particularly connected with Eduardo Mondlane. Second, the archives of the World Council of Churches in Geneva, particularly the material related to the Programme to Combat Racism and the Commission on Inter-Church Aid, Refugee and World Services as well as the General Secretariat. Finally, the archives of the PIDE/DGS held at the Instituto dos Arquivos Nacionais/Torre do Tombo and administered by the Portuguese Ministério da Cultura in Lisbon which contain files on the Protestant leadership in Mozambique and its connections with other Protestant churches in the region and the international ecumenical movement, including the WCC held by the police.

The study also draws on material from informal and more formal conversations with both Mozambicans and foreign missionaries and international co-operants who were actively involved in this period.

## Definitions

It is important from the outset to define the term "Protestant churches." In its broadest sense, it refers to all non-Roman Catholic or Orthodox Christian churches in Mozambique. However, in this study it will refer more specifically to the Christian churches which have grown from non-Roman Catholic mission agencies, primarily from Europe, North America and South Africa. This largely excludes churches which are usually known as "independent" or "Zionist" or "Ethiopian." In general, it will include those churches which were members of the Conselho Cristão de Moçambique (CCM) during and immediately following the liberation struggle.

Throughout this study, reference will be made to the "liberation struggle in Mozambique." It is recognized that indigenous Mozambicans resisted Portuguese colonial occupation in a variety of ways from the earliest contacts with the voyage of Vasco da Gama in 1497 until the time of the *Estado Novo* under António Salazar when Mozambique was fully integrated into the Portuguese state through the *Acto Colonial* of 1930 and the *Carta Orgânica* of 1933. However, in this study, the liberation struggle will refer specifically to the period between 1962 with the founding of FRELIMO in Dar-es-Salam and the independence of the country from Portugal, proclaimed on June 25, 1975.

# 2

# A Grounding in Faith

*Mondlane's Early Life in Mozambique and Integration into the Swiss Mission*

## Introduction

PERHAPS THE GREATEST CONTRIBUTION the Protestant churches of Mozambique, and particularly the IPM, made to the liberation struggle was Eduardo Mondlane. His life and work within the church as a youth in Mozambique were exemplary and when he returned to Lourenço Marques from the United States in 1961 he was welcomed as a hero both of the church and of the nation. His assassination in Dar-es-Salam in 1969, when he was the first President of FRELIMO, deprived the movement and the country of a committed and unifying figure. Many have asked how the liberated country might have been different had Mondlane lived to lead it. Bengt Sundkler has written, "There is a great chapter to be written on the noble company of African freedom heroes who set out to liberate their countries but whose lives were cut short and who were never permitted to complete the march. Eduardo Mondlane, it seems to us, was the greatest of them all."[1]

There is no doubt that many in the Protestant churches believed that Mondlane was leading the country toward a time when the long years of restrictions imposed on them by the Portuguese colonial regime, especially after the signing of the *Concordat* with the Vatican in 1940, would end. Indeed, many probably felt that under Mondlane's leadership, the

---

1. Sundkler, *A History of the Church in Africa*, 986.

Protestant churches would be in a somewhat privileged position, at the very least they would have the ear of the President in important matters of public policy. However, it is equally clear that Mondlane's understanding of the church and Christian faith was changed radically in his time of study and work in South Africa, Portugal and the United States and by the variety of positions on the church and religion present within the FRELIMO leadership. It is not certain that the restrictive and antagonistic policies of FRELIMO toward religion following independence would have been significantly different under Mondlane's leadership. The bulk of the life of the members of the Protestant churches was being lived out in the very closed world of the Portuguese colonial state and under the watchful eye of PIDE/DGS and within the very closed moral and ecclesiastical community of the various missions. At the same time, Mondlane's ideas were being formed in the reality of the armed struggle from its base in Tanzania and within the liberated zones as well as in his interaction with innumerable international organizations and political leaders in his many travels on behalf of FRELIMO. The recently published biography of Janet Mondlane, Eduardo's widow, has shed a great deal of light not only on the development of FRELIMO in its formative years in Dar-es-Salaam and Mondlane's role within it, but also on the development of his thought and relationship with the Swiss Mission and the Protestant churches during his time in the United States.

Yet, despite the unquestioned role the church played in Mondlane's upbringing and in his developing views on the future of Mozambique, there is scant attention paid to it in most of the biographical sketches of Mondlane in histories of the liberation struggle until very recently. Although it is true that he became very critical of the moral and political hypocrisy of the church and of Christian faith as his ideas and engagement in the liberation struggle developed, it can also be argued that his upbringing in the church and his understanding of Christian faith was a significant influence on him, and on his understanding of the liberation struggle, until his death. It will be instructive to look more closely at the influence of the church and Christian faith on Mondlane both as a representative of the vision of national independence from one of the most important children of the Protestant churches and also as a growing critic of the role of religion in the life of the state.

## Chitlangou

In 1946, the Swiss Mission published a little book by André-Daniel Clerc, a missionary in Lourenço Marques and Director of youth work, entitled *Chitlango: fils de chef*. The book was based on the early life of Eduardo Mondlane. Clerc was Mondlane's teacher from an early age and indeed was a father figure to him as he grew up in the Swiss Mission. Although the book is influenced by information gleaned by Clerc from some other sources over his long career in Mozambique, it is based primarily on notes made by Mondlane and passed on to Clerc for this purpose. It was decided not to publish the book under the title of Chivambo, Mondlane's second name, but to modify it to Chitlangou so that he would not be immediately identified by the Portuguese and accused of having spoken too much with foreigners.[2] However, Mondlane and Chitlangou became synonymous, especially as *Chitlangou* was used extensively in Swiss Protestant churches to teach children and youth about the life of young people in Africa. When Mondlane visited Switzerland in 1950, he was billed as the "real" Chitlangou.

Mondlane's early life, as told in *Chitlangou* and as described by him and others elsewhere, was portrayed as typical of African children of the time among the Tsonga. However, it was also emphasized that the character Chitlangou, was the "son of the chief", that is that he did have a certain level of privilege in the traditional African society in which he was raised. Mondlane himself was the son of Nwadjahane Mussengane Mondlane, the local chief, or *Régulo* in the Portuguese colonial administration, and the last child of his third wife, Makungu Muzamusse Bembele. He was born in 1920. His father died before Eduardo was two, and his mother was left to raise him in very difficult circumstances. She chose not to live with one of her husband's brothers or cousins, as she could have done according to custom, but rather to live on her own and to raise her children with the help of her mother. These women had a deep impact on Eduardo's life, in teaching him about their own history and tradition, as well as the devastation wrought by Portuguese colonialism, and in encouraging Eduardo to play a role in rebuilding the community after the death of his father. Like many other boys his age, Eduardo was sent to tend the family's livestock in the pasture land near

---

2. Letter from André-Daniel Clerc to Eduardo Mondlane, June 6, 1946, Archives of the Département Missionnaire des Eglises Protestantes de Suisse Romande (hereafter referred to as DM) 911C.

the village. It was a difficult life in which the boys were left very much to fend for themselves and to survive by their wits without the help of adults; however, it was also a life in which young boys learned to make decisions and to work together in order to survive.[3]

## Mintlawa

It is not without reason that Clerc dedicated so much time to recording Mondlane's and other young boys' experiences as herders. He found this to be a useful model for developing the *mintlawa, patrulhas* in Portuguese, which was the system of organizing the work among children and youth in the Swiss Mission. "The life of the young herder in the bush was extremely interesting. Instead of bringing in European books, I spoke frequently with African colleagues . . . All of them told me about the young African, his life and about the experiences they gained from it. We took all of these teachings into consideration and began to form groups, building a sense of responsibility directed toward the educational field."[4]

Small groups of boys and girls would meet under the guidance of an *instrutor* but with no adult leadership. Conversations within the group were considered confidential and ideas for action would be developed on a consensus basis. A strong sense of loyalty was engendered and these groups became an important part of the youngster's maturation and socialization. Teresa Cruz e Silva in much of her recent work, especially her *Protestant Churches and the Formation of Political Consciousness in Southern Mozambique (1930–1974),* has argued that the participation of Mondlane and many other future militants of FRELIMO in these groups had a profound effect in the formation of political consciousness and in the organization of the developing nationalist movement.

Clerc's use of the model of the groups of young herders in traditional society as the basis for the *mintlawa* groups reflects on the Swiss Mission's respect for traditional culture and its deep desire to plant the

3. See Shore, "Resistance and Revolution," xv–xvii. See also, Cruz e Silva, *Protestant Churches,* 102–3.

4. José Rui Cunha, "A vida de Eduardo Mondlane narrada pelo seu tutor." *Notícias.* May 18, 1975, DM 1291A. *"A vida do pequeno pastor no mato era interessantíssima . . . Em vez de importar obras europeias, dialogava-se frequentemente com colegas africanos . . . Todos eles me falavam do jovem africano, da sua vida, e das experiências que a partir dele se adquiriam. Aproveitámos todos os ensinamentos e iniciámos a formação de grupos, alimentando um sentido de responsabilidade orientado para o campo educacional."*

gospel within the soil of the African context. It seems that it was this, at least in part, that strongly attracted Mondlane to become involved with the Swiss Mission. His mother had enrolled him in the local government primary school in Manjacaze but the teacher knew no Tsonga and Mondlane spoke little Portuguese. Discipline was harsh but ineffective and students were forced to do manual labor. After two years, he enrolled in the Swiss Mission school, in Mausse, near Manjacaze where he finished his rudimentary instruction and also became an enthusiastic participant in the *mintlawa*. Charles Périer and Natala Sumbana, the leaders of the boys and girls programs respectively, continued to have a strong influence in Mondlane's life, long after he left Mausse. He was attracted by the "democratic methods of work within the spirit of comradeship" and "work[ing] rationally instead of resolving problems with violence."[5] Mondlane was to become a model participant and his potential noted by the Swiss Mission. It could be argued that this was one of the significant things that recommended him to Clerc when he travelled to Lourenço Marques to finish his primary education in 1936.

## Gospel and Culture

Despite this attraction, it is very instructive to see the difference in relation to gospel and culture in the thinking of Mondlane and Clerc even at this very early time. In the correspondence between the two, when Clerc was on holiday in Switzerland and writing *Chitlangou,* and Mondlane was attending secondary school in the Swiss Mission in Lemana in South Africa, Clerc pushed Mondlane to describe his experience of conversion. Mondlane wrote,

> So I can summarize in telling you that my conversion did not happen in a day but was an evolution. I think that the beliefs placed in my heart by my grandmother about our ancestors had something to do with my spiritual progress. I believed that there was another life after death because my grandparents live in spirit (even though they are bodily dead). And from this when I heard the story of Christ and God I immediately accepted, and little by little was able to respond to the question which I had always heard within my heart; which one day made me cry (before hearing of Christ) that was this "Where will you go after death?" This idea had entered into my thinking very early on. It was in 1933

---

5. Quoted in Cruz e Silva, *Protestant Churches,* 104.

that I first went to confess before my elders and the congregation in Chalale. After that I entered into a huge struggle with many temptations that afterward went away. I only received baptism in 1939, after Ricatla.[6]

Clearly, Mondlane links his beliefs within his traditional religious upbringing to his understanding of becoming Christian. Although he acknowledges that there was a significant change that occurred in his conversion, there was also a clear line from the traditional belief in the afterlife of the ancestors to the Christian understanding of salvation in Christ. On the other hand, Clerc, while not discrediting the importance of traditional culture writes, "Philosophically the basic idea is this: The pagan life has its advantages but, in the end, it deceives and ends in the total destruction of the individual. 'Civilized' life is another downfall for the indigenous person. Evangelization is not, as many people here think of it, the clarification of a doctrine that the little negro can swallow without understanding. Evangelization is a man's [sic] introduction into a life, a fraternity (Church and Ntlawa) that which is of Christ and is not satisfied with 'painting' but must be deeply embedded in our personality."[7]

It is interesting to note here that Clerc does not believe, as is commonly thought to be the understanding of missionaries of his time, that conversion is synonymous with, or that it even included, accepting

---

6. Letter from Mondlane to Clerc, 1943, DM, 1406A, 3. "No entanto lhe posso resumir por lhe dizer que a minha conversão não foi do um dia mas uma evolução. Penso que as crenças inculcadas no meu coração pela minha avó sobre os nossos antepassados teve alguma coisa que fazer com o meu progresso spiritual. Cria que há uma outra vida depois da morte porque meus avós vivem no espirito (mesmo que estejam carnalmente mortos). E dali quando ouvi a história de Cristo e Deus logo aceitei, e pouco a pouco cheguei de responder à pergunta que sempre se ouvia no íntimo do meu coração; a qual um dia me fez chorar (antes de ouvir de Cristo) que era esta 'Onde irás depois da morte?' Esta idea veio muito cedo no meu pensamento. Foi em 1933 que uma vez fui confessor em frente dos meus superiores e da congregassão [sic] em Chalale. Depois entrou numa luta grande com as muitas tentações que depois sobvieram. Só recebio batismo em 1939, depois de Ricatla."

7. Letter from Clerc to Mondlane, June 6, 1946, DM 911C, 7. "Filosoficamente a ideia de base é esta: A vida pagã tem as suas 'vantagens' mas, a final de contas, engana e leva a ruina total do indivíduo. A vida 'civilizada' é uma outra ruina para o indígena. A Evangelização não é, como muita gente o pensa aqui, o esclarecimento duma doutrina que o pretinho engole sem compreender. A Evanglização é a introdução do homem numa vida, numa fraternidade (Igreja e Ntlawa) que é a do Cristo e que não se satisfaz em 'pintar', mas deve cavar profundamente a nossa personalidade."

European "civilization." Rather, conversion meant the beginning of a whole new life, different from the "pagan" and the "civilized" categories in common use, that is the life in Christ. It is also interesting to note that in the correspondence between Clerc and Mondlane at this time, the "missionary" is also being confronted by the changes in post World War II Swiss society and challenged as to how to present the gospel not only in Mozambique, but also to young people who were living with the legacy of war and who lived by "sport, the radio and parties."[8]

This difference in thinking concerning the relation between Christianity and traditional culture resonates with the earlier difference in thinking between missionaries and African evangelists at the time of the founding of the Swiss Mission in Mozambique. In the earliest community in Ricatla, under the leadership of the evangelist Joseph Mhalamhala and his sister Lois Xintomane, it was clear that the reception of the gospel was within the parameters of traditional African society and charismatic religious experience. The arrival of the Swiss missionary, Paul Berthod, brought rapid change to this situation and a break with what he understood to be pagan culture. In criticizing Joseph Mhalamhala for allowing this to happen, it is interesting to note the language which he uses: he had "a great benevolence, a feminine sensitivity, an infantile faith and a rich imagination."[9] The leadership of women and the "feminine" nature of the approach was to be contrasted with the order and discipline of the, one would understand, "masculine" approach of the missionaries. One of Berthod's first acts after arriving in Mozambique was to prohibit women from preaching.

It can be argued then that this contrast in understanding of the nature of the church in relation to African culture and society is reflected in the difference in thought between Mondlane and Clerc. From this very early time, Mondlane was critical of the missionary model of evangelization in Africa, even the somewhat more enlightened model of the Swiss Protestants in Mozambique. He was clear that his Christian faith grew out of his roots in African traditional religion and that he did not have to become a "civilized" European in order to become Christian. Indeed, as he thinks back to his childhood, he realizes that he became aware early

---

8. Letter from Clerc to Mondlane, April 16, 1946, DM 911C, 4.

9. Butselaar, *Africanos, Missionarios e Colonialistas*, 98, "uma grande benevolência, uma sensibilidade feminina, uma fé infantil e uma rica imaginação."

on that the European, even the European in the church, could be equally pagan as the African:

> In the beginning I thought that the European "mulungu" is a noble, candid, just and sensitive person, but later I had to discover, to my disappointment, that he [sic] is not any more holy than the negro and many times more cruel than Gungunhana. The multiplicity of churches of diverse denominations and the bigotry which each one preaches against the other and the fact that all of them come from overseas convinced me that in the church as well . . . there is corruption. But in comparison with the barbarism about which our elders spoke concerning the past lords of our land I see that the European comes out better. Our indigenous religion could have remained and continued to thrive if there had not been another which offered better answers to the questions of the future. I see a similarity between the Christian religion and the indigenous pagan religion in knowing of the continuation of life after bodily death. The spiritual sentiment was not taught to me by the Christian religion but rather by the religion of my ancestors. When I read the Old Testament concerning the laws which governed the Hebrews related to social life, I do not see any difference. What impedes many people from accepting the Christian life is not the lack of comprehension of religion in general but the lack of faith in the practicality of Christian precepts. There are many churches which preach salvation by Faith in Jesus Christ and nothing more. These churches manage to have a multitude of members who are not any better than the rest of the world's pagans. This is not because the Gospel of Salvation by Faith is wrong but rather because people prefer to live in laziness (knowing that the Lord Jesus Christ will forgive all that they have confessed to him in their hearts). The Christian church has and still will have to struggle against a difficult enemy and this is "European civilization" as it is in Africa. People are in contact with Europeans who teach us that to be civilized and to be Christian is the same thing. Many Africans adapt themselves to European paganism which has dressed itself up in the body of holiness. Never, in the Swiss Mission, have I heard a preacher tell me that our Mission is purer than all the others. I grew up with the spirit that the Christian is the same in all the world. There is not a Christian who is Swiss, American, Presbyterian, Anglican, Catholic, etc. but rather a Christian who is the servant of Our Lord Jesus Christ.[10]

10. Letter from Mondlane to Clerc, April 1946, DM 911C, 3. "No começo pensei

In this lengthy quotation, several important concerns of Mondlane about the church, which would continue into the later stages of his life, can be identified. First, as mentioned above, that the church grows within different and distinct cultural contexts. The church does not need European "civilization" as an antecedent to its existence. Indeed, the so-called European civilization as it is known in Africa, can be a barrier to the development of the church. His own faith began in the traditional beliefs of his African culture. Second, Mondlane identifies the scandal of the denominational divisions of the western churches which were involved in the mission enterprise in Africa. Rather than seeking unity and cooperation in their evangelical task, they focused on their prejudices formed in the contexts from which they had come and translated them into the communities they founded in Africa. These artificial differences then occupied the energy of the African church rather than it struggling with the real challenges of the dehumanizing impact of colonialism. Finally, Mondlane distinguishes between the doctrinal

---

que o europeu 'mulungu' é uma pessoa nobre, cándido, justiceiro e sensível, mas depois tive que descobrir, para meu despontamento, que ele não é mais santo do que o preto e muitas vezes mais cruel do que Gungunhana. A multiplicidade de igrejas de denominações diversas e os prejudícios que cada delas prega contra a outra e o facto de todas elas virem de alem-mar me convenceu de que 'tambem na igreja . . . há corrupção. Mas em comparação com a barbaridade de que falam os nossos avós sobre os antigos senhores da nossa terra vejo que o europeu vem a ser melhor. A nossa religião indígena podia ter ficado e continuado prospera se não tivesse havido uma outra que oferecesse melhores respostas as preguntas do futuro. Vejo uma similaridade entre a religião cristã e religião pagã indígena a saber a continuação da vida depois da morte corporal. O sentimento espiritual não me foi ensinado pela religião cristã, mas sim pela religião dos meus antepassados. Quando leio o velho testamento sobre as leis que governavam os hebreus no que diz respeito a vida social, não vejo nenhuma diferença, o que impede muita gente a aceitar a vida cristã não é a falta de compreenção da religião em gêral mas é a falta de fé na practicabilidade dos preceitos cristãos. Há muitas igrejas que pregam a salvação pela Fé em Jesus Cristo e nada mais. Essas igrejas conseguem ter uma multidão de adeptos que não são melhores do que o resto dos pagãos da terra. Não porque o Evangelho da Salvação pela Fé seja errado mas sim porque gente prefere viver em preguiça (por saber que o Senhor Jesus Cristo lhes perdoará tudo sem que eles lhe admitam nos seus corações). A igreja cristã teve e ainda tem que lutar contra um inimigo difícil e este é a "civilisação europeia" como é na África. A gente está em contacto com europeus que nos ensina que ser civilisado e ser cristão é uma coisa. Muitos africanos se reconciliam com o paganismo europeu que vestiu-se de corpo de santidade. Nunca, na Missão Suiça, tenho ouvido um pregador a dizer-me que a nossa Missão é a mais pura de todas as outras. Cresci com o espírito de que o cristão é um em todo o mundo. Não há cristão suiço, americano, presbiteriano, anglicano, católico etc., mas sim um cristão que é servo de Nosso Senhor Jesus Cristo."

beliefs and the practical application of Christian faith in the life of the community. He had quickly learned that doctrinal differences brought division in the church and impeded the application of Christian faith in day to day life and in the development of the social order. Although he asserts that Christianity provides answers to questions related to the future which are beyond the capacity of African traditional religion, he also asserts that without Christianity's practical and moral application, it does not rise above any other of the world's "paganisms." This emphasis on practicality was to continue to dominate Mondlane's thought concerning the church and his own vocation. Although he often considered ordained ministry in the church, his passion became the social application of Christian faith in the world beyond the walls of the church.

## Lorenço Marques

Mondlane's education, formal and informal, happened largely within the framework of the Protestant mission society of the 1930s, '40s and '50s. His mother died in 1933 when he was enrolled at the Swiss Mission school in Mausse and he came under the care of his older sister. When he finished his Rudimentary Studies in Mausse in 1936 and it was necessary for him to go to Lourenço Marques to continue his Primary School studies, he was already sixteen years of age. When he first arrived in the city, he was employed at the Swiss Mission hospital at Chamanculo where he worked in the laundry. He was noticed by one of the Swiss nurses who suggested to Clerc that he should continue his studies in the mission school and that perhaps he could live in Clerc's home, working as a domestic.

He became a part of the Clerc family and learned French with Clerc's daughters, although Clerc later noted that he would not have approved of this had he known at the time since the Portuguese might have used this to accuse the mission of "denationalization."[11] It is clear in the ongoing correspondence between Mondlane and Clerc after he left Lourenço Marques that Mondlane's relationship with the family became quite intimate although the formalities of the distinction between missionary and African student remained. He usually addresses Clerc as "Dear Teacher, Sir" (Presado Senhor Professor) and often sends greetings to "Mrs. Clerc" (Sra. Clerc). However, he usually signs the

---

11. Clerc quoted in Cruz e Silva, *Protestant Churches*, 104–5.

correspondence with "Your son in Christ" (Vosso filho em Cristo). The sense one has from reading the correspondence and also from talking with other Swiss missionaries who knew the Clerc family is of a loving but fairly rigid family in which the boundaries between European and African were present but being tested and pushed.

It could be argued that within this quite personal relationship the previous clear lines between the European missionary and the African convert were blurred and a new kind of relationship which paralleled and in some ways foreshadowed the more collegial relationship between mission and church could be seen. The later challenges which Mondlane's studies, marriage and work posed for the mission community and where he should be placed within the mission paradigm were often mixed with the more familial relationships which he had developed with Clerc and later, and to a lesser extent, with the family of the white American missionary Darrell Randall. This was not only a challenge for the European and North American missionary community, but also for those in the Mozambican church who were not comfortable with the way in which Mondlane was able to be at home in both cultures and did not conform to the traditional relational patterns between European and African.

## Cambine and the Methodist Church

Mondlane encountered quite a different relationship with missionary personnel when he went to the Cambine mission in 1939. He had finished his primary schooling in Lourenço Marques and, given his age and the colonial education regulations, was not able to continue further formal study in Mozambique. He completed a catechist's course at Ricatla and began working as a catechist and a youth instructor in collaboration with Clerc. The work was very creative and successful despite the restrictions on youth work of the colonial regime and others in the Protestant mission community were interested in developing the *mintlawa* in their own context. This is what took Mondlane to the Methodist Episcopal Mission in Inhambane along with the possibility of him doing an agricultural course at their school. Once again, it is interesting to note that he challenged the traditional relationship and roles of missionary and African convert in being the one who introduced this new program to the American missionary community. It should be noted that Natala Sumbane was also involved in introducing the program for girls in the Methodist mission but because she was not living at the mission as

Mondlane did, her engagement had somewhat less impact. Gender no doubt also played a role in the relative importance given to the girl's program.

This experience for Mondlane was a rich one in terms of his own growth and development and being outside the parameters of the Swiss Mission. At Cambine, he was introduced to a different mission experience, both denominationally and in terms of the origins of the missionaries in the United States. He also met with Africans who had done higher education in the Methodist mission in Rhodesia[12] and read *Aggrey of Africa*[13] which was to have an ongoing influence on him. He learned English and studied music and was also exposed to African American culture. Charles Fuller, writing in tribute to Mondlane in 1969, writes about his motivation to come to Cambine after attending a course with Fuller:

> They sang my translations into Xitswa of some of the finest American Negro spirituals. I lectured on the lives and contributions of great Negro personalities such as Booker T. Washington, George Washington Carver, and Paul Robeson. The recordings of the last, an unquestionably masterful singer, an excellent scholar, and controversial political figure, were heard. Eduardo Mondlane, drinking in everything that was said and sung, begged permission to come to Kambine to learn more about teaching, to discover avenues of further service of practical value to his people, and to learn more about what made these American Negroes go forward.[14]

Mondlane was well liked and his work respected at Cambine. However, the seeds of ongoing tension with the American Methodist mission were also sown at this time. Mondlane wished to continue his studies and he was aware that his age was already working against him. In a letter written to Clerc in October, 1941, he expressed his desire to return to Lourenço Marques by the middle of the following year. Rea, the head of the Cambine mission, however, wanted him to stay there for another three or four years.[15] Over the years, Mondlane would face

---

12. From an interview with Clerc, quoted in Cruz e Silva, *Protestant Churches*, 108.

13. Letter from Mondlane to Clerc from Mucambe, June 9, 1942, DM, 910C, 2.

14. Charles Edward Fuller, "The Making of a Martyr," 1969, Unpublished MS, DM, 1848C, 5.

15. Letter from Mondlane to Clerc from Cambine, October 16, 1941, DM, 910B, 2.

a great deal of resistance to his continuing studies from many of the American Methodist missionaries, as well as some of the Swiss, who felt that his skills and talents should be used in the practical work of the mission rather than risking his being tempted to work abroad after each increase in his level of education. They were afraid that he would be lost to Mozambique and to the development of mission work there. It seems that it was almost impossible for them to look beyond the mission paradigm in which they worked to what Mondlane's education and development might offer not only to the church but also the country as a whole with his broader perspective and contacts.

## Dingane

Perhaps because of his contact with Mozambicans who had studied outside the colony, Mondlane began to formulate an idea to study at the Swiss Mission high school in Lemana in the Transvaal. His passion for education was growing and was well recognized within the mission community. His understanding of English from his time at Cambine also made this a more realistic possibility. Yet as mentioned above, there was resistance to continuing his studies from both the American mission community and some among the Swiss. The Swiss Mission also had very limited financial resources to be able to sponsor his complete secondary education, especially given his age. A decision was made to have Mondlane work for a time in a mission station at Dingane, near Manjacaze, to apply what he had learned at Cambine and also to have some experience in parish work.

This period of time was particularly challenging to the Swiss Mission, and other Protestant missions, in relation to their education programs. The *Concordat* between Portugal and the Vatican signed in 1940, with its *Acordo Missionário* and the *Estatuto Missionário* of April 1941, dramatically changed the role of the Roman Catholic Church within Mozambican colonial society. Although the Colonial Act of 1930 recognized the Roman Catholic Church's particular role as an "instrument of civilization and national influence" within the larger framework of the *Estado Novo*, the *Concordat* and attendant documents gave it exclusive responsibility for the education of the *indígena* population which meant control over all "rudimentary" education, teaching Portuguese and, in theory, preparing students for primary education. The *Concordat* meant that Roman Catholic schools received financial support from the state and became official state schools, while Protestant and foreign Catholic mission schools had to work under severe restrictions. On the other hand, the Roman Catholic Church paid a high price for this privilege in giving over its power for the final approval of appointing bishops to the Portuguese state. It was clear that there was an ideological purpose to this agreement and that the church was co-opted to act as an agent of Portuguese colonial pacification and assimilation policy. Malyn Newitt quotes the principal objective of "rudimentary" education as: "... the perfect training of the *indígenas* in national and moral ideals (*nacionalização e moralização*) and the acquisition of habits and aptitudes for work, in keeping with their sex and condition, and the convenience of the regional economy. Moral ideals being understood to include the abandonment of idleness and the training of future rural workers and artisans to produce sufficient for their needs and for their social obligations."[16]

It can be seen then that all of this proved to be a huge challenge to the Swiss Mission and other Protestant missions operating in Portuguese territory. By law, they were forced to curtail their educational work as new Catholic mission schools became operational throughout the country. In practice, Catholic schools were often targeted to be built in close proximity to Protestant mission schools so that they would have to be closed. In his *"Rapport de l'exercice 41–42 la marche des écoles de la ville & environs,"* Clerc reports that the Swiss mission had been prohibited from teaching the *4a classe*, the final level of primary education in October, 1941 and that the school in Ricatla had been closed. All of this meant that the Protestant missions had to re-think their educational programs to find other ways to engage young people and to be involved in evangelization. Clearly, the further development of the *mintlawa* was one response to this challenge.

This then was the context in which Mondlane began his work in Dingane in 1942. Dingane was named after a chief from the Mondlane clan. It had originally been a Methodist Episcopal Church mission but had been "given" to the Swiss because of an agreement to divide work according to language.[17] In his correspondence with Clerc in this period, he often mentions conflicts with the Roman Catholics, especially in rela-

---

16. Newitt, *History of Mozambique*, 479.

17. Mondlane, "My one and a half year's work in the Dingane Mission Station," unpublished MS, DM 910D 4.

tion to education. However, Mondlane was very creative in establishing a small bush school in Dingane. He befriended the local Catholic teacher in Manjacaze and seems to have led him to believe that he was also a qualified teacher.[18] According to Clerc, he also used his knowledge of the local community and his status as the son of the *Régulo* to enhance and to safeguard the work he was doing from the local colonial authorities.[19] In this placement, he not only encountered the privileged role of the Catholic Church, but also recognized and reflected upon other aspects of colonial society. The exploitative prices in the store run by an Asian trader, the high levels of infant and maternal mortality[20] and the high percentage of men who had gone to work in the Rand[21] all figured in his correspondence. It is interesting to note that Mondlane still saw these issues largely from the impact which they had on the work and growth of the Protestant mission churches and saw the need for a religious revival to overcome many of the problems of the people. However, he was also clear that he was becoming more aware of the impact of the colonial structures on the life of rural people as a whole through his voracious reading and his life experience.

---

18. Letter from Mondlane to Clerc from Manjacase, April 8, 1943, DM, 910D, 1.
19. Clerc quoted in Cruz e Silva, *Protestant Churches*, 109.
20. Letter from Mondlane to Clerc from Dingane, December 25, 1942, DM 910C, 9.
21. Letter from Mondlane to Clerc from Dingane, April 8, 1943, DM 910D, 1.

# 3

## Reformed and Reforming

### *Living Faith in South Africa*

### Lemana Training Institute and Urban Life in South Africa

MONDLANE'S WORK AT DINGANE was highly respected and in 1944 the Swiss Mission allowed him to begin studies at the Lemana Training Institute in Transvaal, probably first going as an evangelist and later, in 1945, on a visa recognizing his student status.[1] Lemana was part of the Swiss Mission in South Africa (SMSA) which developed in parallel to the Swiss Mission in Mozmabique and would become the Evangelical Presbyterian Church in South Africa. Throughout his time of studies in Lemana, Mondlane continued working as an evangelist with a congregation at Shirley. He was well liked and respected in the school and became the Chairman of the "Students Christian Association" in his first year of studies. The move to Lemana represented a major shift in Mondlane's life to a context which presented many new challenges. He moved from the Portuguese colonial context to South Africa with an attendant shift in the cultural and linguistic context. His studies in Lemana were in English rather than Portuguese. In his early correspondence, he wrote that he did not want to lose "my language"[2] and that he had taken his

---

1. Teresa Cruz e Silva has done much to clarify when Mondlane went to Lemana and also some of the history of the secondary school there through conversation with Elizabeth Cuenod a descendent of Swiss missionaries who worked in Lemana. See Cruz e Silva, *Protestant Churches*, 110.

2. Letter from Mondlane to Clerc from Lemana, March 26, 1944, DM 911A, 1. "Minha lingua."

"*Lusiadas*" in his suitcase. Although critical of Portuguese colonial policy, it seems clear here that Mondlane, when placed in this new context, did consider himself to be Portuguese and at some level wished to guard that identity. At Lemana, Mondlane also entered into an environment of secondary education which was less overtly religious in its orientation. He wrote to Clerc, "It is curious. They are so behind in everything! The teachers are professors in the School but don't say anything about Christ. It seems to me that the ignorance which is seen in the people stems from this."³ Despite his great desire to go to Lemana and to be able to continue his studies outside Mozambique, there was a resistance in Mondlane which reflected his more rigid pietistic and moralistic upbringing in the Mozambican Swiss Mission. He was particularly critical of the level of alcohol consumption he saw, especially among the teaching staff. He helped to found a Temperance society and wrote and produced a play about a teacher who was alcoholic.⁴

Beyond the rural life of Lemana, he was also exposed to the urban reality on the Rand. Once again, he was critical both of the life of the city and the way in which the churches had responded to the needs of the people in these burgeoning urban centers. In February, 1947, in a letter to Clerc, he called Johannesburg a "den of all kinds of vices"⁵ and in an earlier letter in 1946, he criticized the Jan Hofmeyer School for having adapted to the ways of the city by having dances.⁶ Although Mondlane had experienced urban life in Lourenço Marques, he seemed to be quite taken aback by life in the city and by the level of what he understood to be moral corruption that he encountered. However, Mondlane also sought to adapt his faith and his understanding of the church to these new realities which he was experiencing. In his years at Lemana, he became convinced that his calling, while still in the church, was not to ordained ministry, especially if he was to work among young people. He did not discount the role of the pastor, but wrote, "there is great reluctance on the part of young people who in general look on the pastor

---

3. Ibid. "É curioso, eles são atrazados em tudo! Os professors são senhores doutores na Escola e não falam nada de Cristo. Pereceu-me que a ignorância que se nota no povo vem dali."

4. Script of play by Mondlane. DM, 911B.

5. Letter from Mondlane to Clerc, February 3, 1947. DM 912A, 3. "cova de vícios de toda a espécie."

6. Letter from Mondlane to Clerc from Lemana, November 25, 1946, DM 911C, 10.

as a criminal looks on a judge and the church as a court. It is not easy for a denominational pastor to help a person who belongs to another church."[7] Mondlane saw the inadequacies of the church in meeting the needs of young people in such a rapidly changing world and began to identify sociology and social work as the direction he would like to follow in meeting those needs. "It seems to me that sociology is a course that relates directly to the people very very much in the large population centers (like in the cities)."[8]

Mondlane's time in South Africa also enabled him to gain a broader perspective on what was happening in the world beyond southern Africa. In an interesting comment on an encounter on the train to Johannesburg he wrote, "In the train I was with Indians (of the Mahomedan [sic] sect) who seemed to rejoice on the news of the death of Ghandi. When I asked them why they rejoiced they answered me saying that Ghandi was one of those who always instigated the Hindus to worry the Mohomedans. I was sorry to hear this obvious lie told by Indians about a man whom all the world respects. I think they do not know Ghandi, they were blinded by their religious fanaticism."[9] With a much broadened world view and capacity for analysis, Mondlane began looking at courses in sociology in the major universities in South Africa as options for continuing his studies after completing his "matric." in Lemana.

## Jan Hofmeyr School of Social Work

At the same time, Clerc and others in the Swiss Mission were also trying to discern what next steps might be for Mondlane. While on holiday in Switzerland in 1946, Clerc attended a conference of the YMCA Executive in Geneva. Despite his discomfort at having to endure six days of listening in English and "American", it seems that he first identified there the possibility of Mondlane continuing his studies with some sort of specialization in youth work and returning to begin a YMCA in Lourenço Marques. This was to continue to be Clerc's dream even throughout all

---

7. Ibid. "há muitas reticências na parte da mocidade que em geral olha para o pastor como o malfeitor olha para seu juiz e a igreja como o tribunal. Não é fácil para um pastor denominacional ajudar uma pessoa que pertence a outra secta."

8. Letter from Mondlane to Clerc, March 1946, DM, 911C, 3. "Vejo que a sociologia é um curso que vai directamente para a vida da gente muito muito nas grandes populações (como nas cidades)."

9. Letter from Mondlane to Clerc, February 2, 48, DM 912B, 1b.

the years that Mondlane would spend in the United States and represented for him one of the most important ways the Swiss Mission could respond to the challenges of urbanization in Mozambique as well as to the great change in the global context following World War II which he was feeling acutely in this time in Switzerland.[10] Although both Mondlane and Clerc at this point discerned a need to use sociology and the other social sciences to adapt the work of the church in Mozambique to the changing context, especially with youth, it seemed apparent that Mondlane was beginning to take a more radical course and was looking beyond the churches to a more fundamental change that would be required to respond to the many challenges facing Mozambique and the region.

In the discussion concerning where Mondlane would continue his studies, the options were the Jan Hofmeyr School of Social Work in Johannesburg, run in conjunction with the YMCA and developed for training native [sic] social workers, or a Sociology course at the University of the Witswatersrand (Wits) or Fort Hare. Although Mondlane agreed that the practical side of the education at the Hofmeyr School would be beneficial[11] he continued to keep the option of a university program open while the Swiss Mission negotiated a place for him at the YMCA school and in fact was disappointed when the decision was made for Hofmeyr.[12] However, the mission connections were quite strong and the Hofmeyr School was willing to provide a scholarship for a student from Mozambique recommended by the Christian Council. Clerc was very clear that he felt this was the best school for Mondlane because of the YMCA connection. In his reference for Mondlane to Dr. Ray Phillips, the Director of the Hofmeyr School, he wrote, "My sincere opinion is that I am backing one of the best and ablest we can find here. My intention is, if circumstances and God permit to see Mondlane trained and seriously trained to be an able Youth Leader for all the youth of Lourenço Marques, starting something new we, as missionaries, we cannot do. This would be one very urgent extension of your work in

---

10. Letter from Clerc to Mondlane from Auvernier, Switzerland, April 16, 1946, DM 911C, 4.

11. Letter from Mondlane to Clerc from Lemana, November 26, 1946, DM, 911C, 11.

12. Letter from Mondlane to Clerc from Lemana, September 10, 1947, DM, 912A, 9.

an important place. May I say that Eduardo Mondlane has gained the confidence of the principal missions working here."[13]

This was clearly the plan of the mission community in Lourenço Marques. In his report for 1946–47, Clerc wrote, "One further difficulty that we have found on our way could be overcome if we would be able to place the young boys who leave the Mintlawa (and the school) to earn their living in a Christian center organized, as well, in communal living groups. The links which connect the youth to the adult Church are missing and we do not have, at the present time, either the people or the funds to forge them. It was while thinking about this deficiency that, on the initiative of the missionaries in the city, steps were taken so that Eduardo Mondlane would be able to do a union secretary course and afterward found a Christian Center in Lourenço Marques."[14]

It did not take long at the Hofmeyr School before the tensions between city life and Mondlane's rural upbringing came into conflict. Indeed, on the first day at the school, he wrote to Clerc, "I do not like the restlessness that is ruling life here in town. I think Lemana will always remain the best place for intellectual undertakings."[15] Yet he could not avoid the hard reality of life in the city and was in fact thrust into the heart of the tensions of life in the townships when in his first semester he was placed for his practical work in the "Missão Anglicana" in Sophiatown, in a boys club held in the evening. Although it is not clear in the correspondence, it is quite possible that this was part of the work of Fr. Trevor Huddleston and the Community of the Resurrection. The only thing Mondlane objected to in the program was that the boys were being taught boxing. He was made an honorary boy scout but again was critical of the low moral standards of the "non-European" leadership

13. Letter from Clerc to Ray Phillips, September 15, 1947, DM 912A, 10.

14. *Rapport sur la marche des Mintlawa de la région de Lourenço Marques Durant l'exercice 46/47*. DM 23K. "Plus d'une difficulté que nous rencontrons sur notre route serait écartée si nous pouvions remettre les jeunes garçons qui sortent des Mintlawa (et de l'école) pour gagner leur vie, à un centre Chrétien, organisé, lui aussi, en groupes de vie communautaire. Les châinons qui relient la jeunesse à l'Eglise adulte manquent et nous n'avons, pour le moment, ni les hommes, ni les fonds pour les forger. C'est en pensant à cette déficience que sur l'initiative des missionnaires de la ville, des démarches sont faites pour qu'Eduardo Mondlane puisse faire des études de secrétaire unioniste et puisse fonder un Centre Chrétien à Lourenço Marques."

15. Letter from Mondlane to Clerc, February 2, 1948, DM 912B, 1b.

who "drink to excess and do not show Christian respect in their sexual life."[16]

Mondlane also very early on came face to face with the increased racial discrimination under the National Party Government, elected in May 1948. In September he was assaulted by a police officer when he would not give him the cane he was carrying. The officer took the cane and beat him with it and slapped the side of his face with his open hand which resulted in the perforation of his eardrum. Mondlane went with a friend to report the assault at the police station where the friend was assaulted for asking the detective to speak in English. Their complaint was taken but the person taking it told them that they did not have enough respect for Europeans. Although the following day the detective came to the school to make an apology, Phillips wanted to send this on to the provincial police because other students had had similar experiences. In commenting on the incident to Clerc, Mondlane wrote, "Teacher, all of this is owing to the interracial relations which are becoming worse here in the Union since the new government has been in power. My case is minor compared with many others. The Boers kill Africans without any remorse and still think that they are Christians."[17] It is interesting to note that Mondlane used this argument to challenge the racist attitudes of the Boers. He would develop this much further in relation to ministers in the National government after his expulsion from South Africa in 1949. Unlike in Mozambique, those in positions of authority in South Africa were Protestants, in the same Reformed tradition as Mondlane. This challenged not only his political but also his ecclesiastical and theological assumptions. In fact, it was his encounter with racism, most particularly within the Protestant missions and churches over the years, which would bring about his disillusion with the church more than any other issue.

It was clear to Mondlane that the course at the Hofmeyr school was inferior to what he would have received at one of the South African universities and he continued to look for alternative programs and for alternative sources of funding. In a letter to Clerc on November 25, 1948,

16. Letter from Mondlane to Clerc, May 14, 1948, DM 912B, 2. "bebem em excesso e não teem respeito Cristão da vida sexual."

17. Letter from Mondlane to Clerc, October 1, 1948, DM 912B, 5. "Sr. professor isto tudo é devido às relações interraciais que se tornaram peores aqui na União desde que o novo governo está em poder. O meu caso é menos comparado com muito outros. Os Boers matam Africanos sem remorso algun e ainda pensam que são Cristãos."

he wrote that he would be able to acquire up to £40 from "European friends" and also that he had been in conversation with the Native Affairs Office which was offering him a scholarship if he would work in South Africa following his studies. His contacts in South Africa were widening and he was willing to look beyond what the Christian Council of Mozambique would offer him in order to enter a university program. An important influence on Mondlane at this time was an American Methodist missionary, Darrell Randall, who taught economics at the Jan Hofmeyr School. Like Clerc, Randall saw Mondlane's potential but given that they were much closer in age, Randall's relationship with Mondlane appears to have been much more collegial than Clerc's. Randall was part of a new generation of western missionaries who were more attune to the political changes afoot in Africa after World War II and were seeking to develop a less paternalistic relationship with African churches and colleagues. It appears that Randall was becoming Mondlane's confidant and that Mondlane was reluctant to express some of his emerging views with Clerc. In his criticism of the Hofmeyr School to Clerc, he uses the argument that the school does not reflect Christian morals as one would think it would: "Before coming here I thought that there would be some insurance against pagan influence, since it is a Christian college. But I have been surprised to discover that on the contrary the place creates hypocrites by not allowing direct criticism of the system of instruction. And as well the fact that the college does not have a residence means that control over the life of the student is beyond the reach of the director. Such that if the student was not truly Christian it would never be possible to have any kind of influence."[18] Yet, what seemed to be truly concerning Mondlane was the obvious substandard level of education at the school compared to that at a university in South Africa. He had been studying the calendars of the various universities and was leaning toward Wits, Cape Town or Natal, those universities that admitted "Africans" and had departments of sociology.[19]

18. Letter from Mondlane to Clerc, November 25, 1948, DM 912B, 7. "Antes de vir aqui pensei que talvez houvesse alguma segurança contra a influência pagã, como é um colégio cristão. Mas fiquei surpreendido em discobrir que pelo contrário o lugar cria hipócritas por não admitir crítica directa ao sistema instrutivo. E também o facto de que não há dormitório do colégio contribute para que o controle da vida do estudante esteja fora do alcance do director. De modo que se o estudante não foi cristão por verdade nunca sera possível influenciá-lo de nenhuma maneira."

19. Letter from Mondlane to Clerc, December 3, 1948, DM 912B, 8.

### Núcleo de estudantes secundários africanos de Moçambique (NESAM)

By the time that Mondlane returned to Mozambique on his vacation at the end of 1948, he was gaining notoriety within the mission community as well as in the larger colonial society, and was certainly under the scrutiny of the police. It was at this time that he joined with other students in forming the Núcleo de estudantes secundários africanos de Lourenço Marques, later de Moçambique (NESAM). In a letter to Clerc, who despite Mondlane's deep desire to have his counsel[20] was on holiday in South Africa while he was in Mozambique, he described the objective of this student organization: "The objective of the 'Núcleo' is to create a spirit of unity and camaraderie among African students which will be expressed in a) the fervent desire to develop spiritual, intellectual and physical culture and b) to serve the African community impartially."[21] The members of the "Núcleo" were all Protestants and most were members of the Centro Associativo dos Negros de Moçambique.

Without a doubt, as Teresa Cruz e Silva suggests, Mondlane's experience in organizing students in South Africa made him a natural leader in the group. As well, it is clear that his thinking was becoming more politicized through his experience in the townships of Johannesburg, his studies at the Jan Hofmeyr School, and his connection with the more liberal thought of church leaders such as Darrell Randall. However, it would appear to be somewhat spurious to suggest that Mondlane at the time saw in NESAM a nascent revolutionary organization and that this thinking had developed through his involvement with the ANC Youth League in South Africa. Cruz e Silva's reference for this connection is in E. Friedland's thesis, *A comparative Study of the Development of Revolutionary Nationalist Movements in Southern Africa—FRELIMO (Mozambique) and the African National Congress of South Africa* which in turn is quoting from the article "FRELIMO, the Real Choice" in the Cuban journal *Tricontinental,* an article which is purported to have been written by Mondlane. There is little evidence other than in this article to support the claim that Mondlane was involved in the ANC Youth

---

20. Letter from Mondlane to Clerc, November 25, 1948. DM 912B, 7.

21. Letter from Mondlane to Clerc, January 18, 1949, DM 913A, 2. "O alvo do 'Núcleo' é criar um espirito de unidade e camaradagem entre os estudantes Africanos que se exprimirá em: (a) o desejo ardente de adquirir cultura spiritual, intellectual e física, e (b) servir a comunidade Africana desinteressadamente."

League or that Mondlane was attempting to establish a similar political organization in Mozambique. On the contrary, in his correspondence with Clerc, Mondlane seems to be most interested in bringing together Protestant young people for mutual support to further the growth of the Protestant churches in Mozambique. Immediately following the first meeting of NESAM, Mondlane went to Chamanculo church to be part of a meeting of another "núcleo" called the *Mancebos Cristãos* led by his close friend Novidades Honwana. This group and the work of Novidades Honwana was at least as important to Mondlane at this time as NESAM and it seems clear that his political thinking was not nearly so developed or revolutionary as has been read back in later accounts of the period.[22] This is not to say that NESAM did not play a significant role in the developing resistance to Portuguese colonial rule. In *The Struggle for Mozambique*, Mondlane himself wrote of NESAM, "It spread nationalist ideas among the black educated youth. It achieved a certain revaluation of national culture, which counteracted the attempts by the Portuguese to make African students despise and abandon their own people; [it] provided the only opportunity to study and discuss Mozambique in its own right and not as an appendage of Portugal's. And, most important perhaps, by cementing personal contacts, it established a nation-wide network of communication, which extended among old members as well as those still at school, and which could be used by a future underground."[23]

According to Friedland, when Mondlane was detained by PIDE before his return to South Africa in February 1949 to begin his studies at Wits University, they were interested to know whether NESAM had any Pan-African financial or political connections. Unfortunately, all records of these early interrogations by PIDE appear to be lost to the archives in Lisbon but one suspects that this detention in 1949 did more to politicize Mondlane than to give PIDE any information concerning his radical pan-Africanist activities. His main concerns in this period seemed to be his studies, his future work in the church and his search for a suitable life partner. In fact he wrote to Clerc in January while still not sure which university he would be attending: "For as I said . . . in Chicuque the environment in which I am living in Johannesburg is not beneficial for either the spiritual or the intellectual life. In the Cape there,

---

22. Cf. e.g. *Eduardo Mondlane*, 19–20.
23. Mondlane, *The Struggle for Mozambique*, 113–14.

where life is quieter and less concerned with the life of racial politics etc. I would be able to concentrate my mental and spiritual efforts toward things that are really worth studying."[24]

## Study at the Univeristy of the Witswatersrand

It is not clear why the plans to study at Cape Town shifted suddenly to Wits when Mondlane returned to South Africa on February 6, 1949. He had been advised by the South African Consul in Lourenço Marques to return before his immigration permit, which he had been granted in 1945, expired since the permit was renewable every six months.[25] He was welcomed and oriented by E. Juillerat, the head of the Swiss Mission in South Africa and wrote that "the university accepted me without any difficulties thanks to Mrs. Jaqueline Eberhardt and Mrs. Violaine Junod."[26] Although there were divisions within the Christian Council in Mozambique and even within the Swiss Mission there concerning Mondlane's continuing studies, it appears that he was well received by the representatives of the mission in South Africa and that his continuing education was given their assistance and their blessing. Darrell Randall had arranged a job for Mondlane before the beginning of term to give him some spending money.

It appears that Mondlane entered wholeheartedly into life at Wits, academically but also socially and within many of the organized student groups. He was popular and made friends easily. In an early letter he wrote that many of his new friends wanted to learn Portuguese. He lived in Douglas Smit House together with a number of medical students from Fort Hare University.[27] This is interesting to note since these students also became a target of expulsion from what the National Party Government understood to be "white" universities.[28] However, in his

24. Letter from Mondlane to Clerc, January 20, 1949. DM 913A, 3. "Porque como... disse em Chicuque o ambiente em que vivo em Johannesburgo não é saudável tanto para a vida espiritual como intellectual. No Cabo ali, onde a vida é mais calma e menos inclinada à vida política racial etc. eu poderei concentrar as minhas forças mentais e espirituais para coisas que vale a pena estudar."

25. Tobias. "A Little known Chapter," 120; and Letter from Mondlane to Clerc, February 18, 1949. DM 913A, 4.

26. Letter from Mondlane to Clerc, February 18, 1949. DM 913A, 4, "a universidade aceitou-me sem dificuldades graças às senhoras Jaqueline Eberhardt e Violaine Junod."

27. Letter from Mondlane to Clerc, March 3, 1949, DM 913A, 5.

28. Tobias, "A Little Known Chapter," 124.

early correspondence with Clerc, Mondlane did not seem to be cognizant of the imminent threat he was under due to apartheid policies. He was chosen by the National Union of South African Students (NUSAS) to represent the first year class of Wits at a conference in Cape Town in the July vacation time of 1949 and was pleased to accept this as a "once in a lifetime" opportunity.[29]

It is clear in Mondlane's correspondence with Clerc at this time, and from other sources, that, although without any doubt his political consciousness was being raised as the apartheid structures of the National Party Government elected in 1948 were being instituted, his primary connections and the lens through which he was watching these developments was in his involvement with the growing ecumenical movement in the country. He was deeply involved in the church; he taught Sunday School in a Swiss Mission church in the "Western Native Township." He wrote that, he had preached in a Baptist Church together with two young European women from the Students' Christian Association. He then went to "the Methodist Hall" afterward to pray for the students of the world. He noted that out of two hundred students present, only four were black. He also recounts the story of attending a picnic with a group of young people at "Enzenzeleni, near Roodepoort" which is very telling of his thinking at the time: "We were a group of young Christians from all the South African races (Indians, Africans, Europeans, Coloreds), of good will and Christian faith. The picnic was organized by some missionaries who belonged to the Christian Council of South Africa. Mr. and Mrs. D.D. Randall were part of the organizing committee. The Rev. Mr. Blaxall, Director of Enzanzeleni (Tiyencelani) Deaf & Blind School, was able to buy a plot of land close to his school to be used for building huts and tents for the use of Christian "campers" who wish to have meetings in which there is no color bar."[30]

29. Letter from Mondlane to Clerc, May 9, 1949, DM 913A, 7.

30. Letter from Mondlane to Clerc, June 1, 1949, DM 913A, 9. "Éramos um grupo de jovens Cristãos de todas as raças Sul-Africanas (Indianos, Africanos, Européus, Mixtos), que creem na boa-vontade e Fé Cristãs. O pic-nic foi organisado por alguns missionários pertecentes ao Conselho Cristão da África do Sul. O Senhor e senhora D. D. Randall foram colaboradores da commissão organisadora. O Senhor Rev. Blaxall, director de Enzenzeleni (Tihencelani) *Deaf and Blind School*, arranjou comprar um terreno perto da sua escola que deverá ser dedicado a construção de palhotas e barracas para o uso dos 'campers' Cristãos que queiram ter reuniões em que não haja nenhuma barreira de côr."

Indeed, at least in his correspondence with Clerc, he identified his life in the church and his Christian faith as the most important thing which sustained him in his times of difficulty: "I must not be prevented from continuing this religious work because it revives my courage to live. There are times when I feel that it is not worth working and even living. When things don't go as they should and the world becomes more confused and irrational than it really is, or should be, there is nothing that gives me more courage to stand up to the facts than to speak about the Man who had more courage and faith than all those beings that have lived on this planet, Earth."[31]

## Expulsion from South Africa

Even the growing crisis around his permit to remain in South Africa was seen through this lens of faith. Mondlane understood that the refusal to renew his visa in June of 1949 was part of the larger plan of "separate development" of the new National Party government. "I suspect that this is a political strategy to satisfy the political desire of the new Nationalist government, that of wanting to force all the Universities which accept Africans to expel them from these universities. I hope that I am wrong in my opinion."[32] However, his critique is voiced not in political terms but rather, as he did at the time of his beating by the South African police officer, in religious or theological terms: "What bothers me in all of this is that Mr. Rev. Dr. D. F. Malan (D.D.) is a Christian, each day that he goes to the parliament to discuss the affairs of the nation he dedicates himself to the same Lord Jesus Christ to ask for the guidance of the same Holy Spirit in which I, his innocent victim, confide. I am in a dilemma. Pray for me if possible."[33]

---

31. Ibid. "Não deve proibir de continuar a fazer este trabalho religioso porque ajuda-me a reaviver a minha coragem de viver. Há tempos em que sinto que não vale a pena trabalhar e mesmo viver. Quando as coisas não andam como deviam, e o mundo se torna mais confuso e irrazoável do que realmente é, ou devia ser, não há nenhuma coisa que me da mais coragem de enfrentar os factos do que falar do Homem que teve mais coragem e Fé do que todos os seres que teem vivido neste planeta, Terra."

32. Ibid. "Eu desconfio que isto é uma estratégia política para satisfazer o desejo do novo governo Nacionalista, o de querer forçar todas as Universidades que aceitam Africanos de tirá-los dessas universidades. Espero que estou errado nesta minha opinião."

33. Letter from Mondlane to Clerc, June 17, 1949, DM 913A, 10. "O que me atrapalha em tudo isto é que o Sr. Rev. Dr. D.F. Malan (D.D.) é um cristão, cada dia que vai ao parlamento discutir os assuntos da nação dedica-se ao mesmo Senhor Jesus Cristo para

By mid-June, 1949, the situation around Mondlane's ability to continue to study at Wits was reaching a crisis point. He had many advocates within the mission and university communities and there was significant interest in the Johannesburg press but he was reluctant to be very public about his situation. His main concern was to be able to complete his term exams at the end of June. He talked with a lawyer, a member of the National Party,[34] and communicated this with Clerc who felt that he should not have done this on his own but should have worked through the leadership of the Swiss Mission.[35] Indeed, they were already working with connections within the Dutch Reformed Church (DRC) and Clerc encouraged Mondlane to go to Pretoria to meet with South African immigration authorities with members of the mission leadership. It is clear that Clerc was depending on the mission network and its connections in both the DRC and the National Party to sway the immigration authorities, a method which had no doubt worked in the past in dealing with problems with the South African government. However, the changed reality in South Africa after the election of the National Party government and the consequent growing rift between those who supported and those who did not support its apartheid policies meant that this network was under considerable strain. Mondlane's situation was quickly becoming a test case to find the limits of the new regulations in relation to visas and immigration policy and he became something of a political *cause celebre* for the primarily liberal students and faculty at Wits. Clerc was somewhat assuaged by the news that Darrell Randell had been involved in consulting the lawyer since this involved someone from the mission community. However, once again it appears that Randall represented a changing understanding of the role of mission personnel with a heightened political awareness and willingness to advocate for political and social change rather than seeking favors from the government. It is of particular interest to note that both the lawyer who took on Mondlane's case, Kay Theron, and the professor from the Social Studies department of the university who advocated for him with the Minister of Immigration were both Afrikaners and perhaps represent the less than monolithic view of Afrikaners at the time

---

pedir a guia do mesmo Espirito Santo em que eu, o seu inocente vítima, confio. Estou num dilema. Ore por mim, se faz favor."

34. Ibid.

35. Letter from Clerc to Mondlane June 26, 1949, DM 913A, 11.

toward the policies of apartheid. Theron's advice to Mondlane not to go to Cape Town for the NUSAS gathering also reflected the increasingly politicized nature of the case with Mondlane explaining that "if the government knows that I am a member of that organization, which is known to be anti-nationalist, I would be victimized."[36]

On August 29, 1949, Mondlane received a final notice from the South African Ministry of the Interior indicating that his permit would not be renewed. From his correspondence with Clerc, it appears that he believed that he would have to leave the country that day. In fact, over the next few days, there was a last ditch effort to convince the Minister to reverse the decision and allow Mondlane to stay. In a story in the *Johannesburg Star*, it was reported that letters had been sent from the Students' Representative Council and from a Professor in his department. In a story in the *Daily Mail* from the same period, it was reported that over seven hundred students had gathered to protest Mondlane's expulsion, fearing that this was only the beginning of a broader threat to students from other African territories studying at the university "using administrative rather than legislative means to impose apartheid."[37] The *Star's* editorial comment states that "this is petty politics and is not really addressing the question of the 'Native land problem' or the 'urban problem.'"[38] The story was also picked up in the Portuguese press in Lourenço Marques, at first asserting that Mondlane was studying on a Portuguese government scholarship but later clarifying the situation. Mondlane visited the Portuguese Consul in Pretoria together with the President of the Student Representative Council and it seems that the Consul was impressed by Mondlane's case, writing a letter to the Minister of the Interior asking to allow him to finish his first year of study at Wits. Although this letter did not achieve the required results, Mondlane was impressed by the attitude of the Consul and appears to have begun a period in which he was willing to work with the Portuguese authorities in order to further his education.[39]

---

36. Letter from Mondlane to Clerc, July 15, 1949, DM 913A, 13, "se o governo sabe que sou membro daquela oranização, que é conhecida anti-nacionalista, seria victimisado."

37. *Daily Mail*, date unclear, DM 913A, 17.

38. *Johannesburg Star,* Date unclear, DM 913A, 23.

39. Letter from Mondlane to Clerc, August 8, 1949, DM 913A, 19.

## Sojourn in Mozambique

Despite all the interest and protest surrounding this decision, Mondlane was forced to leave South Africa on September 3, 1949. On his arrival in Lourenço Marques, he was detained by the police and held for five days. In a letter to Quinton Whyte of the South African Institute of Race Relations, Clerc wrote that Mondlane was held until "he could give proof of his anticommunistic feelings." He also indicated that he himself had been interrogated for three hours until he could prove that "the funds used by Mondlane were not of communist party origin." He concludes that "all this ended well and with declarations of friendship."[40] Reflecting at a later time, Herbert Shore, in his introduction to the 1983 edition of Mondlane's, *The Struggle for Mozambique,* indicates a much more unfavorable report from this interrogation, that Mondlane was considered to be a political threat to the colony and that he had been "contaminated by the communist virus." According to Shore, the Public Prosecutor's office determined that Mondlane needed to be put under close police watch and, if possible, given a scholarship to study in a Portuguese university where he would be separated from the black population and, hopefully, cured of his political and intellectual predilections.[41]

Whether one considers the earlier or the later reading of this interrogation, however, it is interesting to note the articulated concern over communist influence as primary rather than nationalism or the influence of neighboring colonial powers, both of which might have been more significant to the Portuguese at an earlier time. The growth of the perceived "communist threat" in the post World War II context was becoming predominant in the thinking of the Portuguese authorities as it was in South Africa and was able to be used to identify and condemn any challenge to the colonial or apartheid regimes. Whether or not Mondlane had any significantly developed political ideology or affiliation in his time in South Africa, any critical tendency may have been labeled as communist. As is clear in the extensive files of the PIDE concerning the Protestant churches and the ecumenical movement, his involvement with church based organizations which raised any kind or political or social critique could have labeled him as communist as

---

40. Letter from Clerc to Quintin Whyte, October 3, 1949, DM 1172E, 1B.
41. Shore, "Resistance and Revolution," xiii–xxxi.

quickly as his affiliation with student or overtly political organizations such as the ANC.

Again, this is not to deny that his experience in South Africa had a significant impact on Mondlane's growing political consciousness. However, in reading his correspondence from this period it appears that his primary concern continued to be how he could complete his studies, and where, and how he might find a life partner, all within the framework of Clerc's dream of him providing dynamic leadership in a growing church youth movement in Lourenço Marques under the auspices of the Y.M.C.A. After his return to Mozambique, he read for a second time Stanley Jones', *The Choice before Us*. Jones criticized both the capitalist and the communist political options held out for African development and highlighted the value of socio-political Christianity. Mondlane wrote, "This is a document of great interest, especially for people who still aspire to a satisfactory social organization for all people, but based on the Christian religion."[42]

Mondlane was still very much working within the framework of the development of a society based on Christian principles, largely emerging from the Protestant mission vision for Africa that was still very much alive at this time, even though his education and integrationist ideas were pushing the boundaries of that model. His enthusiastic work with the Laubach method of literacy training and his intentional development of relationships within the church on his return to Mozambique in this period highlight his dedication and commitment to the work of the church. Of critical importance to the future was the opportunity to work with Pastor Zedequias Manganhela and the Swiss missionary, Duvoisin, in Catembe. Mondlane seems to have gained a deep appreciation for the work of Manganhela. He wrote in the Duvoisin's guestbook in April, 1950, "Now I begin to understand what has been going around in my head: the zeal that I have found in Pastors Zédéquias and Bernardo Manganhela. I see now that they are the inheritors of their parents, who you are."[43] In the future, this developing relationship between the

42. Letter from Mondlane to Clerc, January 11, 1950, DM 913B, 2. "É um documento de grande interesse actual, especialmente para pessoas que ainda aspiram para uma organisação social satisfatória a todas as pessoas, mas baseada na religião cristã."

43. Mondlane in the guest book of the Duvoisin family in Matutwini, April 30, 1950, DM 474E, 1. "Maintenant je commence à comprendre ce qui me poursuivait dans ma tête: le zèle que j'ai trouvé chez les pasteurs Zédéquias et Bernardo Manganhela. Je vois maintenant qu'ils ont hérité de leurs 'parents' que vous êtes."

two church leaders was to prove fatal for Manganhela. The PIDE was relentless in trying to track what communication passed between the two men and believed that Manganhela provided the primary link and channel for FRELIMO within the country in large part because of this relationship. However, in 1950, these developments were still only in embryonic form. Mondlane was able to complete his first year of studies at Wits through a special arrangement which allowed Clerc to supervise his examinations and his primary concern remained how and where he would be able to continue his studies.

# 4

# Into the Heart of Empire

## Growing International and Ecumenical Connections

AFTER MONDLANE'S DEPORTATION FROM South Africa in 1949, it was left to André-Daniel Clerc to find an alternative way for him to complete his studies in order to be adequately qualified to coordinate the youth work in Lourenço Marques for which the Swiss Mission had been planning for some time. This was not an easy task. Mondlane was part of a first generation of African leaders to be sponsored to study abroad and there were many in the European and North American mission community who were extremely skeptical of this change. Although supportive of Mondlane, the Swiss Mission itself was cash poor and did not have the funds to finance his studies abroad. All of the funds which the Conselho Cristão de Moçambique (CCM) had pledged for Mondlane's studies had been used up in his time at the Jan Hofmeyer School[1] and there was little chance of any further funds being forthcoming from the CCM given the strong opposition of the American missionaries to this project, going back to the time of Mondlane's work at Cambine. In his report to the Administrative Committee of the Swiss Mission on May 15, 1950 Clerc wrote that there was a "very lively discussion in the course of which Mr. Juillerat, the representative of our mission, argued against the common front of the American missionaries."[2] The argument of the Americans

---

1. Letter from Clerc to Whyte October 5, 1949, DM 1172E, 4a.
2. "Rapport sur les études futures de Eduardo Mondlane" from Clerc to La Commission Administrative de la Mission Suisse, May 5, 1950, DM 913B, 9, "trés vive discussion au cours de laquelle M. Juillerat, représentant notre Mission, lutta contre le front commun des missionnaires américains."

was that those who were sent to study abroad rarely returned to work in their churches. However, it also would appear that there was a sectarian concern with Mondlane being a Presbyterian and not from one of the American missions. Despite their opposition, the Americans did agree to allow Mondlane to continue his studies as long as all support came from his own mission.

Clerc's growing divergence with the American missions and his doubts about the American educational system became very apparent in this period. His strong preference would have been for Mondlane to continue his studies in England, and indeed he was looking for a wealthy patron to support his studies there,[3] or elsewhere in Europe. However, it soon became clear that the greatest possibilities for financial support were in the United States. Clerc also revealed his strong anti-communist feelings at this time. When indicating that Mondlane would not be able to get a bursary to study in England because he was not from one of the British colonies, he wrote, "Moreover, it appears that the English communists are successfully eating up the African students."[4] In describing Mondlane's return from South Africa he also wrote that he could not have escaped suspicion since at the time the Portuguese authorities "were about to destroy a nest of communists."[5]

Clerc turned, it appears somewhat reluctantly, to possibilities of funding for study in the United States beyond the usual mission channels. He had extensive correspondence with Quinton Whyte, the Director of the South African Institute for Race Relations and also a member of the Carnegie Foundation. Whyte encouraged Clerc to look for funding through the Phelps Stokes Fund to finance Mondlane's continuing studies in the United States. An interesting aside is that Whyte requested a report from Clerc on the situation in Portuguese East Africa to be included in the Institute's documentation on the region. Clerc was hesitant to respond beyond providing official documents saying that issues concerning assimilation and native labor are "dynamite"[6] but he did provide the information that Whyte had requested.[7] This contact

3. Letter from Clerc to Mondlane, January 15, 1950, DM 913B, 3.
4. "Rapport sur les études", DM 913B, 9. "Au surplus, on s'est aperçu que les communistes anglais cuisinent les étudiants africains avec succès."
5. Ibid. "s'apprêtait à démolir un nid de communistes."
6. Letter from Clerc to Whyte, October 3, 1949, DM 1172E, 1b.
7. Letter from Whyte to Clerc, November 1, 1949, DM 1172E, 7.

with Whyte appears to have pressed Clerc in his analysis of the situation in Mozambique and also to have linked him to those in more liberal ecumenical circles in South Africa who were involved in a deeper analysis and protest of the apartheid policies of the new National Party government.

Whyte was one of the "European friends" of Mondlane in South Africa[8] who had supported him in his studies at Wits, had participated in the protest against his deportation and had pledged support for some alternative for his studies. This group also appears to have included Ray Phillips, the Director at the Jan Hofmeyr School.[9] Through them, Clerc was put in touch with Dr. Tobias, Director of the Phelps Stokes Fund. Through Darrell Randall, also a part of this group and now back in the United States after a brief sojourn in India, Clerc was directed to write to Dr. Emory Ross, the Chair of the Phelps Stokes Committee and someone with whom Clerc and Juillerat had both been in contact previously concerning literacy campaigns.[10] Mondlane himself was not absent in this process. He was in correspondence with Randall and it appears that both he and his wife Mildred were advocating for Mondlane's continuing studies in the United States. Mondlane received a letter from a Nigerian, Chukwunwubah Ezeami, who was already studying in the United States and who had heard of Mondlane's situation in a talk given by Mildred Randall[11], encouraging him to continue his studies. Although not antagonistic to Mondlane's direct connection with Randall, Clerc did caution him not to act alone in this matter.[12]

## A Complicated Plan for Lisbon

By May of 1950, Clerc seemed to have been able to develop a consensus among all parties concerning Mondlane's continuing studies. It was agreed that he would first go to Portugal to gain more grounding in Portuguese culture. Despite his reservations at delaying his studies further during this year of sojourn in Portugal, Clerc agreed to this because Mondlane was being watched closely by the Portuguese authori-

---

8. "Rapport sur les études," DM913B, 9.
9. Ibid.
10. Ibid.
11. Letter from Mondlane to Clerc, February 22, 1950, DM 913B, 5.
12. Letter from Clerc to Mondlane, January 15, 1950, DM 913B, 3.

ties and he clearly believed that they would see that Mondlane was not a threat through this experience. It was proposed for Mondlane to leave Mozambique in June so that he would be able to do a summer course in Coimbra or Lisbon for the *maitre de portugais à l'étranger* and then spend ten months in a course at the Lycée or the University depending on what credit they would give him for his matric in South Africa "without latin or sciences or maths."[13] The trip to Portugal was to be paid for by the money collected by Mondlane's "friends in Johannesburg" and the courses by the Phelps Stokes Fund (PSF). The PSF would also appoint an advisor and a treasurer for Mondlane in Portugal and the Swiss Mission would contribute 5,000 ecus annually as a contribution to his tuition fees. Clerc added that this would be the first time that a black Protestant from Mozambique would study in Portugal and that it would not be easy for him because of his religious convictions.

This somewhat complicated resolution to get Mondlane to Portugal did provide him with the financial and organizational support he would need. However, the paternalism involved was not lost on Mondlane, now a man of thirty years of age who had passed his first year of study in a Bachelor's program and had proven himself in his work in the Swiss Mission. Although he makes no comment on it, the irony could not have been lost on him that Clerc's son Etienne was beginning studies in Johannesburg at the same time[14], significantly younger and with no necessity of such a complicated system of support. It is clear that the parties involved did not feel that Mondlane was able to administer his own personal funds and that he must be, at best, "guided", in his financial decision making. Despite his deep appreciation for the church support for his studies, Mondlane was also made acutely aware of the different procedure which he was made to follow because of his race and his coming out of the paternalistic mission structures. This would become clearer and more problematic for him as time went on.

Mondlane sailed on the *Angola* from Lourenço Marques. He was not able to arrange a 3rd class berth and so shared sleeping quarters with eight "Europeans" and took his meals with the 3rd class passengers.[15] Still, after the initial sea sickness abated and despite getting tired of eating cod and potatoes, he enjoyed the trip. The ship stopped

13. "Rapport sur les études", DM913B, 9, "sans latin ni sciences ni maths."
14. Letter from Mondlane to Clerc, January 20, 1950, DM 913B, 4.
15. Letter from Mondlane to Clerc, June 16, 1950, DM 913B, 10.

in Cape Town, Lobito, Luanda and São Tomé. It is interesting to note that all along this route Mondlane attempted to make contact with the Protestant missions and to learn more about the work they were doing as well as to make comparisons with the mission work in Mozambique. In Lobito, a tourist took him to meet an American missionary who in turn offered to take him to Benguela, probably to the United Church of Canada mission. He was impressed that the Angolan church members had raised money for the travel of three Canadian missionaries to a World Sunday School Conference. He was also impressed that in the mission school children of white missionaries were studying with Angolan children, at least up to *4a classe*. On the train ride back from Benguela to Lobito, Mondlane met some young men who invited him to their home for supper. He was pleased to find out that the family was also Protestant. In Lobito he also commented favorably on the number of cars the mission possessed (three). In Luanda, Mondlane went immediately to what he describes as the "magnificent" home of Dr. Tucker, an American Congregationalist missionary and the head of the Aliança Evangélica in Angola, with whom Mondlane would have continuing contact in the future. He visited a mission school and the offices of the Protestant newspaper, the *Estandarte* and was impressed with both. In São Tomé, he visited an Adventist school.[16]

### Arrival in Lisbon and Connection with the Presbyterian Church

Mondlane was not so impressed on his arrival in Lisbon. Although he says that the rich neighborhoods of Lisbon would rival anything that could be found in Johannesburg or Pretoria, he was horrified by the poverty which he encountered in the streets of the metropole.[17] He was met in Lisbon by representatives of Jose de Silva Barbosa, Michael Testa and Almeida. Michael Testa, an American Presbyterian missionary of Portuguese origin was named as Mondlane's advisor. Testa was also to have an ongoing relationship with Mondlane and would have a significant influence in funding for FRELIMO in later years in his role as Representative in Europe for the Board for World Ministries of The United Presbyterian Church in the USA and The United Church of Christ (U.S.A.) and Consultant on Mozambique for the Commission on Inter-

---

16. Letter from Mondlane to Clerc, July 4, 1950, DM 914A, 1.
17. Ibid.

Church Aid, Refugee and World Service of the WCC. Already some difficulties had begun with the arrangements for funding; monies received were not enough for his upkeep and the PSF had not yet sent any funds.[18] After some conversation with other Mozambicans he had met in Lisbon, Mondlane realized that the housing arranged for him was not adequate. In a move that proved to be very advantageous to Mondlane's stay in Lisbon, at least in his connection with the church there, Michael Testa arranged for him to stay at the Presbyterian Seminary in Carcavelos.[19]

On his arrival in Lisbon, Mondlane received an invitation from P. Fatton to attend the 75th anniversary celebrations of the Swiss Mission in Lausanne between the summer and winter terms.[20] This experience would prove to be one of the highlights of Mondlane's stay in Europe and perhaps one of the first examples of what would become known as "reverse mission", that is someone from the "mission field" being present, even for a short period of time, in the "sending" church community in order to teach and evangelize. Although, rightly, much has been discussed concerning the contact which Mondlane made with future revolutionary leaders from other Portuguese colonies during his time in Lisbon[21], the connections which he made with the leadership of the Swiss Mission and other future leaders of the ecumenical movement were also significant for him and for the support they would lend to the developing independence movement in Mozambique.

## Relationship with Georgette Libombo

It was also at this time that Mondlane's relationship with Georgette Libombo began to become problematic. Mondlane had begun a relationship with her when he was in Lourenço Marques following his year at the Jan Hofmeyr School and she was part of the group of students involved in the formation of NESAM. Her father, Enoque Libombo, was an *assimilado,* and an influential figure in the colonial society of Lourenço Marques. He was an Executive member of the Conselho da Missão Suíça as well as President of the Centro Associativo dos Negros. He worked in the City Hall and was well connected in the Portuguese

---

18. Letter from E. Holden to P. Lombard, MSAS, July 14, 1950, DM 1577B, 1.
19. Letter from Mondlane to Clerc, July 27, 1950, DM 914A, 3.
20. Letter from Mondlane to Clerc, July 4, 1950, DM 914A, 1.
21. Cruz e Silva, *Protestant Churches*, 116.

community. It seems that he wanted his daughter to advance within the colonial society as well and was less than pleased to find out that she was involved with Mondlane. Janet Mondlane writes that Libombo saw Mondlane as a peasant who spoke Shangaan from the countryside rather than the Ronga of the city. In addition, he believed that he was going to become a Presbyterian pastor with an inadequate income. On the other hand, Janet Mondlane suggests that Libombo was threatened by Mondlane's outgoing character, his education and his potential to advance in Mozambican society.[22] So, despite his influential position in the church, he was not willing to encourage his daughter to live the life of a pastor's wife and forbade her to have any contact with Mondlane. Nevertheless, they continued to write and the relationship appears to have developed during the time that Mondlane spent in Mozambique after his deportation from South Africa.

After his arrival in Lisbon, Mondlane was concerned about the lack of correspondence from Georgette and wrote to Clerc to ask him if his wife might intervene.[23] Despite Clerc's hesitations, his family did become involved in the ongoing relationship between Georgette Libombo and Mondlane. Although the melodrama of much of the correspondence, and lack thereof, suggests two people with little experience in romance, their relationship also demonstrated at least two important tensions which would be significant for Mondlane's future. First, the differences with Enoque Libombo demonstrated a division within the Presbyterian Church in terms of collaboration with the Portuguese regime. There were Protestants who were convinced that the future of Mozambique lay with Portugal and that faith should not be used to critique the colonial project. Mondlane's most frequent criticism of Georgette, and indeed of many young Mozambican women, was that they used all their energy and time in fashion and parties and were not concerned with the serious issues confronting the country. Second, Mondlane had to come to terms with what the appropriate intervention of the missionary community should be in his personal relationships. Although he himself opened the door to the Clercs' intervention in this case, his future experience in his relationship with Janet Johnson would be quite different. As was the case with his personal finances, the paternalism of the mission community would be revealed in its interventions in his personal relationships and

22. Nadja Manghezi, *O meu Coracão está nas Mãos de um Negro*, 99–100.
23. Letter from Mondlane to Clerc, July 27, 1950, DM 914A, 3.

indeed would lead in large part to Mondlane's disillusion with much of the mission model of the church in which he had grown.

## Participation in the 75th Anniversary of the Swiss Mission in Lausanne

Mondlane's visit to Switzerland on the occasion of the 75th anniversary of the Swiss Mission was hailed by all as a great success. In addition to participating in the actual celebrations, Mondlane travelled extensively in the *Romande* as well as in German speaking parts of the country and was well covered in the religious and secular press. He was received as the "real Chitlango" and drew crowds wherever he spoke, especially among young people. He spoke three times in St. Francis Church in Lausanne to more than two thousand people on each occasion.[24] Still, in many cases Mondlane was seen as something of an novelty, an African who could communicate within the complexities of European culture. Mondlane may have been pioneering in terms of "reverse mission" but he was still working within the assumptions of the nineteenth century Protestant mission paradigm. An article in *La Vie Protestante*, clearly illustrates this:

> When we talk about work in the mines, Alan Paton's book, *Cry the Beloved Country,* the mix of races in Africa, we are on the same level. Your clear-sighted intelligence weighs the nuances and places you in the larger picture as if you had a long tradition of European thought behind you. And I admire the miracle of Christian communion: yesterday your ancestors were natives dominated by the laws of the jungle, terrorized by the mysterious forces of nature and the tyranny of witchcraft. Today, faced with the problems of contemporary life, you have the reflective and concerted responses of an aspiring philosopher, you ask for the best solutions from your faith and from the culture of the old world; you know how to work, on your part, for a better world in the future, in justice and truth, without pomposity and without wild illusions.[25]

24. Letter from Mondlane to Clerc, November 29, 1950, DM 914B, 5.

25. "Edouard Mondlane" in *Vie Protestante*, October 28, 1950, DM 914B, 7. "Que l'on parle du travail dans les mines, du livre d'Alan Paton: *Pleure, ô pays bien aimé*, du mélange des races en Afrique, nous somme de plain-pied. Votre lucide intelligence mesure les nuances et s'établit sur le plan général comme si vous aviez derrière vous une longue tradition de pensée européenne. Et j'admire le miracle de la communion chrétienne: hier vos ancêtres étaient des indigénes dominés par les lois de la jungle, ter-

Clerc commented on Mondlane's travels in Switzerland from Lourenço Marques, perhaps with a touch of resentment given some of his disillusion on his last visit to Switzerland, that "a Swiss person does not awaken such interest as an African in Switzerland. A prophet is not accepted . . ."[26] However, he clearly saw the importance of this tour for the work of the mission and supported Mondlane's participation. Perhaps Alain Reymond, the General Secretary of the MSAS at the time had the most insightful comment on the impact of Mondlane's visit. In his thank you letter to Mondlane he wrote, "It was extremely valuable that an African Christian established a living contact between the Church of southern Africa and the Church which has sent and continues to send missionaries . . . Thank you for the reflections that you gave in the presence of the Assembly of the delegates from the Mission or from the Council concerning mission work. You know that we are trying hard to adapt the mission work to the new conditions, and that we always want to think more about the preparation of Church officers, about the training of leaders."[27]

For Mondlane himself, his visit to Switzerland was an opportunity to expand his thinking and his contacts beyond the local mission community. He wrote that he "had time to talk with very interesting people about the social, political and religious problems of the world."[28] He was impressed with the knowledge that people in Switzerland had

---

rorisés par les forces mystérieuses de la nature et la tyrannie des sorciers. Aujourd'hui, devant les problémes de la vie contemporaine, vous avez les réactions réfléchies et concertées d'un philosophe en herbe, vous demandez a votre foi et à la culture du vieux monde les solutions les plus favorables; vous entendez travailler, pour votre part, a l'avènement d'un monde meilleur, dans la justice et la vérité, sans grandiloquence et sans chimériques illusions."

26. Letter from Clerc to Mondlane, December 12, 1950, DM 914B, 2, "um Suisso não desperta tanto interesse como um africano na Suissa. Não há profeta . . ."

27. Letter from Alain Reymond to Mondlane, January 25, 1951, DM 1577C, 1. "C'était extrêmement précieux qu'un Chrétien africain établisse un contact vivant entre l'Eglise du sud d'Afrique et l'Eglise qui a envoyé et continue d'envoyer les missionnaires . . . Merci des réflexions que vous avez émises en présence de l'Assemblée des délégués de la Mission ou du Conseil concernant le travail missionnaire. Vous savez que nous nous efforçons d'adapter ce travail missionnaire aux conditions nouvelles, et que nous voulons penser toujours davantage à la preparation des responsables de l'Eglise, à la formation des 'leaders.'"

28. Letter from Mondlane to Clerc, January 28, 1951, DM 914D, 2, "tive tempo de conversar com pessoas muito interessantes sobre os problemas sociais, políticos e religiosos do mundo."

about the situation in southern Africa and the number of people who had read Alan Paton's book, *Cry the Beloved Country*. Although already interpreting the Mozambican situation for colleagues in Portugal, it seems that Mondlane was freer in Switzerland to speak about the needs of the territory and the situation facing the church. Mondlane was also able to visit Paris on his return to Portugal where it seems he met with Jaqueline Eberhardt who was working on a doctorate in sociology.[29] He attended an opera as well as visiting many other cultural sites. His world was expanding and he was beginning to understand his own potential in advocating for his people in this broader context. However, he also continued to experience the limitations which the mission structures placed upon him. The complicated manner in which his finances were organized led to some confusion over how his trip to Switzerland would be paid. The treasurer of the MSAS in Lausanne, Pierre Lombard, assumed that the cost would come from the monies designated for Mondlane's year of studies in Portugal and wrote to Clerc in Mozambique to make up the difference needed for Mondlane's second term. Although this situation was later clarified, the assumptions made were not lost on Mondlane. In a letter to Clerc he wrote, "Look, I never dreamed that my travel to Switzerland would have to be paid by me. But in the end, this is how it is."[30]

## Studies in Lisbon and next steps

Following his trip to Switzerland, Clerc was anxious for Mondlane to get on with his studies and return to Mozambique to take up the work that was waiting for him. There were few Presbyterians going on to higher studies and the mission was suffering for it; one of the few people moving forward with his education was Mondlane's friend Novidades Honwana. Clerc was also feeling the pressure from the American missionaries in Mozambique who believed that Mondlane would not return. They were particularly critical of Darrell Randall; Clerc said that "they become upset every time the name of Mr. Randall is mentioned."[31] He also returned to suggesting that after a stay in Switzerland Mondlane might reconsider

29. Letter from Mondlane to Clerc, November 29, 1950, DM 914B, 5.

30. Letter from Mondlane to Clerc, February, 1950, DM 914D, 3. "Ora eu nunca sonhei que a minha ida para a Suiça devia ser paga por mim. Mas a final vem a ser assim."

31. Letter from Clerc to Mondlane, December 12, 1950, DM 914B, 2, "tornam-se nervosos cada vez que se menciona o nome de Mr. Randall."

studying in a European country rather than in the United States. In perhaps his most damning critique of the American educational system, he wrote: "This bath in classical culture which we have to take in Latin writers offers a great opportunity to measure the distance which separates the cultures of Continental Europe from those of England and, above all, the United States. These differences appear even afterward between Continental and American missionaries who, on a very clear point, can feel and understand in quite opposite ways."[32]

At this point however, Mondlane was more convinced than ever that he should continue his studies in the United States. He continued to correspond with Darrell Randall and by Christmas 1950 he had received word from Randall that everything was prepared for him to enter Oberlin College in Ohio. It is interesting to see how Mondlane turns Clerc's words on himself, particularly concerning the communist influence in European countries when he writes, "Engand and France would not be good places because of politics. The Portuguese would not look at me favorably after some years in London or Paris. Here in Lisbon there are many who think that the English socialist government is a compromise with communism. And in this respect, Paris is worse."[33] In responding to Clerc about the concerns of the American missionaries, that he would not return to Mozambique, he wrote, "Personally and at the present time, I am convinced that the same spirit that forces me to continue my studies at this age rather than beginning to work to earn my living is the same one that will force me to return to my country to work there. I have a mission which I must complete. I feel called to work among 'my' sisters and brothers of color. God help me that I will never waver from the goal I have in sight."[34]

32. Letter from Clerc to Mondlane, April 9, 1951, DM 914D, 5. "Esse banho de cultura clássica que nos tivemos que tomar nos autores latinos oferece-lhe boa oportunidade de medir as distâncias que separam as culturas da Europa Continental das de Inglaterra e, sobretudo, dos U.S.A. Essas diferenças aparecem mesmo, depois entre missionários continentais e americanos que, num ponto claro, podem sentir e compreender de maneira muito oposta."

33. Letter from Mondlane to Clerc, December 24, 1950, DM 914B, 3. "A Inglaterra e a França não seriam bons lugares por causa da política. Os portugueses não me viam com bons depois de alguns anos em Londres ou Paris. Aquí em Lisboa há muitos que pensam que o governo socialista inglês é um compromisso com o comunismo. E neste respeito Paris é peor."

34. Ibid. "Pessoalmente e presentemente estou convencido de que o mesmo espírito que me força a continuar os meus estudos nesta idade em vez de começar a trabalhar

*Into the Heart of Empire* 57

As in South Africa, Mondlane was very dedicated to his studies but also became deeply involved in church and mission life beyond the walls of the classroom. Living at the Seminary in Carcavelos gave him the opportunity to be in contact with a variety of church organizations and movements. In addition to his studies at the University of Lisbon, he registered to do a Religious Education course in the Seminary. He became a member of the Comissão Cultural da Juventude Evangélica Portuguesa and preached regularly at local churches. In addition, he met many of the new missionaries of the Swiss Mission who came to Lisbon to study Portuguese language and culture and often assisted them in Tsonga language learning. It was in this capacity that he met and began a lifelong friendship with Georges and Juliette Morier Genoud; Georges would later become the General Secretary of the Département Missionnaire.[35] Mondlane was held in high esteem by many in leadership in the Presbyterian Church in Portugal. In a letter to Jean Badertscher, the General Secretary of the MSAS, just after Mondlane's arrival in Lisbon, Michael Testa wrote, "He impresses us all as an outstanding young man whose life presents a clear Christian witness . . . He is highly regarded by the twenty or more missionaries who are here for language study, and he attends all our devotional meetings and social events."[36] Later, he wrote again, "We are very happy to have Mr. Mondlane stay here in the Seminary where we feel that he lends a magnificent contribution to Christian fellowship with our students. We do not doubt the admiration for him and we feel that the Swiss Mission is very happy to have chosen such a talented and devoted young man to receive the benefits of advanced study, so that in the future he will be able to make a meaningful contribution to his own people in Mozambique."[37] In yet

---

para ganhar a minha vida é o mesmo que me forçara a regressar para a minha terra para trabalhar lá. Eu tenho uma missão que devo satisfazer. Sinto me chamado para trabalhar entre os "meus" irmãos de cor. Deus me ajude para que nunca me desoriento no alvo que tenho em vista."

35. Ibid.

36. Letter from Michael Testa to Jean Badertscher, August 24, 1950. DM 1577B, 5.

37. Letter from Michael Testa to Jean Badertscher, March 9, 1951, DM 1577C, 5. "Nous sommes bien aises d'avoir Mr. Mondlane demeurant ici dans le Séminaire où nous sentons qu'il prête une contribution magnifique de communion chrétienne avec nos étudiants. Nous n'éprouvons que de l'admiration pour lui et nous sentons que la Mission Suisse est bien heureuse d'avoir choisi un si talentueux et dévoué jeune homme pour recevoir les bénéfices d'un cours avancé, pour qu'il puisse dans l'avenir rendre une contribution expressive á ses propres gens en Mozambique."

another letter to Badertscher two months later he wrote, "I am very happy to inform you that Mr. Mondlane continues to impress us with his marvelous Christian spirit and his excellent qualities as a student. He is set to achieve a good academic record at the University."[38]

## Connections with Other African Students and Scrutiny by the PIDE

Whatever political contacts Mondlane may have had while in Lisbon, it is clear that the focus of his life there was in the church and in preparing himself to return to Mozambique to work with youth in the Swiss Mission. Mondlane met with other black and mixed race Mozambicans in the Casa dos Estudantes do Império and, it seems, was present when the Centro de Estudos Africanos was established in 1951.[39] Cruz e Silva comments on his time in Lisbon from conversations with several other significant independence leaders present at the time that "while many African students coming to Lisbon from Portuguese colonies tried incessantly to *find their African roots,* Mondlane was the only one among them who had no need for such a search. He was imbued with them, maintaining that he had never distanced himself from his origins."[40] It can be argued that, at least in large part, this strong sense of connectedness with his African origins was related to Mondlane's upbringing and education in the Swiss Mission. Although far from embodying what would later be known as "inculturation" in its approach to mission, its longstanding commitment to understanding and respecting indigenous languages and culture meant that Mondlane was never faced with the stark choice of remaining "African" or becoming "civilized" as was so clearly presented in the assimilation process of "Portugalization." At the same time, his deep integration into the life of the Protestant church was perhaps why Mondlane left Portugal without the kind of radical critique of colonialism developed by others. The "mission" church still presented an alternative to him within the colonial structures which could provide

---

38. Letter from Testa to Badertscher, May 7, 1951. DM 1577C, 6. "Je suis bien heureux de vous informer que M. Mondlane continue á nous impressionner avec son merveilleux esprit Chrétien et ses excellentes qualités d'étudiant. Il est en train d'achever un bon record scolaire á l'Université."

39. Mondlane, *The Struggle for Mozambique*, 114–15.

40. Cruz e Silva, *Protestant Churches*, 116.

a certain degree of dignity and advancement without calling for transformation through a revolutionary struggle.

Despite this difference, Mondlane was under scrutiny by the PIDE like other students coming from the colonies such as Marcelino dos Santos, Agostinho Neto, Mário Pinto de Andrade and Amílcar Cabral. On at least two occasions he was interrogated and it is clear that he continued under surveillance during his time in Lisbon. In August 1950, his room was searched and he was taken in for questioning. In a letter to Clerc he wrote, "It is clear that they were sent by the government to see if I had any subversive documents and afterward they took out a citation to go and respond to questions at the International Police."[41] Unfortunately, the second page of this letter is missing where it would seem that Mondlane describes the actual interrogation. While he was arranging his passport to travel to the United States, he was again brought in for interrogation by the PIDE.[42] Finally, he was delayed one day in leaving Lisbon when the police at the airport said that his passport was not in order. It is interesting to note though that this situation was rectified quickly after Mondlane contacted the chief of police.[43] He did not have the same problems with the PIDE as several other students had and the fact that he was allowed to leave and study in the United States would appear to indicate that they did not consider him to be a serious threat at that time. Indeed, in light of his future conversations with Portuguese officials in the United States, it would appear that they felt Mondlane could be co-opted into a Portuguese plan for colonial reform.

Very little of what the PIDE knew about Mondlane, or indeed what they were searching for, is extant in the remaining records.[44] It appears that he was being watched by a person who befriended him during his

---

41. Letter from Mondlane to Clerc, August 1950. DM 914A, 6. "É certo que foram mandados pelo governo para ver se eu tinha documentos subversivos depois levam uma intimação para ir responder perguntas na Polícia Internacional."

42. Letter from Mondlane to Clerc, May 12, 1951, DM 914D, 6.

43. Letter from Mondlane to Clerc, July 20, 1951, DMA 915A, 2.

44. The archives of the PIDE and DGS are housed in the *Instituto dos Arquivos Nacionais/Torre do Tombo* of the *Ministério de Cultura, Arquivo da PIDE/DGS* in Lisbon (hereafter known as TT PIDE/DGS). All of the PIDE/DGS documents in Lourenço Marques were destroyed at the time of the revolution in Portugal in 1974 and the subsequent negotiations with FRELIMO. However, there is some material concerning Mozambique available from files from Lisbon, Luanda and other locations. All of the material which was found related to this present work was dated from 1961 forward.

time in Lisbon. He wrote to Clerc: "This is a colleague of mine called Eduardo Jorge Larcher de Brito, 31 years old, a lieutenant in the army, graduate of the Colonial School and Director at a school for Professional Development for young women graduates of commercial studies. Currently he is a voluntary student in the Arts Faculty."[45] Mondlane added that this man and his wife knew that he was Protestant and they were practicing Catholics but that this was not a problem. He studied in their home and they came to the Seminary to play ping pong, etc. There is no direct evidence naming them as informers for PIDE but given his background it would seem that their interest was not simply in friendship. Either Mondlane was very naïve about this or he knew and was simply communicating the information to Clerc without directly revealing his knowledge of the situation. Michael Testa or others in the Presbyterian Church may have warned Mondlane of this situation as they were also closely watched by the PIDE because of their international connections and Protestant beliefs.

## Departure for the United States

Mondlane left Portugal having been introduced to a much broader range of people and ideas and with a greatly expanded world view. However, he did not leave with clearly defined political views and goals, much less a clear revolutionary path. As Herbert Shore has written, "Mondlane came to the United States still a staunch and dedicated Christian, firm in the belief that the principles and teachings of Christianity, applied to the political and social world, could form the basis for the ultimate liberation of his people.[46]

Beyond what Shore has written, however, it is important to place Mondlane within a particular stream of Christianity to understand what those principles and teachings were and what their application might produce for him. This same statement could have been made about those holding the mixture of conservative theological beliefs and nationalism embodied in the *Concordat* between the Portuguese state and

---

45. Letter from Mondlane to Clerc, June 12, 1951. DM 914D, 10. "Trata-se de um colega meu chamado Eduardo Jorge Larcher de Brito, de 31 anos de idade, tenente do exército, diplomado da Escola Superior Colonial e director de uma escola de aperfeiçoamento professional para raparigas diplomadas do ensino commercial. Presentemente é aluno voluntário da faculdade de letras."

46. Shore, "Resistance and Revolution," xxi.

the Roman Catholic Church. Mondlane, though, was squarely located in the Protestant Christian paradigm and particularly within its mission practice. The Christian vision which he held was one which was clearly connected with modern, progressive thought and which held out the possibility of a more egalitarian society increasingly based on the principles of universal human rights. His experience in Portugal opened him to the emerging global ecumenical movement, grounded in European and North American liberal Protestantism, but also responding to the need for a deeper social and political critique and engagement in the face of decolonization and the Cold War. Many in the Protestant churches recognized his potential as a future leader in this movement and although his sights were still firmly set on returning to Mozambique and living out Clerc's dream, a much larger vision was beginning to emerge both in his own mind and in the minds of those in the ecumenical movement with whom he had come in contact.

# 5

## Study in the United States—Oberlin College

### Arrival in the United States and Participation in Missionary Orientation Program

MONDLANE'S TRANSPORTATION PLANS CHANGED quickly from ship to plane after receiving an invitation to participate in a training program for missionaries in Hartford, Connecticut in July of 1951. According to Mondlane, the money for the plane ticket came from "Dr. Dodge", Ralph Dodge, formerly a missionary in Angola but at that time the Executive Secretary for Africa for the Board of Mission of the Methodist Episcopal Church in the United States. Dodge was considered to be a radical in the mission community and was already providing funding for African students to study in the United States in order to build up indigenous leadership and to move toward independence. His connection with Mondlane would continue during his time in the United States and also when Dodge returned to Africa as Bishop of the Africa Central Conference of the Methodist Church. Dodge would later work with Mondlane and FRELIMO in providing many Mozambican students with bursaries for study in Europe and the United States. The differences with the more conservative missionary community in Mozambique in this regard can be seen in Mondlane's comments after his arrival. "There are Methodist students here in the United States from all parts of the world except Inhambane. I repeat what I said about a year ago: that we Africans of Mozambique will be the 'Kaffirs' of Africa."[1]

---

1. Letter from Mondlane to Clerc, August 3, 1951, DM 915A, 5. "Há aqui nos Estados

It seems that Julian Rea, the head of the American Methodist mission in Mozambique had done everything he could to prevent Mondlane from going to study in the United States including writing to the Methodist Mission Board and holding it against Mondlane that he had been questioned by the police in Lourenço Marques.[2] Once in the United States, Mondlane benefited from a more direct contact with the executive staff of both the Methodist and the Presbyterian Mission Boards and was able to have an influence on their policy on Mozambique that at least rivaled the Inhambane mission community and would continue to cause tension.

In the missionary training program in Hartford, he worked with a "young Canadian university professor" in giving lessons on Bantu languages for new mission personnel planning to work in Africa.[3] Contrary to what Cruz e Silva writes, this was not a program for "experts studying Bantu phonetics,"[4] but rather the usual linguistic and language training that was supplied to any new missionaries preparing for service overseas, similar to the work Mondlane had done for the Swiss Mission personnel in Lisbon. It appears that this was an ecumenical program which also included Congregationalists; he later travelled with a participant, Gilbert Whitney, a Congregationalist going to their mission in Inhambane, to his home in Ann Arbor Michigan en route to Chicago.[5] This program would have given Mondlane a good introduction to the energy of the growing ecumenical movement in the United States and to the changing understanding of world mission which would have been explored in its different sessions. Mondlane too would have made a significant contribution, again, within the concept of "reverse mission" in being a voice from the "mission field." In fact it seems, in light of the tensions between him and the American Methodist missionaries, he felt he needed to be quite critical of the older mission paradigm. "I feel that I cannot give the necessary help to these young missionaries here if I present missionary

---

Unidos estudantes metodistas de todas as partes do mundo excepto de Inhambane. Repito aquilo que disse a quasi um ano: que nós os Africanos de Moçambique sere os 'cafres' da Africa."

2. Ibid.
3. Ibid.
4. Cruz e Silva, *Protestant Churches*, 117.
5. Letter from Mondlane to Clerc, August 31, 1951, DM 915A, 6.

work as a beautiful field of flowers, or if I attribute all the problems of the work to the Africans, shining up the old missionaries with gold polish."[6]

## New York City

This program began a whirlwind tour for him before he ever began his studies at Oberlin College. In New York City, he made his first visit of many to the United Nations building. He also spent time at Riverside Church. Darrell Randall had attended Riverside when he was a student at Columbia University, and, it seems, had planted the idea of helping to build the Youth Centre in Lourenço Marques. Mondlane met with the "Comissão dos serviços de beneficência", the Benficence Services Committee, which promised $1,500 for the project. This money was used to buy the property on which the youth center was to be built east of Chamanculo Hospital in Lourenço Marques.[7] He spent time with the youth group and had supper at the home of Dr. Norris Tibbets, one of the pastors of the church. This began a long lasting relationship for Mondlane with Riverside Church, one of the most progressive Protestant churches in the United States.[8] He also visited the Presbyterian Board of Foreign Mission where his name was well known because of his contact with Michael Testa. He wrote to Clerc, "I haven't forgotten that I am a *Presbyterian!*"[9] However, he also let Clerc know that, like him, the American Presbyterians were surprised that the Swiss Mission was not sending more students to the Presbyterian Seminary in Carcavelos for further study.[10] Here, Mondlane's critique of the Methodists passed over to the Presbyterians and indeed to Clerc himself as he continued to emphasize the need for leadership training for Mozambican Protestants and, consequently, a more autonomous church. Mondlane also visited the offices of the Methodist Mission Board and the Phelps Stokes Fund. He had dinner with Dr. Murray Ross, the Chair of the Phelps Stokes Committee with whom Clerc had been in contact and with a government

---

6. Letter from Mondlane to Clerc, August 3, 1951, DM 915A, 5. "Sinto que não poderei dar a ajuda necessária a estes jovens missionários aqui se apresentar o trabalho missionário como um lindo campo de flores, ou se eu atribuir todas as dificuldades do trabalho aos africanos, polindo os velhos missionários com lustro dourado."

7. Letter from Clerc to Mondlane, October 12, 1952, DM 915B, 11.

8. Letter from Mondlane to Clerc, August 31, 1951, DM 915A, 6.

9. Ibid. "Não me esqueço que sou *presbiteriano!*"

10. Ibid.

official from Uganda, Mr. Mukasa, who was looking at questions of technical education in the United States.[11] Again, it is clear that Mondlane was already held in high regard by the leadership in the Protestant mission boards and the ecumenical movement and, it appears, more in touch with their changing policies and practices than many personnel "in the field" in Mozambique.

## Chicago and the Ecumenical Youth Movement

Mondlane mentions visiting some Presbyterian churches in New England which supported Michael Testa in Portugal but does not elaborate. It seems that shortly after his time in New York, he left with Gilbert Whitney for Ann Arbor and then on to Chicago where he stayed with the Randalls. By this time, Darrell Randall was working on a Ph.D. in Economic Planning. Mondlane was impressed by the city and by the university, particularly by the large African American community and by the number of Nigerians studying at the university and throughout the United States.[12] From Chicago, he travelled to an interdenominational youth conference at Lake Geneva, Wisconsin sponsored by the United Christian Youth Movement, an ecumenical organization that brought together young people from fourteen different denominations. Mondlane describes it as being "under the World Council of Churches."[13] It was here that he first met Janet Johnson who would later become his wife. Mondlane wrote with obvious approval that "the organizers tried to call the attention of the youth of the Protestant churches to the spiritual, social, economic, political and moral problems of our times and to suggest a Christian response to the same."[14] Certainly one of the major issues facing the U.S. churches was that of race and there was discussion of the issue in the camp but more interestingly the camp itself also reflected the problems of racial segregation and discrimination practiced in the United States in its very organization. Janet Mondlane remembers

---

11. Ibid. Mondlane describes him as the Prime Minister of Uganda in his letter. It is not clear who this was, possibly Balamu Mukasa who was Secretary of the Democratic Party in Uganda.

12. Ibid.

13. Ibid.

14. Ibid., "os organizadores tentaram chamar a atenção da juventude das igrejas evangélicas para os problemas espirituais, sociais, económicos, políticos e morais dos nossos dias e indicar a solução cristã dos mesmos."

that on the application form she had to complete for the camp, she was asked if she would be willing to share a cabin with a "negro."[15] Although the camp was broadly ecumenical, only eight participants were African Americans. At the end of the camp, eight young white men "openly decided to fight against the racial prejudices they had before coming."[16] These were the early days of the growing consciousness of the civil rights movement and the churches' involvement, especially through the ecumenical movement and even more particularly through the youth. Mondlane and his future wife found themselves immersed in this dynamic and indeed their growing relationship soon brought them face to face with the deep seated racism of U.S. society.

As well as dealing with racism as manifested in the United States, Mondlane began his campaign to bring a more realistic picture of the African context to American people. "I tried to clean up some of the ideas that many of them—including the blacks—had of Africa."[17] As he would in countless other camps and youth gatherings during his stay in the United States, Mondlane spoke of the reality of life in Mozambique in a way that his audience could understand and with a style that attracted people to listen. Mondlane found in the dynamism of the ecumenical movement, both in North America and in Europe, and especially among the vibrant youth movement of the 1950s, a force which he believed could significantly change the relationship of these continents with Africa and be the foundation of a transformed and racially equal church which would be in the vanguard of a transformed African society. In these gatherings, Mondlane met and influenced many young people who were interested in "mission" overseas but who were also much more profoundly aware of the need to challenge the paternalistic mission paradigm of the past and to work as equals with African colleagues. Indeed, Janet Johnson was interested in being a medical missionary when she met Mondlane but even at that time had a very different understanding of the role of a missionary and emphasized the practical side of what she could do to help in improving the lives of African people.[18] In a letter

---

15. Manghezi, *Meu coração*, 19.

16. Letter from Mondlane to Clerc, August 31, 1951. DM 915, 6, "decidiram-se abertamente lutar contra os preconceitos raciais que tinham antes de vir."

17. Ibid. "Tentei limpar algumas das ideias que muitos deles—incluindo os negros—tinham da Africa."

18. Manghezi, *Meu coração*, 20.

to Clerc, Mondlane said that he met several young women who were interested in being missionaries but does not mention Janet Johnson by name. A relationship did begin at this camp but it would not become more widely known for some time.

Before going on to two other youth gatherings, an American Methodist Youth Convocation in Purdue University and a Conference of the United Christian Youth Movement National Commission, Mondlane returned to Chicago where he went to hear a talk by a Ugandan speaking about the situation in Uganda, Kenya and Tanganyika. After the lecture, he found himself embroiled in a very heated discussion about South Africa. His comments are very telling of where his thinking was at the time in relation to the situation in South Africa: "They attacked the Union of South Africa without understanding what they were talking about. They really over generalized. I indicated to them that they should read more than they have read about South Africa. They didn't like me at all. They thought that I was one of those ignorant people who have never been in South Africa."[19] The next day he had a chance for more conversation and he felt they were more receptive. However, he said that when he spoke again he was going "to try to show that South Africa has many good things that they don't know about."[20] It is clear here that, again, Mondlane was far from espousing a revolutionary political agenda for southern Africa when he arrived in the United States. Indeed, he found himself opposed to many who believed that a radical political transformation was the only avenue to overcome the colonial and apartheid structures. Even after his experience of deportation from South Africa, it would appear that he still believed that the country could be reformed from within inspired by a Christian vision of a just and egalitarian society. Once again, as in Switzerland, he was surprised by the popularity of Paton's, *Cry the Beloved Country* in the United States, and it seems that he often used the book as a basis for a discussion on South Africa.

---

19. Ibid. "Atacam a União da África do Sul sem compreender de que estão a falar. Generalizam demais. Indiquei-lhes que deviam ler mais do que leem sobre a África do Sul. Não gostaram nada de mim. Pensaram que eu era um dos ignorantes que nunca estiveram na África do Sul."

20. Ibid., "tentar mostrar que a África do Sul tem muitas coisas boas que eles não sabem."

## Arrival at Oberlin College

Mondlane began his studies in Oberlin College in September, 1951 after an exhausting summer program. Given his studies in Johannesburg and in Lisbon, he entered the college as a third year student (a Junior). He was warmly welcomed at an evening with the President William Stevenson and his wife Eleanor with whom he discussed his plans for working with youth in Lourenço Marques; they suggested that he should do a full social work program.[21] Once again, Mondlane was popular at the college. He continued to be invited to speak at a variety of youth gatherings throughout the year and often complained to Clerc that he should not do so much beyond his studies.[22] However, it appears that it was these gatherings rather than his studies which were animating him at that time. Again, he spoke primarily about the need to develop mission work in Mozambique. At a Methodist University Youth Conference at Ohio State University, he spoke of the "value of missionary work in my country"[23] and at a UCYM gathering in Columbus Ohio on Thanksgiving Weekend he led a discussion for the "Future Missionaries" group. At this conference, the Governor of the State also spoke and money raised was to be sent to the Youth Centre that Darrell Randall had worked with in Johannesburg.[24] In an article in the *Methodist Herald*, C. E. Fuller, a former missionary in Inhambane who had worked with Mondlane when he was in Cambine, commented on his message in support of Christian missions in this period: "Skeptics in reference to Christianity, normally adamant to religious words, were moved, some to unashamed tears, by Mr. Mondlane's fearless testimony to his own faith and his unparalleled statement of Christian charity and tolerance in terms many copied to quote. His demand for education and religion as the two essentials of African salvation went unchallenged in the face of his clear exposition of the needs . . . His unashamed tribute to missions, his grasp of science, his intense loyalty to his Christian ideals, his humility throughout were the greatest testimony for missions most of his hearers had ever heard."[25] His first semester results showed "C's" and "C+'s" but his popularity in

---

21. Letter from Mondlane to Clerc, September 14, 1951. DM915A, 9.
22. Letter from Mondlane to Clerc, November 28, 1951, DM 915A, 12.
23. Ibid., "valor do trabalho missionário na minha terra."
24. Ibid.
25. *Methodist Herald*, Date unclear, DM1337, 2.

the school and in the ecumenical youth movement overshadowed his grades.

## UNESCO Conference

In his second semester, Mondlane was invited by President Stevenson to participate in a UNESCO conference to be held in New York. He was asked to be part of a panel discussing "Underdevelopment and Dependence in the World" which included Emory Ross, as well as a history professor from Harvard, Dr. Wieschoff from the United Nations and Edwin Munger, a geography professor from the University of Chicago. He was also introduced to Dr. Ralph Bunche at this meeting and was very impressed by him. In the rather extensive quotation which follows, it can be seen that much of what he heard at this conference challenged his very positive view of the role of Christian mission:

> It is a battle to talk about missions here in the United States, because many intellectuals think . . . that the political, economic and social problems that are agitating the societies of the Far East and the Middle East were brought about in large part by the missionaries who went to impose a foreign culture on the natives of those lands. They say that all human cultures are good. Why then try to Christianize the pagan peoples when they too have the right to follow their native and traditional religion? The economic systems of each nation are adequate for the good of these nations. Western people should not impose their cultural superiority on anyone. It seems that this flies very well in words. But no one wants to see what the capitalist and commercial nations of Europe and America have done in recent times in the East and in Africa. They think that the whole heap of economic and racial problems would not have existed if the missionaries had not gone to impose these things on the natives of these lands. I have a good opportunity to suggest to them the error of this way of thinking. Unfortunately, the majority of Asian and African students who are here are anti-missionary. I can understand why. There are many missionaries who accept the status quo without trying to analyze the situations in which they find themselves with enough intelligence.
> 
> In my way of thinking, there is a great danger in overly emphasizing the value of eternal (heavenly) life over the material part of life. Many religious missions have devoted themselves exclusively to the development of the spiritual life ignoring almost completely the immediate needs of the natives. When these

natives are able to acquire some studies, and begin to understand a little about the political-economic life of our times, they lose all confidence in the missionary.

The spiritual life and the material life are intertwined with each other and it appears it is not easy to separate them completely.

My work is to suggest that not all missions preach an exclusively "otherworldly" gospel. On the contrary, there are missions which dedicate themselves to the education of the natives in all respects.[26]

Mondlane clearly defended the important role of Christian mission but had to admit that it could also be a source of continuing colonial subservience when those involved did not understand the context in which people were living. His experience in Mozambique had been augmented by his interaction with people from various parts of Africa and elsewhere in the world where the traditional approach to mission had

---

26. Letter from Mondlane to Clerc, February 23, 1952, DM 915B, 3. "É uma batalha falar sobre as missões aqui nos Estados Unidos, porque muitos intelectuais pensam . . . os problemas políticos, económicos e sociais que efervescem as sociedades humanas do extremo oriente e médio oriente foram ocasionado em grande pelos missionários que foram impôr uma cultura estranha aos nativos dessas terras. Dizem que todas as culturas humanas são boas, todas as religiões são boas. Para que tentar cristianizar os povos pagãos quando eles também tem direito a seguir a sua religião nativa e tradicional? Os sistemas económicos de cada nação são adequados para o bem destas nações. Os ocidentais não devem tentar impôr a sua superioridade cultural a ninguém. Como ve isto voa muito bem na palavra. Mas nenhum quer ver o que as nações capitalistas e comerciais da Europa e América dos ultimos tempos teem feito no oriente e na África. Pensam toda a chusma de problemas económicos e raciais não teriam existido se os missionários não tivessem ido impôr essas coisas aos nativos dessas terras. Tenho uma boa oportunidade de lhes indicar o erro dessa maneira de pensar. Infelizmente a maior parte dos estudantes asiáticos e africanos que estão aqui são anti-missionários. Posso compreender porque. Há muitos missionários que aceitam a status quo sem tentar analisar as situações em que se encontram com adequada inteligência.

No meu ver há tanto perigo em acentuar demasiadamente o valor da vida eterna (do céu) como a parte material da vida. Muitas missões religiosas se teem devotado exclusivamente ao desenvolvimento da vida espiritual ignorando quasi completamente as necessidades imediatas dos nativos. Quando estes conseguirem adquirir alguns estudos, e começarem a compreender um pouco a complexidade da vida político--económica dos nossos tempos, perdem toda a confiança no missionário.

A vida espiritual e a vida material interlaçam-se um a outra, e não parece fácil apará-las completamente.

O meu trabalho é tentar indicar que nem todas as missões pregam um evangelho exclusivamente "doutro mundo." Pelo contrário são as missões que se dedicam no trabalho de educar os nativos em todos os respeitos."

been a hindrance to the emergence of a more autonomous church and movements for political independence.

## Continuing Engagement with Youth and the Broader Ecumenical Movement

Mondlane's second summer in the U.S. carried an equally busy schedule of youth camps and conferences as the first. He attended a "Crusade Scholars Get-together" in Indianapolis in June with forty Phelps Stokes scholars from different parts of the world as well as participating in the North American Assembly on African Affairs sponsored by the Foreign Mission Division of the National Council of Churches of Christ in the U.S.A. where he gave a lecture entitled, "A Message from the Heart of an African".[27] The rest of the summer was spent at various Methodist youth camps. These camps continued to give him a great feeling of satisfaction that he was helping to change the attitudes of those attending: "My experiences in the camps with the Methodist youth were very fruitful. Besides tiring me out a lot, it satisfied me spiritually to know that I am helping to change the attitudes of people who otherwise would not have had the chance to ask themselves questions concerning racial problems. If things continue as they are now it will take very little time here in America before the majority of people consider the Negros their equal in everything. The Christian Church is one of the best strategies."[28]

Indeed Mondlane appeared to be truly caught up in the very optimistic thinking of the American Protestant churches where significant social change seemed possible in the booming post war economy. Post-secondary education was available to many more people and relationships among racial groups were changing with greater contact through improved transportation and communication systems although racist attitudes persisted. After speaking at the influential "Exchange Club" at Oberlin College on "The background of the Political, Economic and

---

27. Letter from Mondlane to Clerc, June 3, 1952, DM 915B, 6.
28. Letter from Mondlane to Clerc, August 22, 1952, DM 915B, 9. "As minhas experiências nos campos com a juventude metodista foram muito frutíferas. Apesar de cansar-me bastante satisfaz-me espiritualmente saber que estou ajudando a mudar as atitudes de pessoas que doutra maneira nunca teriam ocasião de se preguntarem a si próprios em respeito aos problemas raciais. Se as coisas continuarem da maneira presente levara muito pouco tempo aqui na América antes de a maior parte do povo considerar os Negros seus iguais em tudo. A igreja cristã é uma das melhores estrategias."

Social problems of Southern Africa," he wrote to Clerc, "It is very difficult for me not to accept all the invitations to speak, especially at this time when the American Protestant churches are studying Africa. As well there are so many people who are interested in what is going on in South Africa and in Kenya. My stay here in the United States is not only to get good grades in class at the cost of losing all the opportunities to be in touch with the American people who are anxious to know what is happening in other parts of the world."[29]

### Return to Mozambique or Further Studies?

In Mozambique, Clerc was becoming concerned with the very hectic schedule with which Mondlane was faced and the impact that this might have on his studies. He was also becoming increasingly anxious that Mondlane finish his studies and return to take up the work which was waiting for him. There were very few people available to take leadership with youth and Mondlane's presence was greatly missed. The person who was engaged in this work, and in whom Mondlane put great confidence, was his friend Novidades Honwana. His sudden death was a great shock to both Mondlane and Clerc. Mondlane wrote, "Unfortunately, few Mozambicans are going to understand the depth of the loss of this young African."[30]

By the fall of 1952, Clerc had also heard of Mondlane's hopes to continue his studies in a Masters program at Northwestern University in Chicago and wrote that this would be a disaster for the work in Lourenço Marques. He felt that Mondlane should return to Mozambique and be involved with the youth work and return to further studies in five or six years. However, Clerc was also becoming increasingly aware of the complexity of this work in light of the growing number of youth seeking work in the city as industrialization increased rapidly and migration

---

29. Letter from Mondlane to Clerc, January 27, 1953, DM 915C, 1. "É muito difícil para me recusar-me de aceitar todos os convites para falar especialmente nestes dias em que as igrejas Protestantes americanas estão a estudar a África. Também por haver tanta gente que se interessa pelo que se passa na África do Sul e na Kenya. A minha estadia aqui nos Estados Unidos não é somente para fazer boas notas nas classes e perder todas as oportunidades de comunicar com o povo americano que está ancioso em saber o que passa em outras partes do mundo."

30. Letter from Mondlane to Clerc, April 6, 1952, DM 915B, 4. "Infelizmente poucos moçambicanos vão compreender a profundeza da perda deste jovem Africano."

continued from the rural areas.³¹ He wrote to Mondlane about a talk which he gave while on deputation in Switzerland in 1953 which he felt was quite unique in addressing this question: "'Bantus in coveralls'— about the African proletariat of the cities... This final series is illustrated with photos which I took of the life, during only one day, of the factory worker of LM from the time he gets up in the morning, breakfast, life in the factory, and, at home, in the evening, domestic life. This last theme is the most original. I am the first to expose with documents the profound transformation which the African world is now experiencing and how this appears in LM."³² In fact, one of the reasons that Clerc later gives to justify Mondlane continuing his studies at Northwestern was that "he would be 'gathering first hand and unique documentation on the native and social situation in a rapidly industrialisating [sic] African town,'"³³ information which would obviously be very important for them in their work with youth.

Clerc wrote to Darrell Randall to try to convince Mondlane to return to Mozambique when he finished his B.A. at Oberlin College. Randall's response gives some important insight into the person who Mondlane had become through his studies and experiences outside of Mozambique:

> A critical danger exists in the possibility of mission friends in PEA (Portuguese East Africa) under-estimating what has been happening to him. Eduardo is really a young boy who has grown into maturity at a whirlwind pace and with a success that far surpasses most of the people who have been his councillors [sic], teachers, and associates. He is no longer the "boy" whom most of the people in PEA will remember. He is a seasoned thinker who can carry his own with the most scholarly leaders. His capacity continues to astound me. There are over eight hundred African students now in the USA. It can be said that none of them has

---

31. Letter from Clerc to Mondlane, 12/10/52, DMA 915B, 11.

32. Letter from Clerc to Mondlane, June 4, 1953, DM 915C, 7. "'Les bantous en salopettes'—sobre o proletariado africano das cidades... Este última serie é ilustrada por fotos que tomei da vida, num mesmo dia, da pequena operária de LM desde o momento em que desperta de manha, a hora do chá, a vida na fábrica, e, em casa, a noite, o culto doméstico. Este ultimo assunto é o mais original. Sou o primeiro a revelar com documentos a profunda transformação que o mundo africano sofre actualmente e como aparece em LM."

33. Letter from Clerc to Florence Cox, March 11, 1953, DM 916C, 5.

made a greater impact in stimulating American interest in Africa than Eduardo has done.[34]

In relation to Mondlane's participation in the NCCC conference, Randall comments: "It was probably the most representative conference which has ever been held concerning Africa . . . He showed great tact and statesmanship in the association with the former Governor General of Mozambique (Nunes d'Oliveira) and his aide who were there to represent Portugal . . . The day these official colonial representatives submitted to questions from the Assembly will long be a memorable one."[35]

Randall also wrote that Frank Laubach, with whom Mondlane had worked on a literacy project in Mozambique, had commented: "Eduardo was the most outstanding Christian African youth he had known and expressed great hope for his future leadership. The World Christian Youth Council wanted to have him sent to India to the World Christian Conference this year."[36]

In relation to the impact that Mondlane had on American church attitudes toward Africa Randall wrote that he communicated in such a way "so that people might feel and see Africa as a member of the emerging community . . . Few missionaries ever experience the notoriety which has already been bestowed upon this young African."[37]

Randall was concerned over what these changes in Mondlane might mean for the future and his relationship with the church, particularly the mission community. He wrote: "Now what happens to a young man when all of this happens? All of us are anxious to know how it is going to influence his attitude toward his less privileged Africans, towards his mission leaders, toward his government, toward the Christian Church, etc. This cannot be fully visualized yet. He is not a mind that can be controlled by teachers, missionaries etc. He will think and act on his own. We have the faith that God's will may be worked out through his life of service."[38] Randall saw that the plans that the mission community had for Mondlane, even the ambitious and farsighted plans for working with alienated youth in Lourenço Marques, were not enough to hold

---

34. Letter from Darrell Randall to Clerc, September 29, 1952, DM 915B, 10a.
35. Ibid.
36. Ibid.
37. Ibid.
38. Ibid.

him. He warned that the mission community must be careful in how it made decisions concerning his future or he could be "lost" like others with high potential.

In addressing the question of future studies with Clerc, Randall wrote that the President of Oberlin College was trying to get a fellowship for Mondlane to do graduate work. Randall did not take responsibility for encouraging this and said that he believed that Mondlane would be going back to Lourenço Marques after the B.A. However, he understood Clerc's concerns that he might not be able to leave Mozambique again to continue his studies "because of the opposition of the missionaries and the authorities."[39] Clerc's initial reaction to this letter and the possibility of Mondlane continuing with his studies was one of anger.[40] However, in a later letter, he was more conciliatory and encouraged him to return to Lourenço Marques where everyone was anticipating his return and the work he would do: "I would have loved if you, Eduardo, had been able to feel with what friendship and what confidence and pride the missionaries discussed the possibilities of your future. There was nothing of any of the old sentiment of race. What all have in mind and are thinking about are the great services which you Eduardo will be able to make to the cause of the Gospel and the people of Africa—without excluding the Europeans!—and certainly will be able to make full use of your possibilities and qualities."[41]

This was clearly an important moment of decision for Mondlane. He knew the hopes which the Swiss Mission, and particularly Clerc, had put on him for the work in Lourenço Marques and was deeply committed to this work as well. However, he was also clearly aware of his potential to play a larger role in the future of Mozambique as he moved in powerful decision making circles related to mission, and indeed to the larger political scene, in the United States. Further study would involve him more deeply in this larger vision and open new doors for him and

39. Ibid.
40. Letter from Clerc to Mondlane, October 12, 1952, DM 915B, 11.
41. Letter from Clerc to Mondlane, November 1, 1952, DM 915B, 12. "Teria gostado que Eduardo pudesse sentir com que amizade e que confiança e que orgulho (pride) os missionários discutiram das possibilidades de seu futuro. Não há nada de qualquer sentimento atávico de raça. O que cada um tem em vista e considera são os muito grandes serviços que Eduardo poderá prestar a causa do Evangelho e do povo Africano—sem excluir os Europeus!—e certamente poderá fazer pleno uso das suas possibilidades e qualidades."

make the possibility of his taking up the leadership of youth work a more and more remote possibility. His concerns related to being able to leave the country again were certainly valid, but, to some degree, they seem to mask a growing desire to play a different and larger role in determining the future of Mozambique. In the United States, he was in dialogue with many African students in whose countries the process of decolonization was much further advanced. In addition, he had an opportunity to engage Portuguese authorities such as Nunes d'Oliveira about a reformed colonial relationship without fear of reprisal.

It is interesting that at this time Mondlane also considered shifting his studies from sociology to theology at Yale. It is clear that he had read the work of some of the prominent theologians of the time and no doubt was engaged in theological debate in the many encounters he was having with academics and church people in the United States. However, in a similar manner to his considering seeking ordination at an earlier period in Mozambique, he was convinced that his vocation must be active and responsive to the real issues facing humanity and not remain in theological speculation: "Many times I have asked myself if I could be a pastor but I have never received a clear answer. Social work still is my preference. It seems to me that the greatest difficulty is theological above any other reason. I read some of Dr. Brunner's books, and one or two of Rheinhold [sic] Niebuhr but I don't find anything that throws light on the practical problems of people's lives in these days. I agree with a large part of the ideas of Neo-Orthodoxy and the ideas of Kierkegaard have greatly interested me, especially in relation to Love as a divine imperative for all people. But ideas that are not put into practice do not seem to be of great value."[42]

It is also interesting to note that at this time, Mondlane was beginning to raise many questions about some aspects of the mission theology in which he was grounded and particularly the continuing divisions

---

42. Letter from Mondlane to Clerc, January 27, 1953, DM 915C, 1. "Muitas vezes preguntei-me a mim mesmo se podia ser um pastor mas nunca recebi uma resposta certa. O trabalho social ainda toma preferência em mim. Parece-me que a maior dificuldade é teológica do que qualquer outra razão. Li alguns livros do Dr. Brunner, e um ou dois de Rheinhold [sic] Niebuhr, mas não acho nada que me de luz sobre os problemas prácticas da vida de todos os dias. Concordo com a maior parte das ideas da Ortodoxia Nova, e interesso-me bastante pelas ideas de Kierkegaard, especialmente no que diz respeito ao Amor como um imperativo divino a todos os homens. Mas ideas a não ser que sejam postas em prática não parecem ter grande valor."

## Study in the United States—Oberlin College

between Protestant denominations.[43] For his part, Clerc was not at all in favor of Mondlane shifting to study theology. He wrote to Florence Cox at the Crusade Scholarships in New York to say that the Mission would support his continuing studies in an MA program but would not support him in beginning theological studies.[44] Clerc's own interest, as noted above, in a sociological analysis of the migration of labor to the growing industrialized cities in Mozambique and his own experience as a non-ordained person in the mission community may have influenced this perspective.

The discussion around Mondlane's future studies also began to touch on how he was being seen by the Portuguese authorities. It has already been mentioned that Mondlane and others were concerned that his passport might not be renewed if he returned to Portuguese territory. In writing to the Crusade Scholarships in favor of continuing financial support for Mondlane's studies, Clerc also indicated this concern. However, Clerc's concern had gone beyond the issue of a passport. He had received the reports of the NCCC Assembly on African Affairs and realized that Mondlane's intervention might have caused serious concern for the Portuguese authorities in attendance: "The presence, however, of highly placed individuals in the Portuguese world, hearing your talk or many of the declarations of other Africans or individuals could be interpreted as a dangerous sign. What was focused in these assemblies reveals the development of the African peoples, their grounding in justice and a global opinion supporting this grounding. To be sure, a Portuguese nationalist could interpret this as a "Protestant" tendency and very dangerous."[45] It is interesting to note how the political critique is understood in religious terms. Clerc knew that what Mondlane could say while under the protection of the church and the universities in the United States could prove to be very dangerous in the context of colonial Mozambique. In his own work, he was well aware of the tightening restrictions on the Protestant schools in Mozambique and that

---

43. Letter from Mondlane to Clerc and family, March 3, 1953, DM 915C, 4.

44. Letter from Clerc to Florence Cox, March 11, 1953, DM 915C, 5.

45. Letter from Clerc to Mondlane, March 17, 1953, DM 915C, 6. "A presença, contudo, de altas individualidades do Mundo Português, a ouvir o seu discurso ou muitas declarações de outros Africanos ou individualidades, pode ser interpretada como sinal de perigo. O que foi focado nessas assembleias revela o desenvolvimento dos povos africanos, a sua sede de justiça e uma opinião mundial atras dessa sede. Ora um Português nacionalista pode interpretar isto como a tendência 'Protestante' e muito perigosa."

the *Concordat* with the Roman Catholic Church gave the Portuguese government a much freer hand in suppressing the Protestant missions than in other predominantly Roman Catholic countries or colonies.[46] However, he did not seem to be willing at that point either to admit that it might be too dangerous for Mondlane to return to Lourenço Marques nor to counsel him to moderate his political discourse.

### Relationship with Georgette Libombo

These dilemmas around whether or not Mondlane should remain in the United States to continue his studies after he completed his B.A. at Oberlin College were being played out within a deepening crisis in Mondlane's personal life which was not without its links to his understanding of, and participation in, the church and his role in Mozambique. Despite the distance and the tensions with her father, Mondlane's relationship with Georgette Libombo had continued throughout the time he was in Lisbon and after he arrived in the United States. They continued to write to each other but the frequency of correspondence slowed. Darrell and Mildred Randall had attempted to arrange for Georgette to study in the United States and it seems that Oberlin College had agreed to a special course for her.[47] It also appears that she was willing to come to the U.S. but was afraid to confront her father about this possibility.[48] There was a change in Enoch Libombo's attitude in September, 1951 when he wrote to Mondlane to tell him that he could write to Georgette.[49] However, this was at exactly the time that Mondlane had met Janet Johnson and a relationship was developing between them. Mondlane did not tell this to Georgette Libombo nor did he attempt to break the relationship at that time. Indeed, he was still encouraging her to come to the United States and in at least one letter assured her that he was not involved in any other relationship.[50]

Before receiving Enoque Libombo's letter, Mondlane had written to Clerc with reservations about breaking the relationship with Georgette because of her father. "[Enoque] is intimately linked to our government.

---

46. Letter from Clerc to Mondlane, September 23, 1951, DM 915A, 10.
47. Letter from Mondlane to Clerc, August 3, 1951, DM 915A, 5.
48. Letter from Georgette Libombo to Mondlane, August 8, 1951, DM 915A, 3.
49. Letter from Mondlane to Georgette Libombo, September 12, 1951, DM 915A, 3.
50. Letter from Mondlane to Georgette Libombo, April 7, 1952. DM 915A, 3.

It is possible that he could harm the work for me."[51] In his response, Clerc suggests that Fatton, the head of the Swiss Mission in Mozambique, might act as his advocate with Libombo.[52] Mondlane replies that he does not want Fatton to intervene and that perhaps Enoque Libombo is seeing him in a better light only because he is studying in the United States.[53] By June of 1952, Mondlane was admitting that the problem indeed was him and that he no longer loved Georgette. His main concern was the potential consequences of the break, particularly the reaction of her father. He was not sure that he could work in Lourenço Marques if Enoque Libombo was there.[54] Given Libombo's close ties to the colonial government, Mondlane was realizing that the animosity which he felt toward him could severely prejudice any work he might do and indeed potentially be a threat to his life.

## Growing Relationship with Janet Johnson

At the same time, his relationship with Janet Johnson was growing. It seems that Mondlane had been interested in several women he had met during this period.[55] The most serious of these relationships, besides that with Johnson, was with Hope Griswald, a student at Oberlin and the daughter of the Rector of Harvard's Law Faculty. Janet Mondlane says that she was from a "non-religious" family and that the difference in their beliefs sparked many of Mondlane's questions about religion in this period. The relationship might have led to marriage had it not been for these differences.[56]

After their initial encounter at the Youth Camp in Wisconsin, Mondlane did not see Janet Johnson again for a year and three months. However, they began to write to each other on an almost daily basis and the relationship developed over this period. There was a significant difference in their age; Janet was seventeen when they met and in her last year of secondary school while Mondlane was already thirty-one although he did not admit this to her for some time. Although her knowl-

---

51. Letter from Mondlane to Clerc, September 1, 1951, DM 915A, 7. "[Enoque] está intimamente ligado ao nosso governo. É possivel que me venha prejudicar o trabalho."

52. Letter from Clerc to Mondlane, September 14, 1951, DM 915A, 8.

53. Letter from Mondlane to Clerc, November 28, 1951, DM 915A, 13.

54. Letter from Mondlane to Clerc, June 3, 1952, DM 915B, 6.

55. Letter from Darrell Randall to various, September 26, 1953, DM 1268A, 5.

56. Manghezi, *Meu coração*, 95.

edge of Mozambique was quite limited, Johnson was very interested in Africa and became well informed about the situation in the territory through this correspondence.

Johnson had grown up in a Methodist home and was very active in the local church. By the time she met Mondlane, the family was living in Indianapolis. Their politics were conservative and their attitudes toward race were typical of the U.S. mid-west at the time. When Johnson proposed having Mondlane come to their church to speak and to stay in their home to reduce costs, her father's response was, "I will not allow any black man in this house and I don't want anything to do with any black man."[57] The correspondence between Mondlane and Johnson had to be kept secret from her family. This was somewhat alleviated in Mondlane's second year at Oberlin when Johnson began her undergraduate studies at Miami University in Ohio over the objections of her parents who wanted her to study in Indianapolis and live at home.

## Crisis in the Church and mission community

Both Mondlane and Johnson had to keep this relationship secret, he from the mission community and she from her family; both knew that they would face major objections to the relationship because of the race issue. Although Mondlane maintained that the relationship with Georgette Libombo was over in the summer of 1952 when she had returned his photographs and had not written again,[58] he had not told anyone in Lourenço Marques, particularly Clerc, so that there would be no concern about him returning and taking up the work with youth. It appears that Georgette Libombo had said nothing to Clerc nor to anyone else in the mission community and so there was no indication in Mozambique that the relationship was over. However, Mondlane did write to his uncle, Ozias Bila, telling him of his relationship with Johnson and the story spread from there that Mondlane was marrying a white woman from the United States.[59] Several Presbyterian pastors visited Juillerat, the head of the Swiss Mission in Mozambique, to discuss the situation with him and he, in turn, contacted Charles Périer, the Director of the

---

57. Ibid., 51.
58. Monlane to Clerc, August 17, 1953, DM 915C, 12.
59. Manghezi, *Meu coração*, 104.

MSAS in Lausanne who had once worked with Mondlane in the mintlawa in Mausse.

Clerc was deeply hurt that Mondlane had not confided in him concerning the relationship with Johnson and was also very angry that he had not clarified that the relationship had ended with Georgette Libombo. He had received a letter from Randall previous to the word arriving in Switzerland from Mozambique, letting him know of the relationship but Randall did not reveal that Johnson was white.[60] From the beginning, Clerc was very concerned by the race issue and all of the implications of an interracial marriage in the context of colonial Mozambique. In a letter to Randall he wrote:

> If the girl is of the European race: it is obvious that all his folks will feel this as a treason toward the African race. They will not accept her; She would have the worst situation in society. Not among the missionaries, but among the Africans, the Portuguese people, the mulattoes. She would resent it strongly as something unbearable and flee away; Ed's authority as a Christian leader and African leader is cut down; at LM the children would be called: son of a p ... by black and white; Ed has pledged himself for the service of his folks and God in Moçambique. If he marries an American negro, or colored, he chooses a difficult way for himself, his work and his wife. If he marries a white girl, better to stay in the States and abandon all project of work in Moçambique.[61]

In Mondlane's first response to Clerc concerning the relationship with Janet Johnson, he is conciliatory and tries to explain to him why he was attracted to Johnson and why they had to keep the relationship a secret: "What is most important, beside the fact that I am so in love with her, is that she is intensely interested in the problems of my people, and she is a Christian of the type that I really admire."[62] He also assured Clerc that she was in good health and was very intelligent and was studying the social sciences so that she would be prepared for the task of living with him in Mozambique and understanding its context better.[63] However, he also wrote that he was very upset by the fact that he could

60. Ibid.
61. Letter from Clerc to Randall, September 3, 1953, DM 1268A, 1.
62. Letter from Mondlane to Clerc, August 17, 1953, DM 915C, 12. "O que é muito importante, ao lado do facto de que eu a amo muitissimo, é que ela se interessa intensamente pelos problemas do meu povo, e é uma cristã do tipo que admiro bastante"
63. Letter from Mondlane to Clerc, September 5, 1953. DM 915C, 14.

not have a private life and wondered what it was that had so displeased the pastors in Mozambique. He put a great deal of the problem down to the deep seated racism in the United States which was reflected in the American missionaries in Mozambique as well as in Johnson's parents who were threatening to cut off her financial support if she did not end the relationship with him. Clerc did not read the letter in the conciliatory way in which it was written; his response was angry and sarcastic. He could not believe that Mondlane did not recognize the problems that his marrying Johnson would create and felt that he was not taking any responsibility in the matter. He also reminded him of the backlash he was facing in Lourenço Marques because of his not being honest with him concerning breaking the relationship with Georgette Libombo and felt that Mondlane could not put all of the negative reaction down to racism. The normally judicious and restrained Clerc ends his letter with a very scathing criticism of the man whom he considered to be his son but by whom he clearly felt betrayed: "You have overcome the greatest difficulties but you have been overcome by success. In the meantime, this letter makes me sick. Good luck."[64]

The depth of the relationship with Clerc is shown in Mondlane's response to him. Despite their close relationship and despite the love which Clerc had shown for him, Mondlane wrote that there were things which he could not understand because he was not an African. In speaking about the prejudice which he had experienced from some missionaries in Mozambique he wrote, "They have drawn a line of contacts with Africans which does not include the possibility of eating on the same table with an African."[65] Mondlane felt he had to challenge his "father" in order to expose the racism behind the response to his relationship with Johnson, a challenge to the fundamental racism in the mission community which would not permit sexual relations across racial lines: "I still love my people in the same way that I always have. Loving Janet does not change a dot in my love for my own people. The only difference that has taken place so far in me is that I consider all human beings the same and do not consider marrying a person of another race a violation of the love

---

64. Letter from Clerc to Mondlane, September 14, 1953. DM 915C, 15. "Venceu as piores dificuldades mais foi vencido pelo sucesso. No entanto, essa carta torna-me doente. Muitas saudades"

65. Letter from Mondlane to Clerc, September 25, 1953, DM 915D, 1.

I have for my country and people."⁶⁶ This simple statement goes to the heart of the compromise which the Protestant missions had made with the racialized Portuguese colonial structures as well as pointing to the racist attitudes which the missionaries brought from their own contexts. Clerc was forced to examine his own response and, indeed, the mission structures in which he was so deeply integrated for their racist biases.

Périer's response to the news of Mondlane's relationship with Johnson was stronger than Clerc's and again reveals the entrenched racial divisions among the mission community in Mozambique and, indeed, in the structures and attitudes of the MSAS. In his letter to Juillerat, he also used this issue to emphasize the divisions between the Swiss and American missionaries and his sarcasm exposes the very negative attitude of the Swiss toward the Americans:

> So we now know, from a trusted source, that the young person in question is a white woman: about 20 years old, I think that she still has 3 years of study . . .
>
> So, before writing to Mondlane about what we think, not with the purpose of condemning him but in a manner to help him well consider the situation before taking decisions that he might regret, before trying to clarify as we would attempt to do with our own child—being well understood that he would take these responsibilities after having considered all the consequences which might result, for his future, of a marriage with a white woman—before everything else, we would like to correspond with you, in order for us to mutually clarify about this extremely complex case . . .
>
> All this shows us that E. Mondlane seems to have lost his footing. He simplifies the problem and does not take into account the difficulties that he will find for his wife in Lorenço Marques: isolation of his Janet (this is the name of the young heroine of 20 years of age) face to face with the American missionaries of Mozambique, difficulties in receiving the numerous bush relatives zeroing in on their home in the city. Where will she go on vacation, as a white woman? Namaacha? Not sufficient. Transvaal? Impossible. America? And many other points without counting those which question where the little coloreds will stay, their education, etc, etc. It is a little naive to say that this young girl of 20 years of age, moreover an American, so naive, knowing the problems of Africa well after having read the books that talk about them (only in English, so not everything). There is all the

66. Ibid.

rest that we learn from the life lived on the ground and which, you well know, is not given to us without going through a great effort of adaptation and a lot of suffering.⁶⁷

It seems that initially Périer could not see beyond the very delicate compromise which the Protestant missions had established in the Portuguese colonial context in Mozambique. The relationship between Mondlane and Johnson, as Mondlane argued, could have been seen as an important opportunity to challenge the racial assumptions underlying the colonial social structures and indeed the Protestant mission community as well. It is possible that Périer and others in the Swiss Mission at the time did recognize this challenge and chose to draw back from it, recognizing the profound change which accepting this theological truth would force in the life of the mission community and the relation of the Swiss Mission with the Portuguese colonial authorities.

There was a very significant exchange of correspondence between the leadership of the MSAS and Mondlane concerning his relationship with Johnson. Responding to this situation for Périer was somewhat complicated by the fact that Enoque Libombo was on holiday in Portugal at the time and from there went to Switzerland to present his case against Mondlane saying that Mondlane was going to marry a white

---

67. Letter from Charles Périer to E. Juillerat, September 11, 1953, DM 1268A, 3. "Nous ne savons donc que maintenant, de source sûre, que la jeune personne en question est une blanche: environ 20 ans, je pense puisqu'elle a encore 3 ans d'études . . .

Donc, avant d'écrire à Mondlane ce que nous pensons, non dans le but de l'accabler mais dans celui de l'aider à bien considérer la situation avant de prendre des décisions qu'il pourrait regretter, avant d'essayer de l'éclairer comme nous tenterions de le faire pour notre propre enfant—étant bien entendu qu'il prendra ses responsabilités après avoir envisagé toutes les conséquences qui pourraient résulter, pour son avenir, d'un mariage avec une blanche—avant tout cela, nous aimerions correspondre avec vous, de façon à nous éclairer mutuellement sur un cas extrêmement complexe . . .

Tout cela nous montre que E. Mondlane semble avoir un peu perdu pied. Il simplifie le problème et ne se rend pas compte des difficultés qu'il va procurer à sa femme à Lourenço Marques : isolement de sa Janet (c'est le nom de la jeune héroïne de 20 ans) vis à vis des missionnaires américains de Mozambique, difficulté à recevoir la nombreuse parenté de la brousse s'attardant à leur foyer en ville. Où ira-t-elle en vacances, comme blanche? Namaacha? Pas suffisant. Transvaal? Impossible. Amérique? Et bien d'autres points sans compter ceux que soulèveront la venue de petits métis, leur instruction, etc, etc. C'est un peu naïf de dire que cette jeune fille de 20 ans, Américaine par surcroît, donc naïve, connaît bien les problèmes de l'Afrique pour avoir lu les livres s'y rapportant (en anglais seulement, donc pas tous). Il y a tout le reste que nous apprenons par la vie vécue sur place et qui, tu le sais bien, ne nous est donné qu'à travers un gros effort d'adaptation et beaucoup de souffrances."

American woman but had not ended the relationship with his daughter.⁶⁸ However, in his first letter, Périer's principal argument against the marriage appears to be that Mondlane is not being practical about the real situation in Lourenço Marques: "we stay, we live in *a pre-determined, a given world* and we are not able to ignore *this given*.⁶⁹ Although he had the right to marry whomever he chose, Mondlane had to realize that several groups would raise problems with an interracial marriage including many in the African church community. Indeed, at least two pastors, Manganhela and Nhancale, expressed their objections to the relationship saying that Mondlane was not providing a good role model by marrying a white woman and would no longer identify with their situation.⁷⁰ Périer also wrote that although they would not officially admit it, the relationship would also create problems with the Portuguese and would be another way for the Portuguese to demonstrate the negative influence of the Protestants. He also argues that it would destroy Mondlane's credibility within the CCM and embarrass the Swiss missionaries who had defended his cause.⁷¹

Mondlane's response clearly addressed the compromise which the Protestant missions had made with the racialism of Portuguese colonialism which Périer defended so vehemently. He acknowledged all of the problems and difficulties which his relationship with Johnson would create for them in Mozambique. However, after weighing all of this negative impact his mind was not changed:

> I sat down to think about everything I had learned in and outside of the church concerning human life. As you know, I believe with all my heart that relations between individuals and between groups are never ideal. I am in America today because white people in South Africa refused to let me continue my studies in a white school. Many bad things have happened between blacks and whites from both a Christian and a human point of view. My faith in Christ rests on this: all the hurtful things that we believe God does not like in us will leave us only when we fight against them in our lives. I do not believe that we can fight against those

68. Letter from Périer to Mondlane, September 25, 1953, DM 1268A, 6.

69. Ibid., "nous demeurons, nous vivons dans *un monde conditionné, donné* et nous ne pouvons pas faire abstraction de *ce donné.*"

70. Letter from Z. Manganhela to Clerc, December 17, 1953, DM 1268D, 5; and Letter from F. Nhancale to Mondlane, December 10, 1953, DM 1268D, 3.

71. Letter from Périer to Mondlane, September 25, 1953, DM 1268A, 6.

things only in our thoughts. I also do not believe that God only wants us to have peace in heaven. It is my belief that political issues, economic issues and social issues will be rectified only if we humans here on earth receive God's demands and execute God's will. For me, human salvation does not begin in heaven but in this world. If our churches are interested in human problems, it is my conviction that they should take an interest at least in practicing what they know is God's will here in the world.[72]

Mondlane's "practical" Christianity cuts to the heart of the mission compromise with colonialism. It is more important to live out the demands of the gospel in the real challenges of human life than to wait for the perfect life of heaven to overcome those things which alienate people from one another.

In Périer's next letter on October 20, and also in a further letter from the Council of the MSAS sent on December 4, the focus shifted to the inappropriate way that Mondlane treated Georgette Libombo in not clearly telling her that his love for her had ended and that he wanted to end the relationship. The Council was careful to point out both in the letter to Mondlane and in a letter written to Georgette Libombo on December 4, that they had avoided interfering because of the autonomy of the local church in Mozambique to deal with these matters. However they justified their writing by saying that they cannot allow their "grandchildren" to continue to suffer. On this point, their criticism seems to be well founded and Mondlane agrees that he may not have dealt well with ending the relationship with Libombo; eventually he wrote to her expressing this.[73] Even in this regard though, the paternalism of the MSAS response was clear. Neither Périer nor the Council directly addressed Mondlane's critique of the mission's compromise with the racist attitudes endemic not only in Portuguese colonialism but in the wider European colonial project and in the societies in which the missions originated in Europe and North America. However, it is interesting to note one paragraph in which the Council does seem to acknowledge that it is necessary to recognize the complexity of the situation and that there are serious future implications in the decisions they make: "Pharisaic complaints are abundant as well as those who quickly agree just because

---

72. Letter from Mondlane to Bakulukumba ba Secretariado ya Mission Suisse, October 10, 1953, DM 1268B, 1. Translation from original Tsonga by Samuel Ngale.

73. Letter from Mondlane to Georgette Libombo, November 17, 1953, DM 1268C, 4.

they do not want to understand the deep complexities of the issue. They do not have enough love to look at themselves in the future. We do not place ourselves with the former or the latter."[74]

## Clerc's Travel to the United States

In January of 1954, Clerc made his first trip to the United States to attend several meetings but more importantly to meet with Mondlane and Janet Johnson in order to discuss their relationship and its implications for the church. Although the MSAS had already clarified that it was Mondlane's decision to make, the fears concerning the response of the Portuguese and the practical difficulties of life in colonial Mozambique and the mission church for an interracial couple continued. The trip was able to help Clerc see the person that Mondlane had become and the role that he was playing in the United States. In a letter to Charles Périer he wrote that Mondlane was a missionary to the United States and for the first time talks about the possibility of Mondlane doing a doctorate.[75] He genuinely seemed to have liked Johnson and also, remarkably, to have warmed to American culture and life, but after his visit he continued to recommend that they wait for marriage until after Mondlane had been back in Mozambique for some time and to raise concerns about the problems that they would encounter in Lourenço Marques.[76] Concerns continued to be raised by the local church as well; Mondlane was particularly angered by a letter that arrived from Pastor Aldasse and that he seemed to be blocking any possibility of him returning to Mozambique with Johnson.[77] At this time, Mondlane felt that it was almost impossible for him to go back to the work that he had planned to take up for so many years and that he needed to look at alternative possibilities in the United States or in other African countries. He felt a deep sense of betrayal both from the Swiss Mission and from the Mozambican church which caused him to begin to question his own commitment to the church as the instrument that could bring about significant social change: "I do not see why the church does not feel its

74. Letter from the MSAS Council to Mondlane, December 4, 1953. DM 1268D, 2. Translation from original Tsonga by Samuel Ngale.

75. Letter from Clerc to Périer, January 15, 1954, DM 1268E, 6.

76. Letter from Clerc to Janet Johnson, February 19, 1954, DM 1268E, 9; and Letter from Clerc to Mondlane, February 20, 1954, DM 916A, 2.

77. Letter from Mondlane to Clerc, April 15, 1954, DM 916A, 6.

own guilt for this lack of tolerance. I am not accusing individuals here, but I greatly lament the fact of the Church preaching love and tolerance and when the occasion arises to practice these Christian gifts, it retreats and refuses to take on its responsibilities. Either the Christian theory is completely erroneous or it must show that it can correct itself."[78]

---

78. Ibid. "Não vejo porque é que a Igreja não se sente culpada por esta falta de tolerância. Não estou acusando individuos aqui, mas lamento imensamente o facto de a Igreja pregar o amor e tolerância e quando a ocasião se oferecer para praticar estes dons cristãos ela se retrai e recusa-se a tomar as suas responsabilidades. Ou a teoria cristã está completamente errada ou deve demonstrar a sua correcção."

# 6

# Study in the United States— Northwestern University, Chicago

## Masters Work in Sociology

IN THE MIDST OF the crisis provoked in the Swiss Mission and the larger Protestant mission community in Mozambique by the news that he was in a relationship with a white American woman, Janet Johnson, Mondlane began his studies in a Masters program at Northwestern University in Chicago. He was awarded a fellowship from the Sociology Department as well as a further Crusade Scholarship through the Methodist Church. He was attracted to Northwestern by its Sociology department and by several professors including Kimball Young and especially Melville Herskovits[1], one of the pioneers in establishing African studies as a legitimate field of scholarly inquiry in American universities in the postwar years. Herskovits was a student of Franz Boas together with Ruth Benedict, Margaret Mead and A. Irving Hallowell.[2] He was best known for his work *The Myth of the Negro Past* in which he argued that traces of African cultures could be found in African American communities in the United States and other diaspora societies.

Mondlane found himself in one of the principal centers of academic debate concerning the nature and impact of African cultures in the United States and enthusiastically entered into this arena. He was to prove himself a serious student. Herbert Shore remembered that Mondlane wrote extensively concerning Marx and Weber and that he

1. Manghezi, *Meu coração*, 98.
2. Glazer, "Out of Africa."

had a keen interest in the American Revolution and read a great deal about the life and work of Thomas Jefferson and Thomas Paine. He also said that his reading widened to include Marx and Engels, Plekhanov and Mao Tse-tung but "it was again the dynamic rather than dogma that interested Mondlane."[3] Janet Mondlane recalls that at this time Eduardo wrote in a letter that he "was neither a capitalist nor a communist but rather a follower of the Fabian Society."[4] She goes on to say, "Like them, he reacted to the very radical type of Marxism. Socialism should be gradually developed through social and educational reforms without class struggle or revolution. Private property should continue to exist, but the State should control vital areas of production. This would be, very probably, the title of his future political position when he became an active politician as the leader of Frelimo and explains his interest in the Nordic form of social democracy."[5]

Despite the way in which Mondlane was often characterized by the Portuguese authorities and in the broader press as a radical revolutionary, his political thinking was to a large extent shaped in the moderate environment of 1950s American academia. His Masters and Doctoral theses focused on various aspects of the influence of race as a social determinant; his Masters thesis was entitled, "Ethnocentrism and the Social Definition of Race as In-Group Determinants," and his doctoral thesis, "Role Conflict, Reference Group and Race." However, it is clear that in these studies, Mondlane's political and theological thinking was being challenged by the liberal and critical teaching at Northwestern and in the broader academic world. His experience with the church in relation to his personal life and relationships created a new distance from mission colleagues and friends which was not easily overcome. Added to this was his changing theological position which he recognized would put him at odds with most of the missionaries and pastors in the

---

3. Shore, "Resistance and Revolution," xxiv.

4. Manghezi, *Meu coração*, 94, "não era nem capitalista nem comunista mas antes um seguidor da sociedade Fabiana."

5. Ibid. 95–96. "Tal como eles, ele reagia ao tipo de marxismo muito radical. O Socialismo deveria ser desenvolvido gradualmente através de reformas sociais e educacionais sem luta de classes nem revolução. A propriedade privada deveria continuar a existir, mas o Estado devia controlar áreas vitais da produção. Este podia ser, muito provavelmente, o título da sua futura posição política quando se tornou um político activo como dirigente da Frelimo e explica o interesse dele pela social-democracia de tipo nórdico."

Protestant churches in Mozambique and, as already noted, he realized that it would be almost impossible for him to return to Mozambique to take up the work with youth which, in principle, he had been preparing to do. In a letter to Janet Johnson he wrote,

> . . . there are two things that have come to interfere with this "cooperation" with the missions. The first obstacle is my own philosophical position at this time. I have arrived at the conclusion that I cannot, in good conscience, defend and preach the gospel of Jesus as he is presented by many of the missionaries in the field. I am too liberal to be useful in the propagation of any gospel. The theology which I embrace now is too diluted to impress any of the missionaries whom I know . . . I think that, at this time, there is a swelling of the so-called spiritual needs of Africa, neglecting almost completely the other facets of human existence, namely the political, the economic and the social. It is clear that these are all interrelated . . .[6]

His early emphasis on the "practical" in religious life was being developed as his theology encountered, and was being critically challenged by, his study of the social sciences, particularly sociology.

## Participation in the 2nd Assembly of the World Council of Churches

Despite this significant shift in his theological thought, and his disillusionment with the mission community, Mondlane remained deeply involved with the church and indeed expanded his network of contacts and relationships within the churches. One of the most important elements in his evolving relationship with the church at this time was his participation in the 2nd Assembly of the World Council of Churches held in Evanston in August of 1954. The first Assembly had been held in Amsterdam in 1948 and it was significant that the second had moved

6. Letter from Mondlane to Johnson, April 24, 54 in Manghezi, *Meu coração*, 120, ". . . houve duas coisas que vieram interferir com esta 'cooperação' com as missões. O primeiro bloqueio é a minha própria posição filosófica neste momento. Cheguei à conclusão de que não posso, em boa consciência, defender e pregar o evangelho de Jesus como ele é apresentado por muitos dos missionários no terreno. Sou demaisiado liberal para ser útil na propagação de qualquer evangelho. A teologia que agora abraço está demaisiado diluída para impressionar qualquer dos missionários que conheço . . . penso que, neste momento, há um empolar das chamadas necessidades espirituais da África, negligenciando quase completamente as outras fases da existência humana, nomeadamente a política, a económica e a social. É claro que estão todas interligada . . ."

from Europe to the United States. The growing power and influence of the United States in the period following the Second World War was also evident in the WCC which had felt it necessary to establish a secretariat in New York as well as having its central office in Geneva. The economic influence of the United States in the reconstruction of western Europe following the war was also evident in the programs of the WCC, particularly in its aid to refugees, still overwhelmingly understood to be those displaced in Europe by the war and by the tensions between the western powers and the Soviet Union and its allies in the post war period.

The Assembly also met in the immediate aftermath of the Korean conflict and the emerging influence of the Peoples' Republic of China (PRC) as well as in the shadow of McCarthyism in the United States itself. Despite the appearance of a united organization which represented Christian churches in every corner of the globe, the reality of the divisions of the Cold War was everywhere evident. There were no delegates from the churches of the PRC; the WCC had supported the U.N. intervention in Korea as an international policing measure in the face of an act of aggression despite the objections of the Chinese churches which then did not, or were not allowed to, participate in the Assembly.[7] The few delegates present from the Soviet bloc were under pressure to avoid any statement which would be seen to be critical of their respective regimes. On the other hand, the fact that the Assembly took place in the United States and, even more pointedly, that it was addressed by President Dwight Eisenhower, emphasized the close identification of the WCC with the western powers and their policies. The vast majority of delegates were still from the Protestant churches of western Europe and North America and, although often critical of western policy, were indeed representative of their own constituencies and contexts. When a contemporary American observer, James Hastings Nichols, described the tensions at work in the Assembly as that between the "unitive and the witnessing tasks of the church", he sees the "witnessing task", or the "prophetic role" as primarily concerned with religious liberty which, in turn, is almost exclusively related to the situation in communist countries.[8] The threat to religious freedom manifested in the House Committee on Un-American Activities and the work of Senator Joseph McCarthy did not figure high on the agenda. Despite the charges of Carl McIntire and

7. Nichols, *Evanston*, 55.
8. Ibid., 49–59.

his followers in the "International Council of Christian Churches", that the WCC was an instrument of communism, it still, in fact, operated by and large within the framework of western liberal capitalist society and carried many of its assumptions.

## The WCC and Racism

One area of social and political concern manifestly evident in the United States and in South Africa and other parts of southern Africa which did come under scrutiny at the Evanston Assembly was racism. One of the major thematic sections of the Assembly was, "The Church Amid Racial and Ethnic Tensions", and this theme was not able to be ignored in the increasingly racially charged context of the United States of the mid 1950s. Nichols points out that the Assembly itself was held in Evanston, one of the leafy white suburbs of Chicago, while at the same time a police guard of over a thousand had been posted in the Trumbull Park public housing project, an almost exclusively African American community on the south side of the city.[9] Despite the tremendous economic growth in the country following the war, wide economic disparity remained and paralleled the racial divisions of the country. Despite the hope of many African Americans that the promises and ideals of justice, equality and democracy of the victorious allied powers would be made manifest in their lives, poverty and discrimination remained virtually unchanged in the South and in the growing ghettos of the northern cities. Throughout the United States, the civil rights movement was growing, given leadership by the Southern Christian Conference and with strong support from many white Protestant clergy, but, ironically, it was in the local churches, the very churches which were so enthusiastically hosting the Evanston Assembly, that the greatest racial division in the country was still to be seen.

South Africa was also clearly targeted in the Report in the wake of the election of the National Party government and the instituting of *apartheid*. The Dutch Reformed churches had delegates at the Assembly and in fact had been represented in the working group preparing the study paper on "Intergroup Relations" by Dr. B. J. Marais, known as a liberal voice within the Nederduitse Gereformeerde Kerk Van Zuid-Afrika in Transvaal (NGK) and author of *Colour: The Unsolved Problem*

9. Ibid., 144.

*of the West.*¹⁰ Alan Paton, representing the Church of the Province of Southern Africa, was also present at the Assembly and was the primary author of the report on Intergroup Relations. The report affirmed that "any form of segregation based on race, color or ethnic origin is contrary to the gospel and incompatible with the Christian doctrine of man [sic] and the nature of the church of Christ."¹¹ It also called on member churches to "renounce all forms of segregation or discrimination and to work for their abolition within their own life and within society."¹² The right to the franchise was affirmed as was the right to marry across racial lines. This was an enormous challenge to churches throughout the world but especially to those in the United States and in South Africa. The delegates of the Dutch Reformed churches in South Africa abstained from voting on the report but did not dismiss it out of hand. In fact they felt compelled to draft a statement on the resolutions which was included in the official Report of the Assembly. In it they stated, "At this stage we dare not commit our churches either way but wish to keep the door open for further conversation. We wish to place on record that we have experienced at Evanston much evidence of what we truly believe to be real Christian goodwill and an attempt to understand the peculiar difficulties we have to face. In response to that we now pledge ourselves personally to the task of urging our respective churches to apply themselves as urgently as possible to the study of the report."¹³

## Theological Challenges in the Assembly

These were some of the major concerns of the Assembly which Mondlane attended as a "Youth Consultant" from the Swiss Mission in Portuguese East Africa. His participation had been suggested to Jean Fraser, Director of the Youth Department at the WCC office in Geneva, first by Clerc while on deputation in Switzerland and subsequently supported by the MSAS.¹⁴ Of course it was convenient for Mondlane to attend since he was studying in Evanston and it may have seemed only natural to invite him to participate. However, his presence was significant. He was one of

---

10. De Gruchy, *The Church Struggle in South Africa*, 57.
11. Visser't Hooft, ed., *The Evanston Report*, 158.
12. Ibid.
13. Ibid., 328–29.
14. Letter from Jean Fraser to Clerc, December 8, 1953, DM 1678E, 2.

only seven Youth Consultants from Africa and one of only four who was not white South African. He was the only person present at the Assembly from Mozambique or from any other of Portugal's overseas territories. Although by WCC standards still a youth, he was already thirty-four and engaged in writing a Masters thesis. He was also keenly aware of issues affecting southern Africa both from the perspective of the church and the challenges to its understanding of its missional role in the region and of the growing political tensions provoked by the National Party government in South Africa and its alliances with other white minority regimes. In some ways his comments parallel those of other participants and observers of the Assembly while in others he brings his own unique perspective to bear.

It was clearly a very significant event for him. In a letter to Clerc giving some of his impressions of Evanston he writes, "I cannot find adequate words to express what I felt during the Assembly. The people that I met from all over the world, the speeches delivered during the sessions of the Assembly, discussions in committee meetings, etc., all these have left an impact in me that will take years to erase."[15] There were several participants whom he mentions as leaving a deep impression on him: Bishop Lesslie Newbigin from the Church of South India, the Archbishop of Canterbury, Geoffrey Fisher, Pastor Marc Boegner of the Eglise Réformée de France, Archbishop Yngve Brilioth of the Church of Sweden, Bishop Eivind Berggrav of Norway, Bishop Bromley Oxnam of the Methodist Church in the United States, Bishop Barbieri of the Methodist Church in Argentina, and Professor J. L. Hromadka of the Evangelical Church of Czech Brethren. He also mentions meeting Bishop Reeves of Johannesburg, Rev. Ben Marais and Alan Paton from South Africa. Mondlane was being introduced to some of the principal actors in the global ecumenical movement, many of whom he would remain connected with as he took up leadership in the struggle for independence in Mozambique. In this regard, it is interesting to note that Michael Testa was present at the Assembly as an Observer from the Presbyterian Church of Portugal. Testa had been Mondlane's "Advisor" and a mentor in his time in Portugal and later would be deeply engaged with the Mozambican liberation movement in his position as "Representative to Europe" in the Geneva based Europe Office of the United Presbyterian Church in the USA and the United Church of

---

15. Letter from Mondlane to Clerc, September 2, 1954, DM 916A, 13.

Christ (USA)—Board for World Ministries and particularly as staff in the Commission on Inter-Church Aid, Refugees and World Service at the WCC.

Mondlane wrote that he was impressed with the way in which the Assembly spoke to the real life of the world: ". . . there was an honest attempt to connect the main theme of the Assembly, namely, Christ—Hope of the World, with actual present day social, political and economic issues."[16] In addition, he mentions the positive way in which theologians from East and West seemed to be able to communicate within the Assembly, despite the so-called "Iron Curtain" which separated them. However, he also raised critiques of what he had experienced. In relation to theological debate he wrote, "Unfortunately there was too much of theological wrangling going on during the Assembly. As a whole German theologians tend to be too other worldly, while American and British theologians tend to concern themselves with present day problems. The Greek Orthodox theologians were overinterested in problems concerning faith and order."[17] This was put into context later in his reflections but his continuing concern for the necessity of making theology relevant to the real issues of the world continued: "It is no wonder, therefore, why the German theologians (including Swiss) would tend to talk a little too much of what they call the Second Coming of Christ. After the mess in which the Christian churches had put themselves in Germany (with Hitler), they cannot see how hope in Christ could be connected with any worldly affair. Yet in telling people that their hope is solely in the Second Coming of Christ one does not solve the problems of man's [sic] confusion in this world."[18]

His analysis is shared by Nichols in his reading of the theological debate: "It was from among those who had faced the extinction of all earthly hope that there came the strongest emphasis on the hope in Christ's Coming Again, the future consummation denied in history. In this situation, they had discovered, the long disregarded apocalyptic passages in the New Testament take on actuality. 'Then,' said Dr. Schlink, 'they suddenly illuminate the whole of human life and the situation of Christians in the world and become a definite stronghold, by means of which God makes it possible for men [sic] to live, to suffer and to die

16. Ibid.
17. Ibid.
18. Ibid.

joyfully.'"[19] And later, "This experience of the churches 'under the Cross' was chiefly the experience of those who spoke French and German. Those who had not faced such radical trials were generally those who spoke English … The bulk of Orthodox, Anglicans and American Protestants simply did not live in this kind of hope in Christ the consummator. Some could penetrate it to some degree imaginatively, but it played no such central role in their lives and thought as it did for many on the Continent [sic]."[20]

In another reflection, written fifty years after the conference by Norman Hjelm who had been a Youth Consultant from the Lutheran Church in the United States, the same thought is echoed: "The assembly's theme itself, *Christ—the hope of the world*, set off theological fireworks not unrelated to the experiences of war. Europeans tended to view this theme in apocalyptic terms, a view dominated by the world's apparent hopelessness as demonstrated through the war. North Americans, on the other hand, tended to view Christian hope progressively, hailing present efforts towards building the kingdom of God in the midst of human society. The major addresses by Edmund Schlink of Heidelberg and Robert Calhoun of Yale stood in stark contrast to each other."[21] It is clear that the theological debate was primarily among European and North American theologians deriving from their own post-war contexts. In the theological debate, even more so than in the debate concerning the place of the church in the world, the voice of the churches beyond those in the west were scarcely present.

In his critique though, Mondlane goes beyond this internal theological debate to the question of how the church speaks to the world beyond itself. He says that the theme itself is one that can only speak to the church, because of its Christological language: "It seems to me that the theme applies only where people accept Christ completely as their master and lord. And I do not know of too many nations where Christ is the sole lord of the people. Even in the so called Christian nations people follow Christ and something else. And many times this something else is more than Christ. In the Western World people trust more their economic and military strengths rather than God. In the Communist states people trust their military strength and the party machines. Even those

19. Nichols, *Evanston*, 91.
20. Ibid., 93.
21. Hjelm, "Evanston After Fifty Years."

individuals who accept Christ as Lord and Master do not consistently keep in Him."[22] This goes to the heart of Mondlane's growing dilemma with the church. Although deeply committed to the church and still wanting to honor his commitment to return to Mozambique and work in the mission of the Protestant churches there, he was increasingly finding the language of the church and of Christian faith inadequate to address the deeply entrenched political and social questions which he encountered all around him. "Jesus Christ: the hope of the World" could lead either to a new form of pietism as he seemed to see in the European emphasis on the return of Christ and the disengagement from the concrete problems of the world or it could lead to a form of frenetic Christian activism which sought the resolution of political and social problems through the further Christianization of society, as he was witnessing in the United States.

It is interesting to turn once more to speeches from, and contemporary reflections on, the Assembly to understand more fully Mondlane's thinking on this point. In response to an editorial in the *Chicago Tribune* which criticized the Assembly's debate over social and political issues James Nichols wrote:

> There were a few . . . who fell into the opposite error from that of the *Tribune* and the pietists. Some supposed that one could find a "Christian solution," distinct from worldly wisdom, for political and social problems. But the discovery of Christian solutions to specific problems lies neither within the capacity nor the duty of the Church. "Our Christian hope as such," explained a discussion leaflet for the section on social issues, "cannot offer technical answers or specific solutions which statesmen and experts have failed to find . . ."[23]

In the official report on the Assembly, Bishop Eivind Berggrav of Norway is quoted extensively on the churches' engagement in the social and political life of the world:

> The churches must confess their solidarity with the world because they not only share responsibility for creating tensions in the world, but they are in fact the source of the very greatest tensions and divisions. They produce these precisely on the basis of that which Christ offered them as His own life's heritage to make

22. Letter from Mondlane to Clerc, September 2, 1954, DM 916A, 13.
23. Nichols, *Evanston*, 121.

the bonds of unity strong among them . . . Today we can say that unity in Christ has become to some extent a force in the life of the Church. It serves as a constant reminder of, and gives us a bad conscience about, our destructive tensions; it creates a new willingness in us to listen to those with whom we are in disagreement; and it helps us to see that there is no "master church" but a "church family" in Christ. And when this spirit of unity in Christ comes to influence the life of the Church, then it may also influence the tensions between nations. For we must demonstrate love to man [sic] in political relationships also. . . .[24]

In an address by Reinhold Niebuhr, the well known neo-orthodox theologian from the United States, the question of the churches' role in political and social issues and the dilemma which Mondlane was pondering is dealt with in typical Niebuhrian language:

In pronouncing our dependence on God we face two particular temptations. One is to renounce all traffic with the wisdom of the world because to do so might deflect us from the truth of the gospel. We must not bury our treasure in the ground. Ecumenical study and action have helped us to bring the gospel into a fruitful encounter with human experience and culture. The other temptation is to interpret the biblical insight that "all men [sic] are sinners" to mean that Christian faith transcends all political and social struggles. But we are men [sic] and not God and we must distinguish between the moral level of our decisions, where we are required to choose between possible alternatives, and the religious level on which indeed we acknowledge that both we and our most dangerous foes are equally sinners in God's sight and are equally in need of His forgiveness.[25]

Although there is no direct evidence as to what influence these interventions might have had on Mondlane, it seems clear that his participation in the Assembly did provide an opportunity for him to be introduced to the growing conviction of many in the global ecumenical movement that the churches had to speak out on the pressing issues of the day and, indeed, to stand with those who struggled for justice, whether or not they confessed the Christian faith. This was to be significant in Mondlane's understanding of the need of a broad based movement in

24. Visser't Hooft, ed., *Evanston Report*, 58.
25. Ibid., 64.

the liberation struggle which would encompass those of religious faith but not be limited to any one group.[26]

## Continuing Ecumenical Engagement and Exposure in the United States

Despite these changing views, or perhaps because of them, Mondlane remained actively engaged in the American churches in this period. In June of 1954, he had attended and spoken at a large gathering of the WSCS with more than four thousand delegates in Milwaukee. In his speech he was very critical of European and American missionaries in Africa, at one point arguing that it would be two thousand years before control of the African churches would be relinquished by the missionaries. Clerc received a copy of his speech in Lourenço Marques, probably through the American Methodist missionary Ruth Northcott, and wrote to Mondlane criticizing him for exaggerating the reality and arguing that he belonged to a church in which Africans were already leading.[27] In that same summer, before attending the Assembly in Evanston, he participated in a mission conference in Nashville with the Methodist Church. He went to this gathering with Ralph Dodge with whom he was very impressed despite his earlier doubts about the role he played in the controversy around his relationship with Janet Johnson. In Nashville, Mondlane went to attend a Methodist Sunday morning service with Dodge in a white church and was asked to leave; Dodge left with him. They also experienced southern segregation at several restaurants in which they tried to be served. This incident had a great impact on Mondlane and also on Dodge who recounts it in both his autobiography, *The Revolutionary Bishop Who Saw God at Work in Africa* and also in his reflections on the state of the American church *The Pagan Church: The Protestant Failure in America*.[28] Following the Assembly, Mondlane attended the World Council of Christian Education and Sunday School Association at the Methodist Centre at Lake Geneva in Wisconsin.

As in the previous summer, Mondlane worked at a cement factory just outside Oberlin in order to make a financial contribution to his studies; together with his many other commitments, it was no wonder

---

26. Mondlane, *The Struggle for Mozambique*, 71–73.
27. Letter from Clerc to Mondlane, December 26, 1954, DM 916A, 16.
28. Dodge, *The Pagan Church*.

## Study in the United States—Northwestern University, Chicago

that his Master's thesis supervisor was perturbed that he did not finish the thesis over the summer as he had planned.[29] However, this job was significant to Mondlane's broader understanding of U.S. society at the time. Janet Mondlane comments: "He immediately noted that there was absolutely no racial discrimination against the three blacks among the total of 70 workers. Nor were there any differences between Catholics and Protestants . . . the relationship between the workers and the management was excellent. He was there to make money and took on some overtime, he was exhausted and changed his working conditions . . . but his social conscience was always alert . . . as well as his need to know people and make friends."[30] The lack of racial prejudice and religious intolerance among working class Americans as suggested in this commentary seems somewhat exaggerated. However, this job did take Mondlane outside the somewhat rarefied atmosphere of the organizations and conferences of the ecumenical movement and exposed him to working class Americans in their places of work. This further challenged him to seek to make theology, and his studies in the social sciences, relevant to people who were further removed from the center of decision making in American society.

The job had been organized by a good friend and Congregational minister, Ed Hawley. Hawley, like Randall, was close to Mondlane's age and had become a close friend; his support would continue throughout Mondlane's life and in fact his marriage to Janet Johnson was held in Hawley's home and Hawley would preside at Mondlane's funeral service in Dar-es-Salaam in 1969 when he was "Pastor for Refugees" with the Christian Council of Tanzania. At the time, Hawley worked with students in Oberlin and Janet Mondlane writes that Eduardo liked his sermons because, "He tried to tear down the walls between Christians and others and criticized Christians for believing that they were bet-

---

29. Letter from Mondlane to Clerc, December 21, 1954, DM 916A, 15.

30. Manghezi, *Meu coração*, 98. "Notou imediatamente que não havia absolutamente nenhuma discriminação racial contra os três negros que existiam num total de 70 travalhadores. Nem havia diferenças entre católicos e protestantes . . . o relacionamento entre os trabalhadores e a administração era excelente. Ele estava ali para ganhar dinheiro e aceitou uma porção de horas extraordinárias, ficou exausto e mudou as suas condições de trabalho . . . mas a sua consciência social estava sempre atenta . . . bem como a sua necessidade de conhecer pessoas e fazer amizades."

ter than others. He showed how the churches in the United States were institutions full of prejudices against people of color."[31]

Once again, Mondlane's links to people involved in the civil rights movement and other social justice causes was clear. At the same time that his criticism of the approach of missionaries in Mozambique was becoming more developed, so too was his perception and critique of American society through his study and his engagement with people of different classes. In a letter to Clerc in February, 1956 he wrote: "It may not be easy to comprehend this for you because you do not quite understand race relations here in America. South Africans easily compare themselves favorably with Americans in their attitude on Negroes. It is true that the Deep South is as prejudiced against Negroes as most of South Africa and some of Mozambique and the Rhodesias. But Northern whites are not so easily classifiable. Speaking generally, there is no racial problem in Evanston, but for a Negro like myself there are a number of situations of segregation and discrimination, which however subtle, cause embarrassment from time to time."[32] As was being recognized in the civil rights movement, Mondlane understood that racism was not limited to the southern states but rather was endemic in American society as a whole, including within the liberal American church. In fact, his reflections on racial segregation in the United States quoted above were in relation to his experience of being received as an affiliate member at Evanston's First Presbyterian Church in 1956: "I will be the first Negro to be accepted in their church since it began nearly 100 years ago! . . . I can attend services in *any* church here in Evanston, so can American Negroes. But membership in most of these churches is another story. So, although two to three years ago a Chinese student was told to leave the church (by an elder who as a consequence was expelled from the church!), today when my name was presented to the elders, they enthusiastically accepted me, and they even went to the extent of offering me full membership."[33]

---

31. Ibid., 95, "ele tentava derrubar os muros entre os cristãos e os outros e criticava os cristãos por acreditarem que eram melhores do que os outros. Mostrava como as igrejas nos Estados Unidos eram instituições cheias de preconceitos para com as pessoas de cor."

32. Letter from Mondlane to Clerc, February 19, 1956, DM 916C, 1.

33. Ibid.

It is in this period that Janet Mondlane says that both she and Eduardo "lost their Christianity."[34] In September, 1954, Janet transferred to Northwestern from Miami University in Ohio to be with Eduardo. As she describes it, they lived a "bohemian" lifestyle and rarely attended church services except at times at the Unitarian Church which "brings together people of all creeds."[35] In this period, Mondlane's correspondence with Clerc decreased markedly; it appears that Clerc was very disappointed with this and began to feel that Mondlane would not return to Mozambique. He was very upset that Mondlane had supported bringing a young man called Guillerme Mabunda to study in the United States; he called Mabunda a *gaillard* (a chap) and was worried that he would ruin Mondlane's reputation in Chicago.[36]

### Changing Perspectives on Mission

Without doubt Mondlane was deeply engrossed in his studies at this time and the relationship with Johnson was of great importance. However, from his correspondence it does not seem that he lost all connection with the church nor that he was not engaged in significant theological reflection on his experience in the United States. In a letter to Clerc in the summer of 1954 he wrote, "Yet the things that you taught me, the things that my Church has taught me, the things that I got from the Bible and other means of education, are impinging themselves on me. Personal integrity is much more important to me than mere acceptance of the Vox Populi . . ."[37] And further, "There is a real paradox that haunts our Christian Faith. We believe that with Christ things can look different, yet at the same time we prefer to see things not change. When the first white people came to Africa they wished that Africans became good Christians, westernized culturally, and so on. Now that too many Africans are accepting the Western way of life they are wishing that it did not really happen as they wished."[38]

At least with Clerc, it was still through the lens of Christian faith and theology that Mondlane sought to interpret what he was experienc-

---

34. Manghezi, *Meu coração*, 128, "tinhamos perdido o nosso cristianismo."
35. Ibid., 128, "juntam pessoas de todos os credos."
36. Letter from Clerc to Paul Vaucher et. al., September 4, 1955, DM 59C, 2.
37. Letter from Mondlane to Clerc, July 10, 1954, DM 916A, 11.
38. Ibid.

ing and the wider socio-political issues he was encountering. Indeed, with Clerc, he emphasized that his education in the church, and particularly with Clerc, had been integral to his current thinking even though it had become much more sophisticated over the years:

> The Christian churches cannot save the souls of the peoples of Africa and leave them in squalor, slavery and depredation. I believe that there is more in the human being than his soul. *This I learned in my Patrulha groups* . . . There is an intricate relationship between the soul of an individual and his body and mind. This truth you taught me, Mr. Clerc, and I have found nothing in my many years of academic life that has contradicted this simple truth about man [sic]. If there is anything that I have said here in this country which many of the missionaries who disagree with me would have objected to it must be my insistence that the American churches, in their praiseworthy interest in Africa and its people, they should include those things which affect the body and the mind.[39]

What Mondlane objected to most strenuously in the Church in the United States was its dishonesty in dealing with the reality of the life of the people with whom it was engaged in mission in Africa and, indeed, its dishonesty about the reality of racism within American society and the American church itself. He spelled this out clearly to Clerc in this same letter:

> Those of us who have had the chance to read reports by missionaries working in China before the Communists took over, cannot anymore tolerate an overoptimistic view of missionary work. There are many missionaries who criticized young Chinese students who were telling Americans that things were not as smooth as the missionaries were trying to make them be in China. Things became so bad that today the American people tend to go to the other extreme; they tend to blame the missionaries for the success of Communism in China. . . . I believe that the Christians who sacrifice their incomes to support missionary work in Africa are entitled to the whole truth concerning the extent to which missionary work is successful or not. I have heard many American Christians say that they are tired of hearing only one kind of report from most missionaries. I believe that part of

---

39. Letter from Mondlane to Clerc, December 5, 1956, DM 916D, 8.

the trouble is that many of our missionaries believe that one cannot raise money if one tells certain problems to the people . . ."[40]

Rather than losing his Christianity, it would appear that Mondlane was developing a significant critique of the way in which Christian mission was carried out and the inconsistencies between what was preached by western missionaries and what was lived. He was part of a growing number of those in the ecumenical movement who felt that the church must take a much more prophetic position in relation to colonialism which meant that it would have to look honestly at the compromises it had made in its mission work as well as the compromises which the western churches had made with their own governments and economic system in order to maintain their social position. In his continuing engagement with American Christians at this time, he tried to expose these compromises and to suggest that the church needed to examine itself and what its role should be if it was to live the justice and love which it preached. In introducing the film version of Alan Paton's, *Cry, the beloved country* at a Methodist Youth Convocation at Purdue, Indianna in August of 1955, Mondlane spoke of the situation in South Africa as if it was being observed from a space ship. Through this medium, he told the truth of what was happening in the country and challenged young people to make concrete political, ethical, social and economic choices which would address this situation. He also linked this with the situation of racial segregation in the United States.[41]

Mondlane not only challenged the political and economic compromises of the mission work of the western churches but also the cultural assumptions on which it was based. He continued to link traditional African beliefs to his understanding of Christianity and refused to equate Christianity with western culture and civilization. He clearly articulated this in an address to a Missionary Training Conference in Meadville in July, 1956 entitled, "African Religious Beliefs and the Christian Faith":

> Unfortunately, Christian missionaries in the past tended to ignore the African beliefs, considering them as simply primitive. The spirit of community, embodied in ancestor worship, and as it suffuses the rest of life, including economics, politics and social

---

40. Ibid.
41. Text of a speech by Mondlane introducing *Cry the Beloved Country* at Purdue, Indiana, August 23, 1955, DM 916E, 1.

relations, was also basic for the early Christian church. Its revival in the Western Christian church will mark a turning point from crass individualism to cooperative living ... When you Western Christian missionaries come to Africa, you should always remember that we Africans are a people with a traditional religion which for centuries has provided us with the moral codes necessary for a normal human existence. If you, in your eagerness to preach the Gospel of Jesus Christ, destroy this religion without substituting something as concrete, you are likely to do more harm than good.[42]

In this regard, Mondlane had clearly been influenced by Herskovits and others in the early African studies departments in the United States. This thinking also resonated with, and perhaps linked some of this sociological work with, the pioneering writing of the Kenyan theologian, John Mbiti and others in identifying traditional African religion and culture as a starting point for articulating an African theology a decade later.[43] In this sense, Mondlane was pushing the boundaries of both theology and the church's understanding of its mission in the African context.

## Appointment to Belgian Congo Cancelled

Mondlane's first proposal for his doctoral thesis research was to have been done in conjunction with a one year appointment to work with the Methodist Church in the Belgian Congo. The appointment was arranged by George Carpenter from the Africa Committee of the Methodist Mission Council in New York. Despite his conflicts with the churches, particularly with the Methodist Church, over his relationship with Janet Johnson, and his growing differences with many in the church concerning its mission work, Mondlane was delighted to take up the appointment which would have involved him in urban sociological research and finally taken him back to Africa.[44] In the course of his research he also hoped to visit the Protestant missions in Angola.[45] Indeed this appointment would have allowed him to be engaged in mission in a way which

---

42. Paper by Mondlane given at Meadville Missionary Training Conference, "African Religious Beliefs and the Christian Faith," July, 1956, DMA916E 2.
43. See e.g., Mbiti, *African Religions and Philosophy*.
44. Manghezi, *Meu coração*, 132.
45. Letter from Mondlane to Clerc, October 17, 1956, DM 916D, 1.

would have put him in touch with the real life of the people as well as furthering his academic career.

Mondlane had received his visa and ticket and was ready to leave for Congo when he received word that the appointment had been cancelled. The Congo General Conference of the Methodist Church had met and heard a complaint from the delegation of the Methodist Church in Mozambique. Mondlane had married Janet Johnson on October 15, 1956 in the home of Ed Hawley and the Methodists in Mozambique had objected to the appointment on the basis of the marriage, that it was too soon after the marriage for the couple to be separated especially with the added strain of it being an inter-racial marriage. What seems to have been most significant however was that Mondlane had done this against the advice of the mission community in Mozambique. In a letter from Bishop Booth to George Carpenter, the following explanation was given: "A third factor in regard to the marriage is that it has taken place now against the counsel of those who have the best interests of Eduardo very much at heart. Does this mean that Eduardo is being insensitive to the advice of others? Would that be likely to make this work with him more difficult?" He wrote further, "Eduardo could enter into political questions and thereby cause trouble with the government here ... he is embittered so that his influence on the students would be adverse ..."[46] It seems too that it was felt that the appointment would worsen relations between the American Methodists and the Swiss Mission in Mozambique.[47]

Despite all of this internal discussion, however, the only explanation given to Mondlane was that the church was afraid that he would not be given a visa. In a letter to Clerc, Mondlane reacted strongly to this rationale, given that he had already received the permit, "There was also the fear that I might not get a permit to enter the Congo because of my marriage with Janet. Since I already have my permit, it is obvious that the latter is not the problem. Even if I had not yet received my permit, would it not have been more consistent with the basic principles upon which the Christian Church stands on the question of race, to wait until

---

46. Letter from Newell Booth to George Carpenter, October 26, 1956, DM 916D, 4.
47. Ibid.

the Belgian Government takes the act of impeding my entrance instead of the Church doing so for the government?"[48]

Understandably, Mondlane was furious with this kind of paternalism and politicking. In addition to cancelling this appointment, the Christian Council of Mozambique had also withdrawn its support for him to sit on the Africa Committee of the International Missionary Council based in London. Certainly the Methodists were also behind this but it seems that it may have happened in part because of Clerc's growing conviction that Mondlane would not return to Mozambique and that those who had predicted this were right.[49] Mondlane wrote to Clerc expressing his profound disappointment:

> How can Christians judge and condemn a man without giving him a chance to defend himself? This kind of dealing with people is against the very basis upon which Protestant Christianity is built. . . . I am afraid our Protestant *vakulukumba* are doing exactly the same thing which they accuse the Church of Rome of doing, viz., *Intolerance*. . . . Since I came to this country I have *always* worked for the Christian Churches. I cannot remember once when I failed to respond to an invitation to do this or that when churches were involved. . . . The situation in which I am found today in reference to the Christian Church is comparable to some extent with that in which Afonso de Albuquerque was found in when he was governor of India (in the 16th century). Because he loved his Motherland, Portugal, he appeared cruel to the Indians (which he might as well have been) and because of his love for the Indian people, whom he knew and understood better than most Portuguese of his time did, he appeared negligent and doleful in the eyes of his king and master in Portugal. I do not want to imply that I think that I love and understand the Africans better than most missionaries, or that I love and understand the Christian Church better than most non-Christians in the academic field. But I think that I am being misunderstood by the Christian Churches because of my insistence that It (the Church) understand the world in which it exists, and by the non-Christian intellectuals because of my insistence that they try to understand the Church and what it is up to. If I sound bigoted, please, forgive me, I am trying to understand my own dilemma.[50]

48. Letter from Mondlane to Clerc, November 1, 1956, DM 916D, 3.

49. Manghezi, *Meu coração*, 138. Also, cf. Letter from Clerc to Carpenter, Booth and Mondlane November, 11, 1956, DMA916C, 5.

50. Letter from Mondlane to Clerc, November 5, 1956, DM 916D, 5.

Janet Mondlane writes that it was at this moment that Eduardo decided never again to work in the mission of the Church.[51] The simmering hostility of those in Mozambique, particularly the Methodists, who could only see Mondlane in the role of a church worker and who were offended by his growing critique of the Protestant mission project and his obvious influence on the Mission Administrators in the United States, had been made manifestly clear in this decision. Despite all his best efforts, the road had been blocked and Mondlane recognized that his passion for his people would have to be expressed through means other than the Protestant churches.

---

51. Manghezi, *Meu coração*, 139.

# 7

## Discerning the Future

### Possibilities in Mozambique

WHEN MONDLANE RECEIVED THE news that his appointment to the Belgian Congo had been cancelled because of the objections of the Methodist Church in Mozambique, it was not clear what path he might follow. In addition to taking him back to Africa, the appointment was also to have been the site of his research for his doctoral dissertation at Northwestern University. There was pressure on him to finish the dissertation from the university and also his funding from the "Commission on Ministerial Training in Africa" of the Methodist Church was reaching an end.[1] He moved to Boston where Janet was studying and was able to use the library at Harvard to continue his work as well as becoming associated with the growing African Studies Center there.[2]

André-Daniel Clerc still felt that Mondlane should return to Mozambique and take up the work with youth which he had originally planned to do and which the Methodists and some in the Swiss Mission felt was his obligation. Although he had reservations on many fronts about returning to Mozambique at this time, Mondlane was not averse to the idea of teaching at the newly formed ecumenical seminary at Ricatla. The seminary had come into existence, although only after some very heated discussion,[3] as part of the movement to establish one "Church of

---

1. Letter from Theodore Tucker to Clerc, March 3, 1957, DM 1577A, 2b.

2. Manghezi, *Meu coração*, 139. See also "The African Studies Center at Boston University: A Historical Sketch," 4. http://www.bu.edu/africa/about/history/historical-sketch.pdf.

3. Letter from Clerc to Mondlane, August 19, 1955, DM 916B, 2.

Christ" in Mozambique, with all the Protestant mission churches united under this name. As early as the summer of 1955, after some conversation with the Swiss missionary, Gillet, Mondlane had written to Clerc presenting himself as a candidate. According to Janet Mondlane, Clerc denied ever having received the letter[4] and in fact was complaining at this time about Mondlane's long silence.[5] Janet Mondlane conjectures that the letter may have been intercepted by the Portuguese.[6] However, in 1958, when Clerc finally did hear that Mondlane had applied to work at Ricatla through a letter from Bishop Ralph Dodge, he was overjoyed and indeed he felt vindicated in relation to colleagues in the mission community who had said that Mondlane would never return to Mozambique. By that time though, despite his great joy, Clerc agreed that it was not the time for Mondlane to come to Mozambique.[7]

In 1957 Theodore Tucker of the National Council of Churches of Christ (NCCC) based in New York initiated some conversation with Charles Périer, Director of the MSAS in Lausanne, about the possibility of Mondlane going to Mozambique as a "missionary." They sought Clerc's advice who strongly recommended that Mondlane not go at that time because of the many tensions in the mission community caused by his marriage and also the difficult position he would be in with the colonial regime because of what he had been saying publicly in the United States.[8] Périer echoes this in his letter to Tucker, saying that it would be impossible for Mondlane to work in the current colonial situation.[9] This was also the concern in an earlier letter to Frédéric Nolde, Director of the Commission of the Churches on International Affairs of the World Council of Churches based in New York City to whom he wrote that Mondlane might immediately be arrested because of his "free expression or even under false pretexts."[10] It is very interesting to see in this corre-

4. Manghezi, *Meu coração*, 131.
5. Letter from Clerc to Mondlane, August 19, 1955, DM 916B, 2.
6. Manghezi, *Meu coração*, 131.
7. Letter from Clerc to Eduardo and Janet Mondlane with confidential copy to Charles Périer, August 1958, DM 1577E, 1.
8. Letter from Clerc to Charles Périer and Theodore Tucker from Pretoria, February 18, 1957, DM 1577D, 4.
9. Letter from Charles Périer to Theodore Tucker, February 22, 1957, DM 1582A, 1b.
10. Letter from Charles Périer to Frédéric Nolde, February 16, 1957, DM 1577A, 4, "liberté d'expression ou même sous de faux prétextes"

spondence the role being played by highly placed church administrators in the United States and in the Swiss Mission in helping to determine Mondlane's next move. It was clear that Mondlane would have, or could have, played a key role in the churches' response to decolonization in the Portuguese territories and also in the broader African context. They were being very cautious that he not be arrested or killed by the Portuguese before he could fulfill this potential. It is also interesting to note the language which was being used in relation to what he might do in Mozambique; despite the fact that he was Mozambican, he was being referred to as a missionary. Mondlane was challenging the clear dichotomy which had always been drawn between the Protestant European mission community and the indigenous church in Mozambique, even in the relatively progressive Swiss Mission. He did not fit easily into either category because of the time he had been out of Mozambique, his advanced studies and his marriage to a white American not to mention his very clear critique of the contemporary mission structures and policies.

## Possibilities with the Portuguese

At the same time, the Portuguese became much more interested in and concerned about Mondlane's growing profile and his potential as a nationalist leader. The decolonization movement in Africa had begun in earnest with Ghana gaining its independence in 1957 under Kwame Nkrumah. Although it may have seemed to most in Portugal and in Mozambique at the time that there was little likelihood of any serious independence movement gaining ground in the Portuguese colonies, Mondlane was clearly a person to be watched. There were also some challenges to what had seemed to be the almost invincible Salazar regime in Portugal[11] which may have provided some possible areas of change in colonial policy. In the course of pursuing positions at UNESCO and at the UN, Mondlane came into contact with Adriano Moreira, the head of the Portuguese delegation at the UN, a post which he held from 1957 to 1959. Moreira was known as a leftist within the Portuguese regime, in fact he had been arrested in 1947,[12] and appears to have taken a genuinely more progressive approach to dealing with the overseas territories. Janet Mondlane notes that Moreira was about

---

11. Malyn Newitt, *History of Mozambique*, 519–20.
12. Manghezi, *Meu coração*, 140.

the same age as Mondlane and that they quickly developed a friendly relationship.[13] Moreira offered Mondlane a position at the Instituto Superior de Ciências Sociais e Política Ultramarina in Lisbon, what Mondlane calls the *Escola Superior de Ultramar* in his correspondence, as an Auxiliary or Extraordinary Professor with a salary that Moreira indicated was quite generous by Portuguese standards.[14] Moreira was closely connected with the *Instituto* and would become its Director when he returned to Portugal in 1959. He also indicated there would be a position available for Janet Mondlane.

Mondlane was very tempted by this offer. He seemed convinced that Moreira was sincere in seeking him out as a more progressive voice to influence colonial policy and administration, although still, clearly, within the framework of Portuguese nationalism; Moreira describes the task as "honorable and patriotic."[15] Mondlane also believed that he might have been able to influence other professors and students at the School.[16] The position would also have enabled Mondlane to spend several months in Africa each year.[17] Part of Mondlane's interest was to cultivate a positive relationship with the Portuguese authorities which would have enabled him to return to Mozambique even though in the offer to teach at the *Instituto* he would have been explicitly prohibited from going to Mozambique, even as a visitor.[18] In a letter to Charles Périer he wrote, "In the future, we would like to be able at least to visit Mozambique and, if we were able, to help my people in some way as well."[19] Moreira was also holding out the possibility of Mondlane returning to the UN as part of the Portuguese delegation and holding an important position.[20] As tempting as this was, and as sincere as Moreira may have been, Mondlane was also aware of the co-opting agenda which was also at work in this offer. In his letter to Périer he wrote that the

13. Ibid.
14. Letter from Mondlane to Charles Périer, March 17, 1957, DM 1577D, 7.
15. Letter from Adriano Moreira to Mondlane, March 22, 1957, DM 1577D, 9, "honrosa e patriótica."
16. Letter from Mondlane to Charles Périer, March 17, 1957, DM 1577D, 7.
17. Letter from Adriano Moreira to Mondlane, March 22, 1957, DM 1577D, 9.
18. Manghezi, *Meu coração*, 140–41.
19. Letter from Mondlane to Charles Périer, March 17, 1957. DM 1577D, 7. "Gostaríamos de que no futuro possamos pelo menos visitar Moçambique, e se podermos, tambem ajudar o meu povo de qualquer maneira."
20. Letter from Adriano Moreira to Mondlane, March 22, 1957. DM 1577D, 9.

Portuguese were playing with him and he realized that if he did not accept the position there might have been negative consequences for himself or for some of the Protestant churches in Mozambique.[21]

Périer strongly advised Mondlane not to take up the position offered by the Portuguese. In a letter in February, 1957, he wrote, "It is not recommended to go to work in or for Portugal at this time. The power of the Jesuits and anti-Protestantism is too strong to allow you, Eduardo, to do productive work with all the necessary freedom and with sufficient personal security."[22] Later, in March of 1957 after hearing some of Mondlane's arguments in favor of working with Moreira in order later to be able to travel to Mozambique, he wrote, "But we can also consider that this time to serve your country directly has not yet arrived and that it is best not to compromise everything because of a little bit of impatience."[23] Périer argued that he already had a police file and that he had already been called a Communist by the PIDE. Indeed, Moreira's letter to Mondlane offering him the position at the *Instituto* was part of his file with the PIDE.[24] He would have had to defend the Portuguese colonial project and he also might have been pressured to become Roman Catholic, although Périer also sees that it might have been to the advantage of the Portuguese to have a highly placed Protestant to whom they could point as an example.

In a very interesting comment about the Portuguese he writes, "It is a shame, for the Portuguese people are one of the most congenial that I know who have enormous possibilities of Heart and mind. Unfortunate that they are dominated by Roman Catholicism which has certainly stifled them."[25] For Périer, it was not the Portuguese themselves, nor even

---

21. Letter from Mondlane to Charles Périer, March 17, 1957, DM 1577D, 7.

22. Letter from Charles Périer to Mondlane, February 28, 1957, DM 1577D, 6. "Não é indicado ir trabalhar já por ou em Portugal. O poder dos Jesuitos e o antiProtestantismo é grande demais para permitir ao Eduardo um trabalho frutuoso em toda a liberdade necessária e numa securidade pessoal suficiente."

23. Letter from Charles Périer to Mondlane, March 25, 1957, DM 1577D, 13. "Mas podemos tambem considerar que este tempo de servir direitamente a tua Pátria ainda não chegou e que é preciso não comprometer tudo por um pouco de impaciência."

24. Letter from Moreira to Mondlane, 1957, TT PIDE/DGS, SC SR 337/6, 1 30513052, 886–87.

25. Ibid. "C'est dommage, car le peuple portugais est un des plus sympathiques que je connaisse et qui a d'énormes possibilités de Cœur et d'intelligence. Dommage qu'il soit dominé par le catholicisme-romain qui l'a certainement stérilisé."

the dictatorial regime of Salazar, but rather Roman Catholicism which had made them so closed in their colonial policies and attitudes toward people of other races. It was an argument which Clerc had also used. It is interesting in that it can be strongly argued that it was Périer and Clerc's own Reformed tradition which lay at the base of the *apartheid* policies in South Africa. Without a doubt, the narrow nationalist Catholicism of Portugal with its considerable political influence exercised through the *Concordat* with the Vatican was an anti-progressive force in its colonial policy. Yet this influence was no greater than the *volks* Calvinism of the Afrikaners and its support for racial "separate development" in South Africa.[26] Any Christian or religious tradition could be appropriated to justify the racial inequality and oppression of colonialism and white supremacy and conversely any Christian or religious tradition could play a more critical or prophetic role. In the Mozambican and Portuguese colonial contexts, given the role of the Roman Catholic Church, it is true that the Reformed, and more broadly Protestant, tradition was, and was seen to be, subversive to colonial policy and supportive of African nationalism. Yet to some extent the same could be said of the role of Catholicism in relation to *apartheid* in South Africa.[27]

## Possibilities in International Organizations

Périer, Tucker and others strongly advised Mondlane, and also were willing to actively advocate for him, to seek a position in an international organization rather than accept the position which Moreira was offering him. They felt that in this way he could do something toward the decolonization process without, on the one hand, compromising himself with the Portuguese or, on the other, being lost to the African nationalist cause by being identified and eliminated as a subversive force by the Portuguese. The two most likely possibilities were in UNESCO and in the Trustee Section of the UN. Périer, though, also suggested the possibility of working in an international ecumenical organization: "However, one could also envisage . . . that your temporary work in an ecumenical center (World Council, International Missionary Council) or in a training center for the African Elite in Europe or in Africa could

---

26. See De Gruchy, *Liberating Reformed Theology*, 21–29.

27. See Houtart and Rousseau, *The Church and Revolution*, 238ff; and De Gruchy, *Church Struggle*, 95–98.

be equally useful, even if indirectly for the moment, in Mozambique."[28] All were aware that work in UNESCO or the UN also had complications because the Portuguese would have to approve any appointment given that Mondlane was a Portuguese citizen.

The preferred position seems to have been in UNESCO. Périer wrote a letter of recommendation for Mondlane to U. Adiseschah, the Assistant Director of UNESCO in Paris in September 1956.[29] In a letter from Périer to Frédéric Nolde at the WCC office in New York, he wrote, "To have a Protestant black African in the mix seems to us of supreme importance."[30] And in a letter to Theodore Tucker he wrote, "That is why we believe that we have to do our best to found [sic], for a few years, a situation for Ed. Mondlane in one international institution like the UNESCO. In this sphere Mondlane would now be the most useful for his country."[31] Mondlane's list of references were very impressive although, interestingly, all American: Dr. Wendell Bell, Professor of Sociology at Northwestern University, Dr. Melville Herskovits, Professor of Anthropology at Northwestern, Dr. George Simpson, Head of Department of Sociology and Anthropology, Oberlin College, Dr. Darrell Randall, Economist and Dr. Calvin Stillman, Professor of Economics, University of Chicago.[32] Initially Mondlane received a very positive response from UNESCO but then a second letter indicated that there was no work at that time. Clerc, Périer and Tucker all conjectured that it was the Portuguese or the Roman Catholic Church that blocked this possibility especially after Moreira had offered Mondlane the position in Portugal.

The other possibility that arose at this time was to work in the Trustee Section of the UN in New York. Theodore Tucker assisted in approach-

---

28. Letter from Charles Périer to Mondlane, March 25, 1957, DM 1577D, 10. "Mais on peut envisager aussi . . . que ton activité temporaire dans un centre œcuménique (Conseil œcuménique, Conseil International des Missions) ou dans un centre de formation de l'Elite Africaine en Europe ou en Afrique pourrait également être utile, bien qu'indirectement pour l'instant, au Mozambique."

29. Letter from Charles Périer to U. Adiseschah, September 29, 1956, DM 1492A, 1.

30. Letter from Charles Périer to Frédéric Nolde, February 16, 1957, DM 1577A, 1a. "Avoir un Africain noir évangélique dans ce milieu nous apparaît de première importance."

31. Letter from Charles Périer to Theodore Tucker, February 22, 1957, DM 1582A, 1b.

32. Ibid.

ing Dr. Heinz Wieschoff, the head of the Trusteeship Department, in order to secure this position.[33] Again, however, there was the problem of needing the approval of the Portuguese to take up this work. Mondlane was concerned that if he took out U.S. citizenship in order to get the position, he might never be able to return to Mozambique.[34] He attempted to deal with this issue as well as to decline the offer from Moreira to teach in Lisbon at the same time. In a very diplomatic letter, he wrote that he was very tempted by the offer to teach in the Centro de Estudos do Ultramar. However, he said that his difficult financial situation, because of debts from his studies and also because they were expecting a baby, did not permit him to take up the position at the time. He links this financial need with the offer of a position at the UN: "The Secretariat of the United Nations has offered me a job in which I would start working next month. In view of what I have said above, I feel that it is worth accepting it, even though it is a "junior" position. I am doing this in the hope that in the future I would be able to return to Lisbon to take up the functions of Professor in the Institute, or another similar position, if my Government still is interested in my services. . . . I think that this work falls very close to my academic and humanitarian interests. And I hope to be able to represent my Portuguese nation with all honour and responsibility."[35]

Although the position which Mondlane was being offered was not a political one and so did not strictly require the approval of the Portuguese, out of courtesy they were asked and in fact gave their authorization. However, this was before Mondlane's letter was sent to Moreira. He very intentionally did this so that the Portuguese might think that he would refuse the position at the UN, even with their authorization, and go to work in Lisbon. Mondlane also used the letter from Moreira

---

33. Letter from Theodore Tucker to Charles Périer, March 7, 1957. DM 1577A, 3.

34. Letter from Mondlane to Charles Périer, March 17, 1957, DM 1577D, 7.

35. Letter from Mondlane to Adriano Moreira, March 30, 1957, DM 1577D, 11. "O Secretariado das Nações Unidas oferece me um emprego para começar a trabalhar no mês próximo. Em vista do que tenho dito acima, vejo que vale a pena aceitá-lo, mesmo que seja uma posição 'junior.' Fá-lo com a esperança de que no futuro poderei regressar a Lisboa para exercer as funções de Professor no Instituto, ou outra posição semelhante, se o meu Governo ainda se interessar em meus serviços . . . Acho que este emprego cai muito perto dos meus interesses académicos e humanitários. E espero poder representar a minha nação Portuguesa com toda a honra e responsibilidade."

to prove that he was a *persona grata* in Portugal for the UN Secretariat.[36] Finally, in order to confuse the censors and the PIDE about his true intentions, he sent a letter to Clerc in Lourenço Marques saying that he was accepting the position in Portugal and later wrote again to say that he was taking up the position at the UN.[37]

## Working at the United Nations

Mondlane began his work as a Research Officer in the Trusteeship Division at the UN on May 1, 1957. This division was responsible for non-self governing territories, many of which had been held under Mandates established by the League of Nations after the First World War. In Africa, these territories included Tanganyika and very early on Mondlane expressed an interest in this territory and was given work related to it.[38] Also very early on, he was considering the possibility of returning to Mozambique as a member of the staff of the UN which would have allowed him to travel with some degree of protection within Portuguese territory.[39] It was in this position that he developed a strong friendship with Julius Nyerere, a frequent petitioner in the Trusteeship Division, and also came under the influence of Ralph Bunche, the Director of the Division and also a moving force in the National Association for the Advancement of Colored People (NAACP) in the United States. Janet Mondlane asserts that at this time Eduardo's desire to become more actively involved in changing the situation in Mozambique was heightened but also that he was convinced that he could work with Adriano Moreira to change the direction of Portuguese colonial policy and move toward self determination for the overseas territories. She quotes an undated letter to Clerc: "The African world is in great political and social commotion. If the Portuguese do not change their political position they are going to lose their influence in all the territories which they control today. If there is a Portuguese who is willing to make these profound changes in the Portuguese position on Africa, it would be Dr. Adriano Moreira. If he does not succeed in doing anything in this direction

---

36. Manghezi, *Meu coração*, 141.
37. Letter from Mondlane to Périer, April 1, 1957, DM 1577D, 14.
38. Letter from Mondlane to Charles Périer, May 13, 1957, DM 1577D, 19.
39. Letter from Charles Périer to Mondlane, May 23, 1957, DM 1577D, 20.

Portugal will be lost."[40] At the UN, Mondlane was often invited to meetings and receptions organized by the Portuguese delegation and they continued to pressure him to accept a position in Portugal. However, he also recognized that the more he resisted taking up their offer, the more likely it was that they would seek other ways to control or silence him. In a letter to Périer he wrote, "It seems to us that if the Portuguese government does not succeed in persuading us it will be forced to resort to whatever methods necessary (including methods which only dictatorial states know how to use!)."[41]

In this period, Mondlane's correspondence with Charles Périer in relation to his work and seeking advice in relation to the Portuguese increased. Indeed, Périer became his primary point of contact for the Swiss Mission. However, his correspondence with André-Daniel Clerc did not end. After the difficult tensions at the time of his marriage to Janet Johnson and the divisions within the mission community in Mozambique, a reconciliation took place and the affectionate relationship between the two men was restored. At this time though, Mondlane became as much a mentor to Clerc as the missionary had been to him at an earlier time. In a letter written in November 1959, Mondlane clearly stated his growing concern for the independence of Mozambique:

> . . . I personally feel that my best services should be rendered through the United Nations. It is only through the United Nations that I can contribute whatever is within my capacity towards the advancement of the African cause. The work that I am doing here in Trusteeship is extremely challenging to me. I feel that I am helping to develop institutions which will be helping in building states in Africa which might finally be influential in delivering our African people from the present oppressive measures. The independence of Tanganyika for instance, is going to be very important in Moçambique. The people of Tanganyika are not different from the people of Moçambique. So that their

---

40. Mondlane, Undated letter quoted in Manghezi, *Meu coração*, 141. "O mundo africano está em grande comoção política e social. Se os portugueses não mudarem a sua posição política vão perder a sua influência em todos os territórios que hoje controlam. Se há um português que está disposto a fazer mudanças profundas na posição portuguesa sobre África, esse será o sr. Dr. Adriano Moreira. Se ele não conseguir fazer nada nessa direcção Portugal estará perdido."

41. Letter from Mondlane to Périer, October 19, 1957, DM 1577D, 22. "Parece-nos que se o governo português não conseguir persuadir-nos será forçado a recorrer a quaisquer métodos (incluindo métodos que só estados ditatoriais sabem usar!)."

freedom is going to help to enhance the freedom of the people of Moçambique. I feel that I am playing a very important role in providing the necessary information which is helping the Trusteeship Council to make decisions which finally aid the cause of freedom in Africa.[42]

## A Changing Understanding of the Church's Role in Africa

Although he wrote to Clerc that if the circumstances were different he would be willing to come to Mozambique and work with the Swiss Mission, it was clear that he was taking a much more political path. Still, he wished to maintain his connection with the Swiss Mission and wanted to establish a bursary in Clerc's name to assist a high school student in Mozambique to continue their studies. He was in conversation with the International Missionary Council to administer these funds. It is interesting that in response, Clerc suggested that the bursary be called the "Novidades Honuane Fund" after Mondlane's friend who died while still in secondary school. Clerc also suggested that Mondlane be in touch with Michael Testa in Lisbon concerning several Mozambican students studying there whom he would have been able to support.[43] Clerc identified many young people from the Swiss Mission who were either in secondary school in Mozambique or doing further studies in Lisbon who would have been candidates for this support.

While Clerc was on an extended leave in Switzerland, he and Mondlane were able to share a much more open discussion by letter about the role of the church in the contemporary African context. Zedequias Manganhela, who was to become the President of the Synod Council of the Presbyterian Church of Mozambique and was a friend of Mondlane's, was accompanying Clerc in his mission interpretation in Switzerland and had been in touch with several Cameroonian pastors. In his letter, Clerc had made some comments about Felix Moumié, the leader of the nationalist UPC which was fighting against the first independent government in Cameroon, the pro-French regime of Ahmadou Ahidjo, which Mondlane had taken to be anti-communist. In the extensive excerpt which follows, Mondlane outlines in some detail his growing frustration with the lack of support from western governments

---

42. Letter from Mondlane to Clerc, November 21, 1959, DM 917B, 4.
43. Letter from Clerc to Mondlane from Lausanne, December 3, 1959, DM 917B, 5.

for genuine African independence movements and the use of the label "communist" to describe any person or group which opposed western interests, a frustration which was to continue with him while seeking support for FRELIMO over the next decade. He also outlines here his frustration with the churches, particularly those of his own Reformed tradition, which echo this labeling and refuse to embrace the movements for genuine African independence, a frustration that harkens back to his expulsion from South Africa by those who confessed his own Reformed faith. His call for a "revolution" within the Christian churches and a re-positioning of their commitment builds on his previous thinking and also anticipates the call to a more prophetic stance among the churches in Mozambique and throughout the southern Africa region in the growing movements of contextual liberation and Black theologies in the 1970s. His use of Weber's theories concerning the role of Protestant piety in the growth of capitalism is also quite evident:

> It seems to be a fashionable thing among modern man [sic] to label his enemies Communist. It is a much simpler way of disposing with the matter than to lay down all the facts pros and cons. I am afraid it is an expensive habit, for the future of Democracy in the world depends on how earnestly interested in the rights of All Men [sic] the people in power are today. The Government of the Union of South Africa is labelling the African National Congress and the Pan Africanist Movement "Communist"; the United States of America is beginning to label Castro in Cuba "Communist", Singhman Rhee in Korea is justifying his brutalities against those who peacefully protest against this Government "Communists", now Ahidjo is labelling the Union des Populations Camerounienne "Communists", and our Christian missionaries are chiming in with the same charges.
> 
> By the way, the Portuguese Government is beginning to imply that the Protestants in Portuguese Africa are preparing the ground for development of Communism among Africans. And if within a short time from now, some of us begin to organize a *Nationalist Movement in Mocambique*, a not unthinkable idea these days, and the Portuguese will call us Communists, I can hear our spiritual fathers from the Western World call us "Communists" too. I hope this is not going to be the case, for we will need the sympathy of many of the Western European peoples who have helped to educate us through the Christian Churches.
> 
> ... Except for the Anglican Church of South Africa, the Christian Churches of that part of the world have dismally failed

to provide the necessary leadership to solve the racial problems that harass mainly the black people. I must say that I am very much ashamed of my own Church in South Africa. I am ashamed of the part played by the Calvinists of all persuasions—Dutch Reformed, Presbyterian, Swiss Mission, and all! When Rev. [Henri Philip] Junod and his wife were visiting the United States a few years ago, they spent all their time defending apartheid. I know this because I drove them to many places where they spoke while they were in the Chicago area. I am afraid members of the Christian churches which derive from the Reformed tradition are too busy enjoying the material wealth which a large number of them accumulated in their pursuit of frugality and hard labor which they learned so well from Calvin. The Christian Church needs a revolution, a new Reformation! We Africans, it does not matter whether we are Calvinists, Catholics, Methodists, Anglicans, Moslems or Pagans, are now engrossed in a struggle against White Supremacy. In our struggle we shall use every help that we can get. If Americans can be persuaded to give us the help we need, we shall welcome them; if the Russians will come first to our aid we shall accept whatever contribution they may be offering us; if those Europeans who love freedom are interested in sharing that love of freedom with us, we shall welcome them. Our sole aim in the struggle in Africa is to dislodge it of oppressors. . . .

The Christian Churches have done a great deal in giving us a sense of belonging and education. We do not believe that God is on our side, for God is on everybody's side. It's already wonderful that Africans are beginning to believe that God is on Everybody's Side. For only a few years ago, I recall hearing many Africans saying that God is on the White man's side. If the Christian Church had a part in teaching the African to believe that God loves them too, it is good enough.[44]

In his response to Mondlane's letter, Clerc attempted to clarify what he had said about the political situation in Cameroon. He also, though, seeks to remind Mondlane of what it is like to be the church and bear a prophetic witness within the reality of Portuguese and French colonial structures and the ongoing connection which existed, and appeared to exist, between the Protestant churches and African nationalism in both Mozambique and Cameroon.

---

44. Letter from Mondlane to Clerc in Lausanne, April 21, 1960, DM 917C, 4.

I don't know how I expressed myself in my last letter when I spoke of Zedquias Manganhela having contacts with pastors from Cameroon, African pastors. Mr. Njami is bantu [sic] and told me of the great satisfaction he had in meeting Manganhela. Mr. Njami had his cousin assassinated by the French in 58 . . . and, agreeing with your affirmations, declared that Moumié is a member of our Presbyterian Church, that he gives offerings to the Church and that, in fact, a pastor was jailed for having the name of Moumié in the financial books of the Church. Perhaps Ed. you don't know that all of us in M. are taken for communists, I being in the same bag with many others. . . . In Cameroon the backbone of the UPC are the Protestants. Mr. Njami who has many reasons to affirm that the French brought nothing good, does not skimp words to congratulate the missionaries (although subject to sin and error, at times crass—you can rest easy that I am well informed over this point!) for the role that they have played, whether in the time of the Germans . . . or whether essentially, by the Swiss of the Paris Mission and the Americans. . . . We must pray that the Church remains true and faithful. It is a daily problem, but I agree with you thinking that the current situation necessitates a huge spiritual renewal and a formidable vision. But this is a problem not only of the Europeans but, also of the Churches of the whole world. . . . The number 1 problem of our Missions in M. is the preparation of a highly educated elite. We have to confess that the Portuguese system does not favour this task and does everything to discourage those who do not have a strong soul and a very lively intelligence.[45]

45. Letter from Clerc to Mondlane, May 31, 1960, DM 917C, 5. "Não sei como me exprimi na minha carta última quando falei de Zedequias. ou exprimi-me mal ou Eduardo leu-me mal. O que quis dizer é que Manganhela teve contactos com psatores dos Camarões, pastores africanos. O Sr. Njami é bantu [sic] e disse-me a muita boa satisfação que teve em encontrar Manganhela. O Sr. Njami teve o seu primo assassinado pelos franceses em 58. . . . e, concordando com as suas afirmações, declara que Moumié é membro da nossa Igreja presbiteriana, que faz ofertas à Igreja e que, até, um pastor foi preso por ter tido o nome de Moumié no livro das contas da Igreja. Talvez Ed. não saiba que nós todos, em M. somos tidos por comunistas, eu sendo na mesma saca com muitos outros. . . . Nos Cam. a coluna vertebral do UPC são os Protestantes. O Sr. Njami que tem muitas razões para afirmar que os franceses nada trouxeram de bom, não poupa em palavras para felicitar os missionários (embora sujeitos ao pecado e ao erro, às vezes crasso—fique descansado que estou muito bem informado sobre este ponto!) pela actuação que desempenharam, seja no tempo dos alemães . . . seja essencialmente, pelos suíços da Missão de Paris e os Americanos . . . Devemos orar para que a Igreja seja leal e fiel. É problema de cada dia, mas, concordo consigo pensando que a situação actual necessita grande renovação espiritual e uma visão formidável. Mas isto é problema não só dos Européus mas, também das Igrejas do mundo inteiro. . . . O problema No 1, das

## The broader debate

This would be an ongoing tension between those involved in the liberation movement outside the country, including those in the global church who acted in solidarity with FRELIMO, and those who struggled to resist and to live faithful lives within Mozambique, especially as the repression increased with the growth of FRELIMO and its penetration into the country. Although this included the European and North American missionaries, it was the local African churches which faced this threat in all its brutality and was perhaps best illustrated in the ongoing harassment and eventual imprisonment and death of Zedequias Manganhela. The critique of the local church from the outside often did not adequately take into account the enormous pressure to remain silent in the face of repression and atrocities and did not recognize the risk and witness that the church made within its limited possibilities.

This debate had also been playing itself out in correspondence between Theodore Tucker and Charles Périer in 1958 and 59 in regard to a report on Mozambique by the American anthropologist Marvin Harris from Columbia University entitled *Portugal's African "Wards."* Harris was a friend of Mondlane's who did fieldwork in Mozambique in 1955–6. In his report, he denounced the plight of Africans under Portuguese rule and it has been argued that this report decisively influenced the abolition of the forced labor system a few years later.[46] The report was published by the American Committee on Africa in which the Africa Committee of the National Council of Churches of Christ in the USA, where Tucker was Executive Secretary, was a member. Périer wrote to Tucker because he was concerned about the response the Portuguese would have toward the Protestant churches because of the report. He compared it to the "Ross Report" which had been written some thirty years earlier and which had had serious consequences for the Protestant missions in the Portuguese colonies. Périer opened the discussion:

> We deplore this type of petard in a colony which is so very little open to Protestant Missions. We have already great trouble to
> nossas Missões em M. é a preparação duma elite altamente educada. Devemos confessar que o sistema português não favorece essa tarefa e faz tudo para desanimar os que não tem alma forte & muito viva inteligência."

---

46. "Marvin Harris," *Cultural Materialism*: http://www.cultural-materialism.org/cultural-materialism/harris.asp

do our work there, and without some gentlemen, of course very sympathetic, still complicating our work with their blunders . . .

Diplomatically, and in the actual world-wide political conjuncture, there is nothing to do against the Portuguese Government. We are simply asking to continue our work in peace.

The most sure and unfailing way to be really useful—and in eternity—to the population of this colony is to preach and to give them the Gospel and to make haste in erecting the Church of Christ whilst there is still time.

Now, all we do get with this demeanour—as it is the case of professor Harris—is stiffness on the part of the Authorities, greater difficulties in obtaining the visa of entry and in renewing or increasing the European staff.[47]

Although sympathetic to Périer's position, Tucker pointed out that the Harris report was published by an independent committee and that it was not directly connected with the Protestant Mission Societies.[48] Tucker had been a missionary in Angola and understood the Portuguese colonial context well; he also had lived the compromise which had to be made with the colonial authorities in order to be engaged in that missionary work. He writes, "For many of us the silent acquiescence in the system of government while we attempted to preach the gospel and do works of mercy was a very heavy burden."[49] He also knew that for many in the African church, this compromise was seen as essential to their survival. "More than once when our African teachers have complained of their lot I have asked them, 'Do you want us to make a public protest, and be excluded from Angola? For me personally this will be a relief to an uneasy conscience'. The reply was always, 'No, stay here and help us.'"[50] However, he responds to Périer's phrase "whilst there is time" with a challenge not unlike that of Mondlane in calling for a revolution among the Mozambican churches:

> There is the rub. Do you not think it possible that in such a time as this, our resolute non-involvement in political matters, our careful refraining from criticizing the Portuguese authorities, our attempt to work within a Roman dominated system, may

47. Letter from Charles Périer to Theodore Tucker, February 5, 1959, DM 1577A2, 3.
48. Letter from Theodore Tucker to Charles Périer, February 9, 1959, DM 1577A2, 4.
49. Ibid.
50. Ibid.

mean that in a very short time, African Christians will reject us because we have refused to apply the gospel to the realm of citizenship? In 1955 and 1956 old bush Africans said to me more than once, "Your relatives are doing thus and so to us." When I protested that Portuguese Roman Catholics and North American Protestants were not closely related they said, "You're all white men [sic], aren't you?" I have the uneasy feeling that perhaps Harris has said what we Christians ought to have said. In our understandable desire to maintain the laudable work we have already begun our silence may possibly have been a denial of our Lord. On the other hand it may be part of the way of the Cross to keep silent, to bear the reproaches of men like Harris, when he says, (in private conversation) "I wish missionaries had made these facts known long ago. They really understand the system better than any one else."[51]

Périer's reply elicits a very pietistic view of mission in Mozambique, one which does not seem representative of the Swiss Mission, especially in a context such as this where he could have been open and honest about the political situation. He wrote,

> I notice that the answer you have received from coloured [sic] people of Angola (No, stay here and help us) is exactly the same I received from coloured people in Mozambique. Quite recently, an African from the Transvaal has said, concerning the intervention of certain Anglican people or from our colleagues who are tempted to interfere in the apartheid politics: "There is a fight which you White people, you cannot do it at our place. That is a work which we, Natives have to do." And he added: "We know very well if the cause of your abstention is from cowardice or from prudence." For the heathen, the Whites are all in the same basket, but not for the christians.
>
> Those who have to interfere directly are the christians, whites and blacks *of the same nationality as the Authorities*. . . .
>
> I think that if we have followed the opinion of Mr. Harris (I wish missionaries had made these facts known long ago) no more evangelical Mission would be accepted in Mozambique. Several hundred thousand souls would never have heard about Christ during these 50 years of Mission. The Church of Christ would not have been born either. And if we know how to value the huge benefit of the salvation for all and even for only one soul, who in favour of this benefit have been out of perdition, of

---

51. Ibid.

ignorance, of the cruel witchcraft, of all the anxious dramas of paganism; in that case, we are rather hesitating to compromise again the results by using an attitude opposed to the apartheid politics.[52]

If this was representative of the Swiss Mission under Périer, it is clear that it was in sharp contrast to Mondlane's thinking about the role of the church and its mission in Mozambique and the other Portuguese territories. It is revealing to contrast their opinions about the Anglican Church in South Africa and its, albeit limited, stand against apartheid. Despite the "winds of change" blowing across the African continent, Périer did not seem to be able to look critically at the compromise which the Protestant churches had made with the Portuguese colonial system and to "read the signs of the times" that called for the churches' solidarity with the movements for political liberation in Mozambique and elsewhere.

## A Rapidly Changing Context

The years 1960 and 1961 marked an important milestone in this movement for political liberation, and the reaction to it. In 1960, seventeen African countries became independent and fifteen took up seats in the United Nations where they joined with many Asian countries in promoting decolonization in the remaining territories of Africa and sought to isolate Portugal because of its determination to maintain its "overseas provinces." This bloc also led a more concerted challenge to South Africa and its system of apartheid and the accommodation of western countries to it. In March of 1960, the massacre at Sharpeville and the subsequent banning of the ANC and the PAC, took the struggle in South Africa to a different level in which it was no longer possible to advocate only non-violent resistance against the National Party government. In June of 1960, Portuguese troops opened fire on unarmed peasants peacefully petitioning the Administrator in Mueda in Cabo Delgado in the north of Mozambique. The resulting massacre of more than five hundred people helped to politicize the Makonde people and to catalyze MANU, one of the founding organizations of FRELIMO.[53] In February of 1961, a violent uprising began in Angola with the Movimento Popular de Libertação de

---

52. Letter from Charles Périer to Theodore Tucker, February 24, 1959, DM 1577A2, 6.
53. Newitt, *History of Mozambique*, 521. See also, Mondlane, *Struggle*, 117–18.

Angola (MPLA), attacking prisons where political prisoners were held in Luanda and in March in the north near the border with Congo with the União dos Povos de Angola (UPA) under Holden Roberto attacking several large Portuguese farms. The subsequent fighting left more than 20,000 Africans and more than 1,000 European settlers dead.[54] In Portugal itself, the Salazar regime was experiencing its greatest challenge since its inception in 1932 with the attempted coup under the direction of the Minister of Defence, General Julio Botelho Moniz, with the complicity of the American Embassy, in large part a response to the uprising in Angola and Salazar's decision to defend Angola "at once and on the largest scale."[55]

In November 1960, John F. Kennedy was elected President of the United States. Kennedy was seen as a liberal despite his weak voting record on domestic issues such as civil rights in Congress.[56] It was in foreign policy that Kennedy sought a much more independent approach for the United States; the so-called "Africanists" within the administration wished to extricate the country from its tacit support for European colonial policies and sought to support political independence movements friendly to the West, and particularly to the United States, as an alternative to communist inspired and supported movements which were growing throughout the continent.[57] For Portugal this would mean an end to U.S. support or abstention in the United Nations on issues related to its African territories. As late as December 14, 1960, still under Eisenhower, the United States had abstained, together with Great Britain, France, Portugal and South Africa on a proposal put forward by the Soviet Union for "a speedy and unconditional end to colonialism in all its forms and manifestations."[58] Kennedy had pledged in 1956 that a Democratic Administration would not continue this policy of abstention and on March 15, 1961 the new U.S. ambassador to the United Nations, Adlai Stevenson, voted in favor of a resolution on Angola put forward in the Security Council by Liberia, Ceylon and the United Arab Republic on which Britain and France abstained. Again on April 20,

---

54. Schneidman, *Engaging Africa*, 16.
55. Ibid., 16–19.
56. Ibid., 12.
57. Ibid., 11–13.
58. Ibid., 2.

the U.S. voted in favor of a resolution in the General Assembly urging Portugal to move toward self determination in its overseas territories.[59]

This then was a time of significant transition not only in Mondlane's life but also in global politics, with the continuing movement of decolonization and the growing power and influence of the United States and its "cold war" with the Soviet Union. It was also a time of transformation in the global ecumenical movement. In 1961, Pope John XXIII opened the Second Vatican Council which was to have a profound impact on the life of the Roman Catholic Church, its relationship with other churches and its role in international politics. In the same year, the 3rd Assembly of the World Council of Churches met in New Delhi, India, the first to be held outside the West. In itself, this reflected the changing face of the WCC to become a truly global organization. Twenty-three churches became members of the WCC at this Assembly, eleven from Africa (two of which were Pentecostal) and four Orthodox from eastern Europe and the Soviet Union. Also of great significance was the merger of the International Missionary Council with the WCC. Since 1948, they had been closely associated but had maintained separate identities; now the three major streams of the modern ecumenical movement which had emerged at the Edinburgh Missionary Conference in 1910 had come together and the mission of the church was to be much more closely integrated with its understanding of faith and order as well as its life and work. In his memoirs, W. A. Visser't Hooft quotes Sam Cavert in his report on the Assembly, "[The churches] were not only determined to stay together (as at Amsterdam) and to grow together (as at Evanston) but to move out together into the world's struggle for social justice and international peace."[60] This was to have great significance for the role which the WCC would play in the struggle for liberation in southern Africa, including Mozambique, and the connection Mondlane would have with it.

---

59. Ibid., 15–16.
60. Visser't Hooft, *Memoirs*, 317–18.

# 8

# Return to Mozambique

## Doctoral dissertation

MONDLANE WAS CLEARLY ENGAGED with all of these events from his vantage point within the Trusteeship Commission of the United Nations and it was within this charged context that he made his decision to return to Mozambique on home leave after his work as part of the UN monitored plebiscite in the former German colonial area of Cameroon. In 1959 he completed work on his PhD at Northwestern University during a leave from the UN and with the help of a further bursary from the PSF.[1] The title of the dissertation was "Role Conflict, Reference Group and Race" and the research focused on a questionnaire with students based on a hypothetical situation in which the student was a proctor in an examination and found someone cheating. Response was documented based on the race of the proctor and the one cheating as well as on whether the university authorities would be likely to know of the action or not. Results were plotted on a Universalism-Particularism continuum. The work is interesting in attempting to gauge racial attitudes of whites and blacks in the northern and southern United States at the time. However, one is also tempted to wonder whether this topic attracted Mondlane because of his own conflicted understanding of so-called reference groups and belonging given his long stay outside Mozambique and his integration into U.S. society, not to mention the growing tension between the possibilities of an academic career and a

---

1. Manghezi, *Meu coração*, 147.

more engaged political life in seeking liberation for Mozambique from Portuguese colonialism.

## Complications in preparing to return to Mozambique

Although, as noted above, Mondlane did feel that his work at the United Nations contributed to the growing independence movement in Africa, he was also increasingly frustrated that it seemed he could do little to advance the cause of independence for Mozambique. In his letter of June 1, 1960 to Clerc he wrote, "My next letter will deal with my new *dreams* about Moçambique. I still hope to return to that enchanted land to play my part in delivering the people from Portuguese oppression. Next year Janet, the children and I will visit Moçambique for two months. Now that I have finished my PhD dissertation I shall definitely go to Mocambique for at least a visit, regardless of the consequences."[2] This trip had been in Mondlane's plans for many years but only at this time, with the protection of travelling as an employee of the United Nations, did it become a real possibility. The trip was organized in cooperation with the IPM and the Swiss Mission as well as with his family.

It is interesting to note the concerns that were expressed about the visit and how much emphasis was still centered on Mondlane's marriage to a white American rather than on the potential political difficulties which Mondlane might have with the Portuguese. In a confidential letter from Clerc to M. E. Juillerat, the head of the Swiss Mission in Mozambique, these concerns are clearly expressed: "a) It is impossible to refuse this visit of Janet's which honors the trust that we placed in Ed. in the sense that he would return to Moz. b) But while visiting New York, I should draw her attention to the fact that it is in Moz. that the real difficulties resulting from her marriage will be able to be seen: the personal reaction of the Libombos, the reaction of African women ... but more seriously, the reaction of the common Portuguese. With the agitation brought on by these events, certain behaviors could become quite annoying. All the more after he has joined her."[3]

---

2. Letter from Mondlane to Clerc, June 1, 1960, DM 917C, 6.

3. Letter from Clerc to M. E. Juillerat, August 3, 1960, DM 917C, 13, "a) Il n'est pas possible de refuser cette visite de Janet qui honore la confiance que nous avons mise en Ed. en ce sens qu'il reviendrait au Moz. b) Mais je devrai la rendre attentive lors de ma visite á NY que c'est au Moz. que les vraies difficultés résultant de son mariage peuvent se manifester: réaction personnelle des Libombos, réaction des femmes africaines ...

It was clear as well that this trip was being made on Mondlane's initiative, not on the initiative of the missionaries. Clerc wrote, "In any case, they seem quite determined to come and they are not asking me if another time would be more suitable."[4]

## The Edelweiss Program

Mondlane had also arranged for Clerc to visit the United States previous to his travel to Cameroon and Mozambique to be involved in the discussion of the scholarship program, originally to be named in his honor but later known as the Edelweiss program.[5] As noted earlier, this concern for educating a future African elite was certainly at the heart of Clerc's understanding of his involvement in mission in Mozambique and would be an ongoing concern for Mondlane and for his wife Janet as they became more and more engaged in the struggle for Mozambique's liberation from Portuguese colonial domination. However, in this endeavor it was also clear that Mondlane was taking the initiative and moving beyond the bounds of the mission community in establishing this program and making it clear that it could not be identified primarily as a church project. He wrote to Clerc, "I should like to ask you to refrain from discussing it with anybody except the most reliable persons among your friends. If the scholarship arrangements succeeded they would not be a part of the missionary training program, for the organization that is interested in giving the money is not a church related body. However, the director of the organization knows that the Clercs are Christian missionaries."[6] Mondlane was also consulting with Theodore Tucker and Emory Ross in establishing this scholarship program[7] but the people involved also included those from his academic and diplomatic circles of contacts. Still though, it is interesting to observe that Mondlane understood Clerc

---

mais plus graves, les réactions des Portugais de la rue. Avec l'énervement provoqué par les événements, certains comportements peuvent être assez ennuyeux. Surtout quand lui l'aurait rejointe, elle."

4. Ibid. "En tous cas, ils semblent bien déterminés à venir et ne me demandent pas si une autre époque conviendrait mieux."

5. Manghezi, *Meu coração*, 147.

6. Letter from Mondlane to Clerc, Undated, DM 917C, 7bis.

7. Ibid.

and Tucker to be the "experts" because of their long missionary service in Mozambique and Angola respectively.[8]

## Pushing the boundaries of the mission paradigm en route

Mondlane was able to have only a short stop in Switzerland en route to Cameroon in order to be in touch with members of the Swiss Mission. His wife Janet went from England to Switzerland and then on to Portugal and Mozambique. For her, it was an opportunity to gain some knowledge of these parts of Eduardo's background and begin to understand more clearly the issues at stake in relation to both the Protestant missions in Mozambique and Portuguese colonial policy. She was warmly received in Switzerland by the leaders of the Swiss Mission and in Portugal she not only met with members of the European mission community but also with many of the students from Mozambique and Angola and other Portuguese territories studying in Lisbon. While in Portugal, Janet wrote regularly to Eduardo in Cameroon as well as to people in the Swiss Mission in Lausanne, including Alain Reymond, its new General Secretary with whom she had stayed, expressing her impressions and opinions. She seems to have been very naïve about the level of scrutiny which the Portuguese, particularly the PIDE, would have had over this correspondence. In a letter to Reymond dated November 8, 1960 she wrote, "It is my turn to thank you again for forwarding Eduardo's letters to Lisbon. On Oct. 29, he received *one* letter from me which I had written on Oct. 13th. I am curious as to the whereabouts of the other letters. I believe the UN is being quite negligent!"[9] Perhaps she was just being sarcastic, knowing that the PIDE would be reading this letter as well, but even so, her discussion of the Edelweiss fund and other issues showed some indiscretion. Clearly, the correspondence was being read; in the archives of PIDE still extant there is a copy of at least one letter from Eduardo to Janet dated January 11, 1961.[10]

Janet Mondlane's encounter with students from Mozambique and other Portuguese territories in Lisbon indicated something of the radicalization that was taking place among them. Just before her ar-

---

8. Ibid.

9. Letter from Janet Mondlane to Alain Reymond, November 8, 1960, DM 1577G, 4.

10. Letter from Eduardo Mondlane to Janet Mondlane, January 11, 1961, TT PIDE/DGS SC SR 337/6 1 30513052.

rival, Agostinho Neto had been exiled to Cabo Verde and many of the students had gone to the airport and applauded him as he crossed the tarmac. For this act, many had been detained and fingerprinted and the leadership in the Protestant mission community was becoming very concerned about what implications this might have for them.[11] In an encounter between students and future missionaries doing language training in Lisbon, Janet Mondlane summarizes the students' interventions as follows, which also perhaps mirrors some of her own thinking at the time: "We are fed up with you preaching the gospel of Jesus Christ to us without any relation to our daily life. We hear your gospel, but what do you do? You treat us like children, you do not train us for your work—you want to be the only authorities in the mission. You make us do the same work as you but for half the salary, too many times you have taken the white side rather than the right side. Help us to achieve our dreams and don't try to make religion a sleeping pill. Give us courage, work with us as equals."[12]

These students were to form part of the core of the emerging liberation movements in Mozambique and in other Portuguese territories. It is interesting to contrast this sentiment with at least part of the rationale which the Swiss Mission was still using for supporting students studying abroad:

> There is moreover another side to the problem. The Russians are making an enormous effort to attract the Africans. The financial situation of the leadership of the Church and of the schools is completely inadequate. Because of the lack of leadership in Mozambique the few that we train are sought with salary offers which cause them serious problems. We must at least double their salaries. . . . We cannot do it. And many risk leaving us with bitterness. The good leadership are at risk of getting away from

---

11. Manghezi, *Meu coração*, 153–55. Janet Mondlane felt that she was not allowed to stay at the student residence because of these tensions and because she might have exacerbated them.

12. Ibid., 158. "Estamos fartos que nos preguem o evangelho de Jesus Cristo sem uma relação com as nossas vidas do dia a dia. Ouvimos o vosso evangelho mas que fazem vocês? Tratam-nos como crianças, não nos formam para o vosso trabalho—querem ser os únicos mandões na missão. Põem-nos a fazer o mesmo trabalho que vocês mas por metade do salário, demasiadas vezes tomam o partido do branco em vez do partido da justiça. Ajudem-nos a conseguir os nossos desejos e não tentem fazer da religião um comprimido para dormir. Dêm-nos coragem, trabalhem connosco como iguais."

us and this is a win for the anti-white and pro-Moscow camp.
... [T]he best means to avoid this sliding away, full of difficulties
for the future, would be to have sufficient financial means to train
very well, technically and spiritually, those who will be tomorrow's Mozambican elite, and who would be able subsequently
to master the forces of anarchy by which all the instincts try to
break free when an opportunity, good or bad, presents itself.[13]

While in Portugal, Janet Mondlane also had contact with Adriano Moreira, by then a Deputy-Secretary in the Ministry for Overseas Affairs. Eduardo had written to him in June and in August of 1960, first to inform him that he had completed his doctorate and that he was going to Cameroon and in the subsequent letter attempting to persuade him to create a position in Mozambique in which he could direct a program which would accelerate the system of public education in "that overseas province."[14] In Lisbon, Janet Mondlane continued to be very impressed by Moreira and continued to believe that he was genuinely interested in change in the overseas territories. He also seemed to agree that a great deal of the fault for the worst of Portuguese overseas policy was to be located in the Roman Catholic Church.[15] However, there does not appear to have been any further discussion of a position in Mozambique for Eduardo. Janet Mondlane also encountered the growing anti-Americanism in Portugal with the election of Kennedy as President of the U.S. She recalls: "One day in Lisbon we were walking through the streets and ... they were going to have a rally in one of the large squares, in which it

---

13. Letter from Mission Suisse dans l'Afrique du Sud to Janet Mondlane, November 14, 1960. DM 1577G, 6. "Il y a du reste un autre côté du problème. Les Russes font un énorme effort pour attirer les Africains. La condition économique des cadres de l'Eglise et des écoles est complètement insuffisante. A cause du manqué de cadres au Mozambique les quelques-uns que nous formons sont sollicité par des offres de traitement qui leur posent de graves problèmes. Il faudrait que nous puissions doubler au moins leur traitement, ce qui représente ... Nous ne le pouvons pas. Et plusieurs risquent de nous quitter avec amertume. Les cadres de qualité risquent de nous échapper et c'est autant de gagné pour le camp anti-blanc et pro-Moscou ... le meilleur moyen d'éviter ce glissement, gros de difficultés, pour demain, serait d'avoir les moyens financiers suffisants pour former très fortement, techniquement et spirituellement, ceux qui seront l'élite du Mozambique demain, et qui pourront ainsi maîtriser les forces anarchiques par lesquelles tous les instincts tentent de se libérer lorsque l'occasion, bonne ou mauvaise, s'en présente."

14. Letters from Mondlane to Adriano Moreira, June 22, 1960 and August 8, 1960, DM 917D, 1 and 2, "aquela província ultramarina. "

15. Manghezi, *Meu coração*, 156–57.

was usual for Salazar to appear on a balcony. . . . I was really impressed because there was Salazar and all his group lined up, exactly as you see in the German films. . . . There were slogans on the walls: *Down with the Americans.*"[16] It appeared that the accommodation which the U.S. had made with the Portuguese dictatorship in order to maintain its air base in the Azores was coming to an end with Kennedy's changing foreign policy and that the U.S. might stand more fully behind the movements for liberation in the African territories, especially those which were not overtly identified with communism. On the other hand, this would mean an end to any more moderate policy toward decolonization, as represented by Moreira, and a hardening of Salazar's determination to resist independence at any cost.[17]

### Janet Mondlane's Arrival and Encounter with a Changing Church

Janet Mondlane arrived in Lourenço Marques with her two children on November 20, 1960. They were met at the airport by André Clerc and a welcoming party from the Swiss Mission. It seems that there was also a government car waiting for her but this is not clear.[18] While awaiting the arrival of Eduardo, she was hosted by the Swiss Mission and stayed in accommodation at the Mission center at Khovo in Lourenço Marques. Here she was exposed first hand to the reality of life in Portuguese colonial Mozambique as well as to the life of the Protestant missions. In her biography, she recounts her shock and dismay at the depth of racism and racial segregation in the Swiss Mission and the difficulties she faced because of being married to Mondlane. Once again, the couple did not fit easily into the racial categories nor into the dichotomy between European mission and indigenous church which still provided the framework for relationships in the Protestant churches. It seems that she was particularly disappointed in Florence Clerc, André-Daniel Clerc's wife, who typified for her the European missionary in Africa: "[Janet]

16. Ibid., 155. "Um dia em Lisboa andávamos pela rua e . . . ia haver uma manifestação numa grande praça, em que era costume Salazar aparecer numa varanda. . . . Eu estava realmente impressionada porque no edifício estava Salazar e todo o seu grupo alinhados, precisamente como se vê nos filmes alemães. . . . Havia frases nas paredes: *Abaixo os Americanos!*"

17. For a full account of the dilemma of the American airbase at Lajes in the Azores, cf. Schneidman, *Engaging Africa*, esp. chapter 1, "Kennedy and Salazar: Africa versus the Azores" and Costa Pinto, *O Fim do Império Português*, esp. 16–19.

18. Manghezi, *Meu coração*, 164.

truly could not learn much from Mrs. Clerc, who had had a good and traditional Swiss education and whose role in life was to be a good companion for her husband. She was white, was a woman and was a missionary. With her role well defined, [she was] friendly but clearly superior in her relation with blacks whether they were evangelists or servants."[19] In her short stay, even before Mondlane's arrival, Janet began to challenge the traditional role of the missionary and also the relationship with indigenous Mozambicans. However, in her account of this period, it seems that in her attempt to define her own role and relationships, she also fell into a certain missionary arrogance of knowing what was best in the Mozambican context. Despite being married to Mondlane and feeling a kinship with her Mozambican family, she also brought with her the norms and attitudes of her upbringing in the United States. Also, because of her relationship with Mondlane she was in a different situation from the Swiss missionaries who had to continue to live and to work in the Portuguese colonial context in the longer term.

In fact, the mission church which Janet Mondlane encountered had already taken many steps on the road to autonomy and some form of "Africanization".[20] In 1948, the Swiss Mission had become the Igreja Presbiteriana de Moçambique—Missão Suiça (IPM-MS) with African leadership alongside Swiss missionaries; the first Mozambican President of the Synod Council was Gabriel Macávi who remained in office until 1963. From that time on, financial responsibility for the church, including the salaries of pastors, was taken on by Mozambicans.[21] Although a significant differential in the salaries of Swiss missionaries and Mozambican pastors and other personnel was maintained, about which Janet Mondlane and indeed many Mozambicans were disgruntled, it set the stage for a further step toward full autonomy with the transfer of all property to the IPM-MS achieved through two further conventions signed in 1962 and 1970.[22] This period was called *Lumuku* and in itself

---

19. Ibid., 173. "[Janet] realmente não podia aprender muito com a sra. Clerc, que tinha tido uma boa e tradicional educação suíça e cujo papel na vida era ser uma boa companheira para o marido. Era branca, era mulher e era missionária. Com o seu papel bem definido, simpática mas claramente superior na sua relação com os negros quer eles fossem evangelistas ou serventes."

20. Cf. Teresa Cruz e Silva's interesting comments on the use of this term: Cruz e Silva, *Protestant Churches*, 92 n. 47.

21. Ibid., 90–93 for more information about this period.

22. Ibid., 135. Cf. also Biber, *Cent ans*, 112.

presented a serious threat to the Portuguese colonial authorities. The creation of the Conselho Cristão de Moçambique (CCM) in 1948, the joint efforts of the Protestant churches through the CCM in the training of indigenous leadership at Ricatla and elsewhere and the move toward creating one "Church of Christ" in Mozambique ran completely contrary to the Portuguese colonial project of "Portugalization", assimilation and the predominance of the Roman Catholic Church. Already the leadership, both Swiss and Mozambican, were being highly scrutinized by the Portuguese authorities, including the PIDE, and further moves toward autonomy would clearly have led to further repression.

### Changing Mission Personnel and Understanding of Mission

In addition to the changes in Mozambique, the missionary personnel coming from Switzerland, and indeed those in other Protestant missions as well, was changing. A new generation of missionaries, educated in the post war period in Europe and North America and influenced by the neo-orthodox theology of Barth, Brunner, Bonhoeffer, Niebuhr, and others with its critical engagement with the world, as well as by their exposure to the social sciences, was replacing the earlier generation of Clerc and Périer. In Mozambique, these included George Morier-Genoud and Georges Andrié. The Morier-Genouds had received lessons in Tsonga from Mondlane while they were in Lisbon in 1950 and preparing to go to Mozambique. In a significant paper which Morier-Genoud presented at the Ecumenical Centre in Bossey in December 1957 entitled, "Eglise et Nationalisme", he looked critically and theologically at the rising tide of African nationalism. In this paper, he was critical of those Europeans, including those in the church, who saw nationalism in Africa only as a threat, the "demon of nationalism", and said that "our first duty as European Christians" should be "to try to put a positive judgment on nationalism. To try to put ourselves in the skin of the Africans, to understand what can push them to want freedom."[23]

However, despite calling for this initial positive assessment of African nationalism, he also writes, albeit still in a somewhat paternalistic way,

23. Morier-Genoud, "Eglise et Nationalisme," 3, "démon du nationalisme," and says that "notre premier devoir de chrétiens d'Europe" should be "essayer de porter sur le nationalisme un jugement positif. Essayer de nous mettre dans la peau des Africains, pour comprendre ce que peut les pousser á vouloir la liberté."

> The most useful, the most necessary thing that we can do ... *is to submit ourselves together, them and us, in an effort at biblical, theological development.* ... For us Reformed, this recourse to the revelation of God, attested to in the Bible, goes more or less without saying. ... Only this effort at theological development, conceived in itself as an act of submission to JC [sic] is able to allow us, is able to allow the African Church, to not place on the nationalist movement a questionable judgment. By this act of faith, abandoning all political or other pretentions, the African Church will be able to make a political witness. It will be able to overcome the very real temptation of confusing its autonomy with political autonomy. The missions must generate and constantly sustain this development effort, even if it risks attracting to themselves the bad feelings of the Whites as well as many Africans. It is for them the only way to serve each other.[24]

This deeper reflection should also alert Christians to the dangers and the limits of nationalism, no matter where these might be found. Morier-Genoud refers to the linking of nationalism by the Afrikaners in South Africa to the doctrine of election to justify *apartheid*. He says that this is "blasphématoire et anti-chrétien." In every case, nationalism must be tested by the salvific work of Christ and can only find its justification in that work: "The important thing is that the Church discovers the fullness of the work of JC [sic], and the significance of Christian witness in all spheres of the life of a people: that she captures to what extent patriotism, nationalism is an ambiguous thing which man [sic] seeks to use in his revolt against God, but which JC [sic] reintegrates in his service. Hence the necessity for her to remain vigilant."[25] For Morier-Genoud

---

24. Ibid., 6–7. "La chose la plus utile, la plus nécessaire que nous puissons faire ... c'est de *nous soumettre ensemble, eux et nous, à un effort d'approfondissement biblique, théologique* ... Pour nous Réformés, ce recours à la révélation de Dieu, attestée dans la Bible, va plus ou moins de soi. ... Seul cet effort d'approfondissement théologique, conçu lui-même comme un acte de soumission à JC [sic] peut nous permettre, peut permettre à l'Eglise africaine de ne pas porter sur le mouvement nationaliste un jugement équivoque. Par cet acte de foi, d'abandon de toute prétention politique ou autre, l'Eglise africaine pourra avoir un témoignage politique. Elle pourra vaincre la tentation très réelle de confondre son autonomie avec l'autonomie politique. Les missions doivent provoquer et constamment soutenir cet effort d'approfondissement, même s'il risque de leur attirer la mauvaise humeur des Blancs comme de beaucoup d'Africains. C'est pour elles la seule manière d'être au service des uns et des autres."

25. Ibid., 11. "L'important c'est que l'Eglise découvre l'ampleur de l'œuvre de JC [sic], et la signification du témoignage chrétien dans toutes les sphères de la vie d'un peuple: quelle saisisse à quel point le patriotisme, le nationalisme est une chose ambigüe, que

and others of his generation, then, the role of the European missionary was to walk with the African church in seeking to discern the will of God in the midst of the turbulent process of decolonization on the continent and to stand with the African church in its call to challenge injustice wherever it might be found.

It was with these families, among the European mission community, that Janet Mondlane found most in common. Part of this connection was also the fact that the Morier-Genouds had a young family. She was impressed that they were sending their son Claude to school in Mozambique rather than sending him to South Africa or elsewhere abroad as most missionaries had done in the past.[26] Although this did send a strong signal to those in the church in Mozambique, it was not without its problems; his family remember him dressed in the uniform of the Portuguese youth organization, marching and saluting for his *pátria*, Portugal.[27] Throughout the 1960s, '70s and '80s, both Morier-Genoud and Andrié and their families would play crucial roles in accompanying the IPM-MS, both in and outside Mozambique, as it sought to define its role in the struggle for liberation and following independence.

## Mondlane Returns to Mozambique

Eduardo Mondlane joined Janet and their children in Lourenço Marques in February, 1961 after finishing his work with the United Nations in Cameroon. He was received as a hero by his church and by most black Mozambicans. He was also welcomed as an honored citizen by the colonial government and was treated as a visiting dignitary. On the other hand, he was closely watched by the PIDE with every movement and meeting being recorded. The transcript of at least one speech given in Vila João Belo (now Xai Xai) is in the archives of the PIDE/DGS.[28] In an article in the daily *Notícias* newspaper, he was described as "the illustrious U.N. bureaucrat."[29] However, they were quick to add that his work had to do with "trust territories and non-autonomous territories" and

---

l'homme [sic] cherche à utiliser dans sa révolte contre Dieu, mais que JC [sic] réintégre à son service. D'où la nécessité pour elle de rester vigilante."

26. Manghezi, *Meu coração*, 182.

27. Informal conversation with Michelle and Juliette Morier-Genoud, Bienne, 2003.

28. Transcript of speech given by Mondlane in João Belo (Xai Xai), November 24, 1961. TT PIDE/DGS SC SR 337/6 1 30513052.

29. *Notícias*, February 23, 1961, DM 817C, 1, "o ilustre funcionário da ONU."

that "Clearly the overseas Portuguese provinces do not fit this case, nor are they included in the designation non-autonomous territories once they are considered integral parts of the Portuguese nation ... since Portugal is and always will be his only homeland."[30]

## The Ricatla Meeting and Its Importance

Mondlane was constantly surrounded by people seeking to talk with him. He was interested in meeting with everyone he could but especially with the leadership of the church to know what their position would be in relation to the struggle for liberation. Janet Mondlane records what happened in an important meeting with church pastors at Ricatla as remembered by Georges Andrié and Pastor Casimiro Matié who would have been present at the meeting: "The meeting took place in absolute secrecy. He wanted to know how the pastors would position themselves in the struggle and asked them directly who would join him outside the country if he organized a liberation movement. The attitude was what he had hoped. There was a general consensus of total support for what he had planned but none of the pastors would leave the country. They felt, very strongly, that their role was to remain in the country and to help with the work that had to be done from inside."[31]

Perhaps nowhere else is it so clearly stated that there was an understanding that the church had a role to play in the liberation struggle from inside the country. Difficult as this might have been, both Mondlane and the church leadership agreed that it was important to maintain the presence of the Protestant church as a key instrument of resistance to Portuguese domination from within the colonial state. According to Georges Andrié,[32] the PIDE-DGS knew that this was the case but were

30. Ibid., "claro que as províncias ultramarinas portuguesas não estão neste caso, nem incluídas na designação de territórios não-autonomos, uma vez que são consideradas partes integrantes da nação portuguesa ... pois Portugal é e sera sempre a sua única Pátria."

31. Manghezi, *Meu coração*, 189–90. "O encontro decorreu em absoluto segredo. Ele queria saber como se posicionavam os pastores na luta e perguntou-lhes directamente quem se juntaria a ele no estrangeiro se ele organizasse um movimento de libertação. A atitude foi a que ele esperava. Houve um consenso geral de apoio total ao que ele planeava mas nenhum dos pastores abandonaria o país. Sentiam, com muita firmeza, que o seu papel era ficarem no país e ajudar com o trabalho que tinha que ser feito de dentro."

32. Interview with Georges Andrié at his home in Lausanne, April 2, 2003.

never able to extract from people exactly what was said at the time of Mondlane's visit, although clearly they had informers who were aware of the meeting. Several people were detained after Mondlane left the country and members of the IPM-MS were much more closely watched.[33] In a memo from the *Chefe da Brigada* of the DGS in the *Província de Moçambique* dated November 3, 1972, the meeting with Mondlane in 1961 is given as a primary reason for the arrest of the pastors and members of the IPM-MS in 1972 in *Operação Vendaval* (including Manganhela):

> The course of investigations is gradually giving us a more objective knowledge of the focus of potential subversion which the Swiss Mission represents in Mozambique. For a better appreciation of these facts, it helps us to go back to the months of February and March in the year 1961 at the time of the visit to Mozambique of Doctor Eduardo Mondlane. It is known that the Presbyterian Swiss Mission was the intellectual cradle of Doctor Mondlane and precisely in this city. In this sense and during his visit, he was the guest of honour of the Governor of this Province, but he went more to the Swiss Mission, where already at that time, he outlined his political intentions before the noted national and international members of that Mission. In this outline, Doctor MONDLANE already referred to the creation of the FRENTE DE LIBERTAÇÃO DE MOÇAMBIQUE, for which he asked for help, which was promised to him, although they did not agree fully with using the means of armed subversion. This position of the Swiss Mission was held only in the knowledge of those members of higher rank and leaders of the Church, without passing it down to the knowledge of the less responsible people in that community, but in the meantime they contributed with their offerings, part of which went to help the subversion via Switzerland. Among these members of higher rank were present those who now have led to all these arrests.[34]

33. Cruz e Silva, *Protestant Churches*, 124.
34. Memo from Chefe de Brigada of the Direcção-Geral de Segurança of the Província de Moçambique, November 3, 1972, TT PIDE/DGS SC C1(2) Proc. 19639, NT 7844, 43–45. "O decurso das investigações vai-nos dando gradualmente um conhecimento mais objectivo do foco de subversão potencial que representa em Moçambique a Missão Suiça.

Para uma melhor apreciação destes factos, convem-nos recuar até aos meses de Fevereiro e Março do ano de 1961 e quando de visita a Moçambique do Doutor Eduardo Mondlane.

Sabe-se que a Missão Suiça Presbiteriana, foi o berço intelectual do Doutor MONDLANE e exactamente nesta cidade. Deste modo e quando da sua visita, foi

## Return to Mozambique

Mondlane had convinced his colleagues in the church that in order to make their mission relevant to the reality of the country they had to abandon the compromise which they had made with the Portuguese colonial project and actively work to subvert it, although this would have to continue to be in a covert manner and without violence. It could be argued that the PIDE more clearly recognized the importance of this understanding and the role of the Protestant churches within Mozambique in the struggle than did many in FRELIMO and those in solidarity with the liberation movement.

Mondlane travelled throughout what are now Maputo, Gaza and Inhambane provinces visiting Protestant mission stations all along the way. He also spent two weeks in the home of his cousin, João Mapangalane in the district of Maxekahumo in Gaza. Janet Mondlane notes that the PIDE had offered to post a military guard around the house for their protection, which of course was refused.[35] This was in Eduardo's home area and he made many visits to relatives and friends and consulted with them concerning the liberation struggle. In Inhambane, he visited the Methodist missions at Chicuque and at Cambine where he had attended the technical training school. Here too he was warmly welcomed and hosted. Although Mondlane did not go beyond the south of the country, it is generally agreed that his message went beyond his own ethnic group to become a national call for liberation.[36]

### Mondlane's Speech in Chamanculo

Perhaps Mondlane's most famous speech was at Chamanculo Church in Lourenço Marques; significantly the service had been moved from

---

hóspede de honra do Governo desta Província, mas foi-o mais da Missão Suíça, onde, já nessa altura, definiu as suas intenções políticas, perante os membros, nacionais e estrangeiros de mais evidência daquele Missão.

Neste definição o Doutor MONDLANE referiu-se já à criação da FRENTE DE LIBERTAÇÃO DE MOÇAMBIQUE, para a qual pediu auxílio, que lhe-foi prometido, apesar de não concorderem plenamente com os meios a empregar a subversão armada.

Esta posição da Missão Suíça manteve-se somente no conhecimento daqueles elementos de mais prestígio e orientadores da Igreja, sem baixar ao conhecimento daquela comunidade menos responsável, mas no entanto contribuia com o seu óbulo, cuja parte ia auxiliar a subversão através da Suíça.

Nestes elementos de prestígio, contam-se aqueles que agora causam toda essa apreensão."

35. Manghezi, *Meu coração*, 204.
36. Cruz e Silva, *Protestant Churches*, 124.

the church at Khovo which was the headquarters of the Swiss Mission to Chamanculo which is where the African pastors and other workers lived. The church was filled to overflowing and it was necessary to use a megaphone for the people outside to hear. The service began with a long poem recited by Pastor Macávi, the President of the Synod Council, praising Mondlane and welcoming him home.[37] Mondlane thanked the people present for their support during the time that he had been outside the country. To conclude, he told the parable of the eagle which had been used extensively by James Aggrey in his travels in Africa on behalf of the Phelps Stokes Trustees forty years previously with much the same effect. Mondlane had first read the story of Aggrey when he was a young man studying at Cambine in 1942[38] and it had clearly remained an inspiration for him. In summary, the story is about a man who raises a young eagle among his domestic fowl and feels that he has convinced the eagle that it is a chicken. A naturalist visits the farm and tells the man that this is an eagle, not a chicken but the man says he has trained it to be a chicken. After two unsuccessful attempts on the part of the naturalist to convince the eagle of what it truly is, he takes the bird to a mountain and points it toward the sun at which point the eagle flies away, never to return. In relation to this story, Aggrey is quoted as saying, "My people of Africa, we were created in the image of God, but men [sic] have made us think that we are chickens, and we still think we are; but we are eagles. Stretch forth your wings and fly! Don't be content with the food of chickens!"[39] For many in the congregation, there must also have been a resonance with the well known words of the biblical prophet Isaiah, "But those who wait for the Lord shall renew their strength, they mount up with wings like eagles; they shall run and not be weary, they shall walk and not faint."[40] Janet Mondlane records that Eduardo elaborated on the parable with these words: "It is true that people of our race, many among us, think that we are not people. Really, many, many people think this. They think that we are a kind of people who are a little bit inferior to the rest of humanity . . . I want to say . . . I say because I have had the experience of studying and living with people of other nationalities, with people of other races, . . . that we are all human beings. We are all

37. Manghezi, *Meu coração*, 191–92.
38. Letter from Mondlane to Clerc, June 9, 1942, DM 910C, 2.
39. Smith, *Aggrey of Africa*, 137.
40. Isa 40:31 (New Revised Standard Version).

... human beings. We are all children of God!"[41] Mondlane's presence and the recounting of this parable had a powerful impact on many gathered in the church and outside it and was the catalyst for many to be involved in the liberation movement.[42]

As many have written, this visit of Mondlane to Mozambique in 1961 took on some mythic proportions so that it is sometimes difficult to separate fact from fiction. Janet Mondlane's biography has helped somewhat in this regard. However, the visit's importance to Mondlane's renewed engagement with the growing movement for liberation in Mozambique and in solidifying his role as a catalyst in building up this movement cannot be minimized. In addition, although it cannot be denied that his contacts in his travels went beyond the community of the Protestant churches and that his political vision for the country had already grown beyond the confines of that community, it did still constitute the core of his network of support. In addition, by this time the Protestant community had played a significant role in raising political consciousness among its members, particularly in the IPM-Swiss Mission, as so well documented by Teresa Cruz e Silva in her work, and that because of this, and particularly through its program of scholarships, it would provide a very important segment of the militants who would form and be added to the FRELIMO ranks in Tanzania and the liberated areas. It cannot be denied that at this very important juncture in the developing liberation movement that the Protestant churches, and Mondlane's place within them, played a crucial role in enabling it to begin to mobilize against the Portuguese colonial project.

## Status Confessionis

What is key for this present work, is that at this time a significant number of people in the leadership, and it would appear in the membership, of the Protestant churches, especially in the IPM-Swiss Mission, began

41. Manghezi, *Meu coração*, 194. "É certo que gente da nossa raça muitos entre nós pensamos que não somos gente. Realmente muitos, muitos, pensam! Pensam que somos um tipo de pessoas que são um poucochito inferiores ao resto da humanidade ... Eu quero dizer ... Digo porque tenho tido experiência de estudar e viver com pessoas de outras nacionalidades, com pessoas de outras raças ... Que somos todos seres humanos. Somos todos ... seres humanos. Somos todos filhos de Deus!"

42. See Cruz e Silva, *Protestant Churches*, 124; and Manghezi, *Meu coração*, 190–95, especially the comments of Lina Magaia who would later leave the country and become a FRELIMO militant.

to understand that they as church could no longer maintain their ecclesiological compromise with the colonial state. In order to be the church, to be faithful to what they understood to be the good news of liberation in Jesus Christ, they had to transform their understanding of God's mission in their context to go beyond building up the life of the church and to take a prophetic stance in the face of the Portuguese colonial project. Although never explicitly labeled as such, this is consistent with the understanding in the Reformed tradition of a *status confessionis*, that is, a moment when the church must resist absolutely the tyranny of any political, or for that matter ecclesiastical or economic, system which it discerns to be contrary to God's will for humankind. Indeed the sixteenth century Reformation was based on this theological premise. This same status was claimed by the confessing church in Germany in its resistance to the Nazi regime and the state church's collaboration with it. Later, it was also invoked by the World Alliance of Reformed Churches in its meeting in Ottawa in 1982 in condemning any theological justification for the institutionalization of racism in the *apartheid* policies of the National Party in South Africa and in suspending two South African Dutch Reformed churches from its membership. Against the power of the colonial state, and indeed the racist assumptions underpinning European colonialism and the racialist policies which pervaded life in southern Africa at the time, this small community of faith took a confessional stance. The fact that it did not use this language nor the fact that not all Protestants were in agreement, does not negate the changed position which the churches, particularly the IPM-MS, assumed after Mondlane's visit. Indeed, if the measure of this changed stance was to be seen in repression, it began in earnest immediately following his departure[43] and continued until the end of the armed struggle in 1974. This was the "revolution in the church" about which Mondlane had written and it set the stage for the larger movement which would coalesce around him in the following year.

Although this visit was crucial to the development of the movement for liberation in Mozambique, it was not clear after Mondlane's departure what his next steps should be. It is interesting to note that before he arrived in Mozambique he had written to his wife that he

---

43. See Cruz e Silva, *Protestant Churches*, 124. "Nationalists like Albino Maheche, Amaral Matos or Virgilio de Lemos were detained by the police after Mondlane's departure, and Protestants, particularly Presbyterians, were watched more carefully."

had decided to accept a professorship at Columbia University in New York[44] although nothing more came of this. On their return flight, the Mondlanes stopped in Salisbury for one day and Eduardo was able to meet with the Methodist Bishop, Ralph Dodge, whom they had known in the United States, and Uria Simango, a Mozambican Congregational pastor who had studied at Ricatla.[45] Both of these men were to play key roles in the emerging movement. They also stopped in Switzerland for two weeks where Mondlane was able to have discussions with members of the MSAS and others. In an interesting article in the *Feuille d'Avis de Lausanne* from this time, Mondlane challenged the Swiss and Europeans to begin to think differently about their role in Africa and indeed their position in the world, from the perspective of Christian faith: "I became a Christian by conviction. But how can you wish that we believe in the purity of the religious message when the missions are flanked by commercial, industrial neighbors, who only think about doing their business on our backs? . . . I would like Europe to rethink its attitude, its place in the world which is changing, in which you are not aware that you are playing a part. You have to think much bigger, much broader, if you want to survive."[46] His revolution in the church clearly had to do not only with Africa and those who were oppressed but also with Europe and those who were the oppressors. The transformation in the understanding of mission and of the relationship between Africa and Europe had profound implications for both sides in the relationship. As time went on, Mondlane would be as engaged with seeking to break through the intransigence of the West, both in the church and in the broader society, as he would in convincing Mozambicans to break free of their submissive role in the church and in the wider colonial project.

---

44. Manghezi, *Meu coração*, 185.
45. Ibid., 211.
46. Madeline Chevallaz, "Eduardo C. Mondlane" in *Feuille d'Avis de Lausanne,* April 22, 1961, DM 1848A, 3. "Je suis devenu un chrétien convaincu. Mais comment voulez-vous que l'on croie á la pureté du message religieux quand les missions sont flanquées de voisins commerçants, industriels, qui ne pensent qu'à faire des affaires sure le dos des nôtres? . . . Je voudrais tant que l'Europe repense son attitude, sa place dans le monde qui change, dont vous n'etes pas conscients de faire partie. Il faut penser plus grand, plus large, si vous voulez survivre."

## What Next?

On arrival back in the United States, Mondlane found that he had been transferred within the UN to the Economic Commission for Africa to do research on urban development in Africa, a position for which he had applied the previous year. It was a two year appointment, based in Addis Ababa. Initially Mondlane accepted the position thinking that he would be able to continue to develop contacts and support for the liberation struggle in Mozambique. In a letter to the Périers and the Clercs written in April, 1961, Janet Mondlane wrote, "Eduardo is very enthused with the project. It means that probably he will be traveling throughout Africa, and certainly it will bring him much closer to groups he wanted to get in touch with in regard to the Portuguese situation."[47] At this time, they were also hopeful that with the new Kennedy administration in power in the U.S. pressure could be brought to bear on the Portuguese to institute major reforms. In her letter, Janet Mondlane wrote, "Washington has an open ear to him now and he is making full use of it. We are all racking our brains for a brilliant way to get around the Portuguese without the loss of thousands of lives. Awful to say, that presents a difficult problem. The U.S. government has offered lots of money to the Portuguese to help develop and educate the 'provinces' but the Por. refuse."[48] Friends in the Swiss Mission were surprised at this development but realized that the path for Mondlane was not clear. Périer wrote, "You know how often we think, we too, about the future of Mozambique. We know your firm hope to be directly useful. How? When? I will not come back again to our interviews, but I insist on saying to you that in this too if not above all, we surround you with our friendly thoughts, and particularly with our intercessions, asking that God himself, in the complexity of human situations, helps you to see clearly, to take wise decisions."[49]

---

47. Letter from Janet Mondlane to "Our two Swiss families," April 27, 1961, DM 1577G, 8.

48. Ibid.

49. Letter from Charles Perier to Mr. and Mrs. Ed. C. Mondlane, May 19, 1961, DM 1577G, 9. "Vous savez combien souvent nous pensons, nous aussi, á l'avenir du Mozambique. Nous savons votre ferme espoir d'être directement utiles. Comment? Quand? Je ne reviens pas sur nos entretiens, mais je tiens á vous dire qu'en cela aussi sinon surtout, nous vous entourons de notre amiable pensée, surtout de notre intercession, demandant que Dieu lui-même, dans la complexité des situations humaines, vous aide á voir clair, á prendre les sages décisions."

In the end though, Mondlane did not take up this new position because of the continuing political restrictions that would be placed on him as an employee of the UN. Instead he accepted a teaching position with the Committee on East African Studies at what was then known as the Maxwell Center for the Study of Overseas Operations (later the Maxwell School of Citizenship and Public Affairs) at Syracuse University in New York state. This was certainly an institution which was sympathetic to the cause of African liberation and the position provided a good deal of flexibility to allow for other work and travel.[50] Indeed the Edelweiss Fund was rapidly developing and assisting Mozambican students including Pascoal Mocumbi (future Minister of Health and Prime Minister) and Joaquim Chissano (future Minister of Foreign Affairs and President) and demanding a great deal of time from both Eduardo and Janet Mondlane. During their time in Switzerland and Mozambique they had established the procedures for granting these bursaries with Périer and Clerc. The selection committee in Mozambique included Clerc and one other member of the Swiss Mission but also four others from outside the mission. Bursaries were given on merit and were not dependent on the student being a Protestant. Mondlane travelled to Switzerland in August and again in December to be in contact with students in Europe and to consult with Périer about the fund. In France, the Mozambican students had created an organization called the União Nacional dos Estudantes Moçambicanos (UDEMO).

By late 1961, the changing policies of the Kennedy administration were becoming more visible as was the reaction of the Portuguese. The American public relations firm of Selvage and Lee was hired on a one million dollar contract to put the Portuguese case to the American government and people. They sponsored the "Portuguese-American Committee on Foreign Affairs" which countered nationalist arguments for independence in the American press and upheld the "civilizing" role of Portugal in Africa. In a move which was designed to put a more moderate face on Portugal's policies, Adriano Moreira was named the Minister for Overseas Affairs and brought forward much publicized reforms in colonial policy, most importantly the abolition of the

---

50. Letter from Janet Mondlane to Mr. and Mrs. Clerc, June 23, 1961, DM 917D, 5. "It is a fantastic offer: an excellent salary, Eduardo will teach one course the first semester and two courses (one a seminar) the second semester plus research grants and, we hope (are quite sure) ample travel funds. We can scarcely believe our good fortune."

Native Statute of 1954 and with it the classes of *indigene* and *assimilado*. Although in practice this did not significantly change the situation for most Mozambicans, it did enable more African children to attend elementary school and to move on to secondary education. Clerc noted the impact of this reform for the Protestant mission schools in his circular letter of January, 1962 but he was also skeptical about the depth of these changes.[51] In March 1962 a Swiss nurse was denied a visa to enter Mozambique to work with the IPM-Swiss Mission and Périer wrote to Mondlane of his concern for the growing importance which Salazar was giving to the PIDE, often in defiance of his own ministers.[52] It did appear though that Portugal was responding, at least to a small degree, to international pressure and the time seemed ripe for increasing that pressure through a more unified and organized Mozambican movement.

51. Lettre cirulaire de M. A.D. Clerc, January 1962, DM 1369E, 2.
52. Letter from Charles Périer to Mondlane, March 7, 1962, DM 793B, 4.

# 9

# Faith in FRELIMO

## Groups Involved in the Formation of FRELIMO

THE INDEPENDENCE OF TANGANYIKA in 1961 provided new possibilities for the growing Mozambican liberation movement. Several embryonic groups made their headquarters there among Mozambican refugees and Julius Nyerere, the first President of Tanganyika, was openly disposed to providing a place for the movement to develop. Mondlane had known Nyerere at the Trustee Division of the UN and had cultivated a close personal friendship. In fact, Nyerere and Kwame Nkrumah of Ghana put a great deal of pressure on these movements, and on Mondlane, to come together in a unified force.[1] When the UN "Committee of Seventeen", the General Assembly body that monitored the decolonization process, decided that it would meet in Dar-es-Salaam in June of 1962, Mondlane sought to make representation before it. As noted previously, he still had hope that Mozambican independence could be negotiated with the Portuguese without a protracted armed conflict. With Moreira as Minister for Overseas Affairs, and what seemed to be a growing movement of moderate resistance within Portugal,[2] Mondlane's hopes were increased that such a solution might be possible. He realized though that it was important to present a united front; already the re-

---

1. MacQueen, *Decolonization of Portuguese Africa*, 21.

2. Schneidman, *Engaging Africa*, 42. In this group, Schneidman links Moreira with Marcello Caetano, who had been ousted from the position of university rector in Lisbon at the time of a student strike, Craveiro Lopes, a former President of Portugal, and the former Minister of Defense, Botelho Moniz who had been removed from his position after a coup attempt.

gional, ethnic and ideological divisions between Holden Roberto's UPA and the MPLA, initially under the leadership of Mário Pinto de Andrade and Viriato da Cruz and later, after his escape from exile, Agostinho Neto, had weakened the liberation movement in Angola and allowed the Portuguese to play one off against the other. This was complicated even further with the formation of the União Nacional para a Independência Total de Angola (UNITA) in 1966 under Jonas Savimbi.[3]

In fact, the potential for that kind of division in the Mozambican movement was high given the nature of the organizations which came together to form FRELIMO. The União Democrática Nacional de Moçambique (UDENAMO) had been founded in 1960 in Salisbury (now Harare) in Southern Rhodesia and was led by Adelino Gwambe. UDENAMO had represented Mozambique at the Conferência das Organizações Nacionalistas das Colónias Portuguesas (CONCP) at its first congress in Casablanca in 1961. The General Secretary of CONCP, Marcelino dos Santos, whom Mondlane had known in Lisbon, identified himself with UDENAMO. Uria Simango, the Congregational pastor from Beira whom he had met in Salisbury, was also part of the leadership group of UDENAMO.[4] His exit from Salisbury and presence in Tanganyika was well known to the Portuguese and was the subject of an article in the Lourenço Marques daily *Notícias*.[5] It was perhaps the most organized of the groups with the broadest base of support. The Mozambique African National Union (MANU), already a coalition of other smaller groups, was founded in Tanganyika in 1961 and was made

---

3. For a discussion of the development of these movements in Angola, See Costa Pinto, *Fim do Império*; and MacQueen, *Decolonization of Portuguese Africa*, particularly "The War in Angola," 28–36. Of particular interest to this study is Henderson, *The Church in Angola* and Schubert, *A Guerra e as Igrejas*. In part, Schubert's exhaustive work examines the way in which Angolans from different Protestant missions, (Methodist, Baptist, and Congregationalist) based in different ethno-linguistic groups supported different liberation movements.

4. In Mondlane, *The Struggle for Mozambique*, 119–20, he identifies Simango as the leader of UDENAMO. This seems to be a bit of revisionism after the struggle with Gwambe.

5. "O Cônsul-Geral de Portugal em Salisbúria desmente que o desaparecimento de um missionário metodista esteja relacionado com a actividade da polícia portuguesa," *Notícias*, 1962 (exact date not clear), DM 1339D, 7. ("The Consul General of Portugal in Salisbury denies that the disappearance of a Methodist missionary is related to the activity of the Portuguese police.") The article is about Simango even though his denomination and first name ("Willie") are not correct.

up largely of Mozambicans working in Tanganyika and Kenya, most of them belonging to the Makonde ethno-linguistic group. Its leader was Matthew Mmole, a Makonde born in Tanganyika who did not speak Portuguese. Another key figure in its leadership was Lázaro Kavandame who had been part of the agricultural cooperative movement in Cabo Delgado in the 1950s and had fled to Tanganyika after Portuguese repression increased in the early 1960s following the massacre at Mueda. The third group was the União Africana de Moçambique Independente (UNAMI) which had been founded in Malawi by exiles from the Tete region and was led by Baltazar Chagonga. Although this group had little representation in Dar-es-Salaam, it was Chagonga who had invited Mondlane to come to this meeting and to take a more active role in the independence movement.[6] The Mozambican students' group in France, UNEMO, was also represented in the person of Joaquim Chissano.[7]

## Mondlane's Role

Although generally portrayed as a unifying force among these movements, Mondlane brought his own perspective into this complex mix. He was from the south, he was a Protestant and he was a well known international figure educated in the United States and with international contacts through his work with the United Nations. Mondlane constantly tried to downplay the distinctions of race, ethnicity and religion in the movement but these differences clearly played a role in the ongoing divisions which were to plague FRELIMO. In fact, Norrie MacQueen sees Mondlane as representative of the weaknesses in FRELIMO's structure, rather than being primarily a force of unity:

> [FRELIMO] emerged from external pressure rather than a clear indigenous commitment to a unified national liberation struggle. The choice of leader was indicative of this weakness. Its first president was Eduardo Mondlane, an American-educated

---

6. Costa Pinto, *Fim do Império*, 40. Also cf. Mondlane, "La lutte pour l'Indépendance au Mozambique," 19. Translation of a lecture given by Mondlane in Washington on April 11, 1963 at a conference organized by the American Society on African Culture with the theme "Africa in Transition." The date seems more likely to be November 4 when Mondlane was in the United States according to the schedule given by Janet Mondlane in Manghezi, *Meu coração*, 243.

7. Manghezi, *Meu coração*, 220. Chissano would become Prime Minister in the transitional government in 1974, Minister of Foreign Affairs under Machel and then President after Machel's death.

United Nations official and perhaps the most distinguished black Mozambican of his generation. Mondlane was clearly an individual of great ability and his nomination as Frelimo leader owed at least as much to his national and international standing as his commitment to nationalist struggle. Almost immediately he returned to the United States and his post at the UN. These weaknesses in Frelimo's initial construction would only be resolved after a protracted series of internal struggles and schisms fought out in parallel with the war against Portugal.[8]

Janet Mondlane notes that Gwambe, the leader of UDENAMO, immediately felt threatened by Eduardo because of his level of education and his immense popularity. In fact he resisted meeting with Mondlane initially and because of this reluctance the meeting of the organizations which founded FRELIMO, and Mondlane's departure from Tanganyika, were delayed.[9] Despite all this though, FRELIMO was founded on June 25, 1962.

In many ways it appears that Mondlane was not prepared for the internal conflicts and intrigues which were endemic in the developing liberation movement. Although many welcomed his presence, as was seen in his being feted on his return to Dar-es-Salaam in September of that year to arrange the first Congress of FRELIMO,[10] his reception was not as it had been on his trip to Mozambique in 1961. There, he was coming home and his base in the IPM-MS and NESAM was well known to him. In Dar-es-Salaam, he had a great deal to learn about the different groups that were coming together, their motives and their objectives as well as the personalities and motives involved in the leadership, and he could not assume the same level of trust and recognition of his leadership that he had experienced in his travels in the south. The possibility

---

8. MacQueen, *Decolonization of Portuguese Africa*, 21–22. MacQueen here is drawing on Newitt, *History of Mozambique*, 522. However, he does record an error in fact in that by this time Mondlane had resigned from the United Nations and had been appointed to the Maxwell Center in Syracuse. Cf. also, Costa Pinto, *Fim do Império*, 40, "... o nacionalismo anglófilo da África do Sul, da Rodésia e da Tanzânia, foi muito mais marcante [na FRELIMO], como o seu primeiro presidente tinha uma marca norte-americana forte, o que aliás iria provocar a desconfiança de alguns dos seus pares." (... anglophile nationalism from South Africa, Rhodesia and Tanzania, was much more evident [in FRELIMO], just as its first president had a strong North American influence, and would provoke mistrust among some of its partners.)

9. Manghezi, *Meu coração*, 218–19.

10. Ibid., 223.

of infiltration by the PIDE was facilitated by the lack of identity with and loyalty to any established organization. In a letter to Charles Périer from Janet Mondlane while in Dar-es-Salaam, the assessment of the leadership in UDENAMO and MANU is stated in a very blunt fashion:

> We have found that the relationship between the two is a dangerous one, the first party being headed by a dictator who is uneducated but extremely clever in obtaining money and keeping all power in his own hands, the second party headed by an uneducated and rather slow-witted fellow who has a very large following among the thousands of workers here in Tanganyika who come from Moz. It seems that the two parties may unite through the clever manipulations of the head of UDENAMO, Mr. Gwambe ... Mr. Gwambe is supported by a small and integrated group of foreign interests and we are sure he has committed himself to them far beyond what may be for the good of Moz. So while we are here we are trying our best to rearrange this situation so that the Moz. Party is united by democratic means, and that its future will be based on democratic procedures.[11]

In this letter, concern is also expressed for the students in Dar-es-Salaam who had been promised bursaries by UDENAMO with nothing forthcoming. These concerns for democratic organization and for education reflect Mondlane's deep convictions for the shape that the movement, and the future country, should take and reflect, at least in part, the values he developed from his integration in the life of the IPM-Swiss Mission.

In replying to this letter, Périer expressed the support of the Swiss Mission for Mondlane's engagement with the independence movement and the new role which he was taking on in mediating the various perspectives which were present in the movement. He also expressed his confidence in Mondlane's ability to accomplish the task:

> This is a very difficult time, and one filled with heavy responsibilities, that is opening up for you. The ministry of reconciliation ... seeks to avoid the disasters caused by the ambition and the vanity of men [sic]. ... Differences of opinion are not bad in themselves. It is normal. But where they become difficult is when they are transformed into dissensions. Only unity brings strength. Well, unity, it is a complete apprenticeship. It is more difficult, it demands more personality, patience, sacrifice than

---

11. Letter from Janet Mondlane to Charles Périer, June 18, 1962, DM 793B, 8.

division. . . . In this field as in others you are called to attend to urgent and delicate tasks.[12]

In this letter, Périer also tells the Mondlanes about the recent travels of Alain Reymond, the General Secretary of the MSAS, in Mozambique. He was there to attend the 75th Anniversary celebrations of the mission to Mozambique and the signing of the new convention with the IPM. This happened just prior to the formation of FRELIMO, a fact that was most likely not lost on the Portuguese.

## The complexities of securing support for FRELIMO

It was clear to Mondlane that this work could not be done on a part time basis while living on another continent but, on the other hand, his commitments at Syracuse and his lack of a secure personal financial base meant that he could not commit himself fully to the movement at that time. He was under significant pressure from Nyerere to return and take control of FRELIMO[13] and he began to seek ways to provide a stable financial future for himself and his family as well as for the movement. One possibility was to seek a two year appointment as a visiting professor at the university in Dar-es-Salaam through Syracuse[14] but this did not materialize. Mondlane and his wife sought support among organizations in the United States including the Quakers, the Phelps-Stokes Fund, the Rockefeller Foundation, and the Ford Foundation;[15] this of course was in addition to the support they were receiving, and seeking, for the Edelweiss Foundation. Although its exact nature was not clear, Mondlane made an arrangement with Jean-Paul Widmer to organize and oversee his personal finances. Although in 1962 not directly connected with the Swiss Mission, Widmer had known Mondlane in

12. Letter from Charles Périer to Eduardo and Janet Mondlane, July 11, 1962, DM 793B, 7. "Voilà une ère bien grave et chargée de lourdes responsabilités qui s'ouvre pour vous. Le ministère de la réconciliation . . . cherche à éviter les catastrophes dues à l'ambition et la vanité des hommes . . . Les divergences de vue ne sont pas un mal en elles-mêmes. C'est normal. Mais où cela devient grave, c'est qu'elles se transforment en dissensions. Seule l'union fait la force. Or l'union, c'est tout un apprentissage. C'est plus difficile, ça exige plus de personnalité, de patience, de sacrifice que la division . . . Sur ce terrain comme sur d'autres vous êtes appelés à des tâches urgentes et délicates."

13. Manghezi, *Meu coração*, 221–22. Cf. also Mondlane, "La Lutte pour l'indépendance au Mozambique," 25.

14. Letter from Janet Mondlane to Charles Périer, June 18, 1962, DM 793B, 8.

15. Manghezi, *Meu coração*, 224.

Mozambique when he stayed at Clerc's home and later on Mondlane's visit to Switzerland in 1950 as well as in Mozambique in 1961. He was to remain a close friend of the family and provided accommodation for Mondlane and his family whenever they were in Geneva. He later became Mozambique's Consul General in Switzerland[16] and was also key to developing the archives in the DM in Lausanne which documented Mondlane's life.[17]

In February, 1963, Mondlane met with Robert Kennedy, then the U.S. Attorney General in his brother's administration and with Fritz Rarig, a Philadelphia businessman who knew both of them. He also had the support of Averell Harriman, who was to become the Under Secretary of State for political affairs. Robert Kennedy was very impressed with Mondlane and sought to provide support to him both personally and to FRELIMO through covert American support. Within three months, Mondlane received sixty thousand dollars from the Central Intelligence Agency (CIA), channeled through the African American Institute (AAI) in New York. In addition, almost one hundred thousand dollars was given to the AAI by the Ford Foundation (FF) to assist refugees at the Mozambique Institute (MI) in Dar-es-Salaam.[18] In a confidential letter to Robert Kennedy, cited by Witney Schneidman, Fritz Rarig wrote, "The money should not be given on the assumption that we can control Mondlane. In fact, it would be rather foolish to attempt to control him because the attempt would impair his usefulness to us. The truth of the matter is that we cannot control him; we can only trust him ... Support for Mondlane would be a good investment for us because his program represents the best and only hope of a relatively peaceful solution of the Mozambican problem."[19]

Ironically, this covert support came at the same time that the U.S. was decreasing its pressure on Portugal to allow political self determination in its overseas possessions. This was largely because of the American air base in the Azores. Even though Portugal was a member of the North Atlantic Treaty Organization (NATO), and so a military ally, the air base had been used as a significant negotiating tool with the U.S., especially

---

16. Ibid., 222 and 234.

17. Various documents in a binder entitled MOND. MEMORIAL J. P. Widmir in the Basler Afrika Bibliographien, Basel, Switzerland.

18. Schneidman, *Engaging Africa*, 43–46.

19. Quoted in ibid., 45–46.

with the less sympathetic policies of the Kennedy administration and particularly after the lack of U.S. support for Portugal when India invaded Goa in December, 1961. The agreement with Portugal for the use of this base came to an end on December 31, 1962 and Portugal refused to renew it or sign another agreement. After this date, Portugal could have withdrawn its permission for the use of the base at any time and the U.S. had to be very cautious about its criticism of Portugal in the UN and about voicing any overt support for the liberation movements in Africa if it did not wish to put its use of the base in jeopardy. The Americans were particularly sensitive about the use of the base at Lajes because of the growing tensions with the Soviet Union in Berlin and over Cuba. In addition, Salazar moved at this time to harden his stance and removed many of the more moderate officials in the government and civil service, including Adriano Moreira, in December 1962. Although still officially committed to support for self determination in the Portuguese overseas territories, the U.S. administration felt that this had to be done in a much more covert manner and with more deference to Portugal. In July of 1963, the U.S. abstained in a vote in the Security Council condemning Portugal, despite the obvious support of the U.S. ambassador, Adlai Stevenson.[20] With the assassination of John Kennedy in November of 1963 and the escalation of the war in Viet Nam under President Lyndon Johnson, the importance of the Azores base increased. So despite Robert Kennedy's interest and concern, U.S. government support for the liberation movements in the Portuguese African territories would decrease even further.

## Fulltime with FRELIMO on the World Stage

In 1963, Mondlane took a two year leave of absence from his position at the Maxwell Center and in March returned to Tanganyika to take up full time responsibilities with FRELIMO. On his return, he found the movement in complete disarray. Gwambe had left the country when he had not been chosen as President in the elections at the founding in June. By March, 1963, both Paul Gumane and David Mabunda who had been elected to the Central Committee had abandoned the party

---

20. Ibid. The relationship between the U.S. and Portugal in relation to the air base at Lajes and the liberation movements in Africa is discussed fully in chapter 1, "Kennedy and Salazar: Africa versus the Azores," 1–58. cf. also Costa Pinto, *Fim do Império*, chapter 1, "A Guerra Colonial e a Cena Internacional," 13–33.

and the country and were attempting to gain support for themselves as the continuing representatives of UDENAMO. It was imperative that Mondlane establish his leadership within the movement and be seen to be its legitimate leader internationally.

In this early period, Mondlane was seen by Portugal, and indeed by many others, as being supported by the U.S., even an agent of the CIA.[21] In a report on FRELIMO by the PIDE in 1962, Mondlane is seen to be an agent of the U.S. and Gwambe as a representative of the U.S.S.R. It is interesting to note in this report that this connection to the U.S. includes Mondlane's links with American churches as well as the American Committee on Africa.[22] Another factor in this attachment with the U.S. was that Mondlane put a great deal of confidence in an American who posed as a Mozambican refugee, Leo Milas (later to be revealed as Leo Aldridge from California)[23] who was often in conflict with other members of the Executive Committee,[24] particularly those who challenged a more narrow nationalist understanding of the movement.[25] Yet another American connection was the arrival of Ed Hawley, the Congregational minister who had married Eduardo and Janet in Oberlin, as a Chaplain to the Mozambican refugees in Dar-es-Salaam, working with the Tanganyikan Council of Churches, early in 1964.[26]

Without doubt, Mondlane had been influenced greatly by more than ten years in the United States. In the face of this criticism, he dedicated himself to diversifying support for FRELIMO and to not being seen to be allied with any one country or bloc. On his return to the United States after FRELIMO's First Congress, he made representation to the Fourth Committee of the UN. His work in the Trusteeship Division ensured that he had many contacts and that he could garner support for FRELIMO from many quarters. In May of 1963, Mondlane

21. Manghezi, *Meu coração*, 226 and Newitt, *History of Mozambique*, 523.
22. Report on FRELIMO. TT PIDE/DGS SC SR 337/6 1 30513052, 640–43.
23. Newitt, *History of Mozambique*, 522–23.
24. Manghezi, *Meu coração*, 227–28.
25. Isaacman and Isaacman, *Mozambique*, 86ff; also cf. Newitt, *History of Mozambique*, 522.
26. Manghezi, *Meu coração*, 245; also cf. Maro, "The Last Rites for Dr. Eduardo C. Mondlane," archives of the World Council of Churches, Programme to Combat Racism (Hereafter known as WCC PCR), File 5/2, Box 4223.3.11. "When . . . an official of the Christian Council of Tanzania mentioned to the freedom fighter that the Council was actively looking for a pastor for refugees, Dr. Mondlane did not think of anyone else."

represented FRELIMO at the first meeting of the Organization for African Unity in Addis Ababa. He was warmly received by most of the Heads of State present, including Kwame Nkrumah who he met for the first time, despite the best efforts of Gumane and Mabunda to paint him as an American imperialist[27] and the sympathetic hearing they had had with Nkrumah. In the last three months of the year, he travelled extensively in North America, Europe, and Asia where he visited the People's Republic of China and India.[28] The punishing schedule continued into 1964, including a trip to the Soviet Union in which he sought funds to initiate the armed struggle.[29]

Other members of FRELIMO including Marcelino dos Santos and Uria Simango also travelled extensively on behalf of the movement but it seems that Mondlane had growing questions about both of them, according to Janet Mondlane. He saw Simango as being very ambitious with the potential of trying to replace him as leader.[30] Marcelino dos Santos he saw as being distant from the reality of the struggle, wanting to spend most of his time in Europe, with a very romantic and ideological view of "the people".[31] Dos Santos was also identified with a growing number of young, more strongly ideological Marxists who were joining the movement including Jacinto Veloso and João Ferreira[32] and Jorge Rebelo.[33] Although Mondlane had certainly moved to the left politically and was increasingly disillusioned with the U.S. and its allies because of

27. Manghezi, *Meu coração*, 228–29.

28. Notes from Eduardo Mondlane, "The Mozambican Liberation Front: The Crystallization of a Struggle for Freedom." No date, probably 1964, DM 1339C, 3; Also cf. Manghezi, *Meu coração*, 243.

29. Manghezi, *Meu coração*, 249. In a letter to Janet from Tunisia on April 10, 1964, he wrote, "A minha intenção é extrair dessa gente alguma ajuda financeira e material . . . a mesma razão que me leva a visitar a União Soviética agora e não mais tarde. Precisamos desse dinheiro agora ou senão não conseguimos realizar a fase seguinte do nosso travalho." ("My intention is to extract from these people some financial and material help . . . the same reason that is taking me to visit the Soviet Union now and not later. We need this money now and if not we will not manage to realize the next phase of our work.")

30. Ibid., 249.

31. Ibid., 244–45.

32. Ibid., 227. They arrived in Dar-es-Salaam in a high jacked Portuguese Airforce plane.

33. Ibid., 247. He joined the movement in Europe after finishing a course in law at Coimbra University in Portugal.

their refusal to hold Portugal to account for intransigence in its colonial policy, at this time he was not a committed Marxist, nor an apologist for the communist states. He strongly believed that Mozambique should remain non-aligned but once again the shifting policy of the United States, including its increased involvement in Viet Nam and its inability to stand categorically with the movements for liberation throughout southern Africa, meant that it was difficult not to be identified with the Soviet bloc in the Cold War mentality of the time. He consistently argued that the struggle for liberation in Mozambique should be fought according to the needs of the Mozambican people and should not be bound to any ideological position.

### Relation to Protestant Missions and Religious Pluralism

In this process, Mondlane also publicly distanced himself from his connection with the Protestant missions, in order to emphasize the broad base of the movement but also, it would seem, not to raise their profile any more than was necessary because of the level of repression within Mozambique.[34] Despite his continuing connection with the Swiss Mission and the Protestant churches in Mozambique, and strong financial support for the Edelweiss program from the Protestant churches, Mondlane always emphasized that the movement was religiously diverse and that the Portuguese claim that nationalism was simply a product of Protestant teaching could not be sustained. In *The Struggle for Mozambique* he wrote,

> ... for many years the Protestant missions in Mozambique have been hampered and quite often thwarted by a powerful combination of the Portuguese Catholic clergy and officials of the colonial government. From time to time, public statements are made by high officials of the colonial government attacking Protestant missions, accusing them of fomenting anti-Portuguese sentiments amongst the African population. ... In fact, the leadership of the nationalist movements in [Mozambique and Angola] is religiously mixed. In our own Mozambique Liberation Front, most of the members in the Central Committee ... either are Roman Catholics or come from Catholic families. ... The largest number of our students

---

34. See Mondlane, "La Lutte pour l'Indépendance au Mozambique." In this speech, Mondlane narrates his personal history without once mentioning his connection with the Protestant churches.

abroad, who have run away from Portuguese schools either in Mozambique or Portugal, are Roman Catholic . . . [35]

In June of 1964 Mondlane participated in the *Congrès* méditerranéen pour la culture in Florence, Italy, and presented a paper entitled "Le mouvement d'émancipation au Mozambique".[36] According to Janet Mondlane, this was a church conference and a significant portion of Mondlane's paper deals with the role of the Roman Catholic Church in Mozambique. In fact, it appears that the material in this paper, including the section on the role of religion, was the basis for a good deal of what he would later include in *The Struggle for Mozambique* in 1968. Janet Mondlane indicates that this speech was widely publicized and raised the profile of the Mozambican struggle considerably in Italy and that it was suggested by some that Mondlane should meet with the Pope.[37] It is significant that this conference took place at the time of the Second Vatican Council. Mondlane appeals to the more liberal period of Portuguese Catholicism, before the advent of the *Estado Novo*, when he suggests that a more comprehensive and secular approach to the education of African children might indeed have assisted in transplanting Portuguese culture into the African context.

> There was a time, before the establishment of the Salazar regime and for some years after, where the policy of the Portuguese government was to educate as many African children as possible and also as quickly as the economic power of the Portuguese would permit. This policy was sustained by those of the leaders of the Portuguese line who had believed in the possibility of creating a Portuguese culture among the Africans and were convinced that the only way to arrive at this objective was to furnish educational facilities to as many of the African youth as possible. This policy was in part inspired by the liberal spirit that reigned in the democratic Europe of that time, and which disappeared under the assault of the fascist movements in Germany, Italy and Portugal.[38]

35. Mondlane, *The Struggle for Mozambique*, 71–72.

36. Eduardo Mondlane, "Le mouvement d'émancipation au Mozambique." Travail présenté au *Congès méditerranéen pour la culture*, June 20–24, 1964. Unpublished manuscript. DM 1848A, 5.

37. Manghezi, *Meu coração*, 250.

38. Mondlane, "Le mouvement d'émancipation au Mozambique," 9. "Il y eut un temps, avant l'établissement du régime Salazar et quelques années après, où la politique du gouvernement portugais était d'éduquer autant d'enfants africains que possible et aussi rapidement que la puissance économique du Portugal le permettait. Cette poli-

Of course by this time this kind of reform would have come too late but it does seem that in this paper, Mondlane holds out the possibility for a more progressive role for the Roman Catholic Church in an independent Mozambique and within the spirit of Vatican II.

## The Mozambique Institute

As well as building up the credibility of FRELIMO among African and other world leaders and ensuring a broad base of international support, it was necessary to establish a program of education for the growing membership of the movement in Tanganyika. In August, 1963, Janet Mondlane joined Eduardo in Dar-es-Salaam and laid the foundations for the Mozambique Institute (MI), with the funding received from the FF. For more than a year, fifty Mozambican students attended the Kurasini International Education Centre, which had been built by the AAI and funded by United States of America International Development (USAID).[39] By the end of 1964, the Mozambique Institute was housed in its own buildings and was receiving its own students. Not only did the MI provide education for the most promising among the Mozambican refugees in Tanganyika, it also provided the groundwork for establishing a system of rudimentary education among the peasants in the areas that would come under FRELIMO control. The influence of Mondlane's early years and the emphasis on organization and education through the *mintlawa* and literacy programs in the Swiss Mission can be seen to be at work here.[40] Together with the continuing program of bursaries for study overseas through the Edelweiss Fund, the Mozambique Institute, under Janet Mondlane's leadership, was to play an indispensable role in the formation of an educated leadership and a commitment within FRELIMO to the need for education for Mozambicans.

---

tique était soutenue par ceux des chefs de file portugais qui avaient cru à la possibilité de créer une culture portugaise parmi les Africains et que étaient convaincus que la seule manière d'arriver à ce but était de fournir des facilités d'éducation à autant de jeunes Africains que possible. Cette politique était en partie inspirée par l'esprit libéral que régnait dans l'Europe démocratique de ce temps-là, et qui disparut sous l'assaut des mouvements fascistes en Allemagne, en Italie et au Portugal."

39. Manghezi, *Meu coração*, 237.

40. Cf. Cruz e Silva, *Protestant Churches*. Although Cruz e Silva does not specifically mention the influence of this experience on the development of the Mozambique Institute, it seems a logical conclusion to her extensive study on the role of the Swiss Mission in the development of political consciousness in Mozambique.

The MI was established as an independent organization under the laws of Tanganyika although its links with FRELIMO were clear.[41] This separation was intended to enable foreign donors, particularly American, to contribute to the MI without being seen to be supporting armed liberation movements. As U.S. foreign policy shifted to be more accommodating of Portugal, however, the obvious connection with FRELIMO caused pressure to be brought to bear on the FF and the AAI to withhold further funding. Support from the FF was cut in 1964 and it was necessary to seek out other sources of funding. Among other donors, Janet Mondlane was able to secure a grant of $52,000 from the WCC in support of the MI. This was to be the first of many grants from the WCC and other ecumenical organizations which would continue throughout the liberation struggle and beyond.

### The Churches and the Use of Violence

Indeed, although the link with the WCC and other ecumenical groups was minimized in any public documents, the accompaniment which these organizations provided to FRELIMO grew throughout the 1960s, even before the inauguration of the Programme to Combat Racism (PCR) in 1969. The size of the file on the WCC in the extant archives of the PIDE provides some indication of the importance that Portugal placed on the role of the global ecumenical movement in supporting FRELIMO.[42] In 1964, the WCC's Department on Church and Society, the Mindolo Ecumenical Foundation (in Kitwe, Zambia) and the South African Institute on Race Relations held a consultation at Mindolo on "Christians and Race Relations in Southern Africa".[43] Mondlane attended and made a significant contribution. By this time, Z.K. Matthews had become Secretary for Africa in the WCC Commission on Interchurch Aid, Refugee and World Service (CICARWS). He was the former Principal of the University College of Fort Hare in South Africa who

---

41. Manghezi, *Meu coração*, 238.

42. See TT PIDE/DGS SC CI(2) 5898 7407, File on WCC. Also, references to the WCC and other church organizations and the role of Bishop Ralph Dodge are extensive in the file on Eduardo Mondlane, TT PIDE/DGS L Gab 295 8032 and TT PIDE/DGS SC SR 337/61 30513052.

43. Visser't Hooft, *Memoirs*, 291–92. This is the title which Visser't Hooft gives but Z. K. Matthews in his autobiography *Freedom for My People*, 209, recalls the theme as "Christian Practice and Desirable Action in Social Change in Southern Africa."

had been forced to resign because of his leadership role in the African National Congress (ANC). The major concern of the conference was the Christian response to the use of violence in the liberation struggles in southern Africa. Matthews gave an address entitled, "The Road from Non-Violence to Violence" in which he reflected on the decision within the ANC to accept the use of violence and the formation of *Umkonto weSizwe* after the banning of the ANC by the South African government in 1960. Although Matthews did not advocate the use of violence he made it clear that he understood why this decision had been made.

Mondlane spoke in similar terms concerning the decision of FRELIMO to enter into an armed struggle against Portuguese colonialism. Visser't Hooft, the General Secretary of the WCC, attended the conference and was clearly moved by Mondlane's words. In his reflection, he summarizes the issues which were to dominate the discussion within the WCC for decades to come concerning support for the liberation movements:

> He was very ready to discuss the moral and spiritual problems with which he was now confronted. He said that he and his friends had not chosen violence. They were reacting to a form of oppression which was in fact a form of violence. At any time they were ready to enter into negotiations with their opponents. I spoke to him of the dangers of violence. But I did not feel free to condemn his choice. Was he not a striking illustration of what Calvin had said about the role of "lower magistrates" in resisting oppression? Could we Dutchmen continue to sing our national anthem with its praise of William the Silent for his commitment to the cause of "removing tyranny" and say to Mondlane that he was wrong? And had I not approved the actions of my friends Dietrich Bonhoeffer and Adam von Trott, when they had made a similar choice?[44]

By this time it appears that the use of violence in the struggle for liberation was accepted by Mondlane[45] given his frustration with the in-

---

44. Visser't Hooft, *Memoirs*, 293–94.

45. Cf. Isaacman and Isaacman, *Mozambique*, 88–89; Newitt, *History of Mozambique*, 523; Manghezi, *Meu coração*, 250. There had, however, been extensive debate within FRELIMO concerning the nature of the armed action. The question was whether it should follow a similar path to Cuba, the so-called "focal theory" in which it was assumed that peasants would join an uprising whether politicized or not, or Algeria with random attacks on the European community or the Chinese model of low intensity, prolonged guerilla warfare.

transigence of the Portuguese to negotiate. In fact, FRELIMO had been involved in military training since January 1963 in Algeria. Its first military camp was established near the village of Bagamoyo in Tanganyika and arms were transported into Mozambique by May 1964. The first military action was taken on September 25, 1964 when FRELIMO forces attacked the Portuguese administrative post in Chai in Cabo Delgado.

As Visser't Hooft mentions, Mondlane and others in the liberation movements could not understand the reluctance of the churches to support legitimate struggles against colonialism when they had for centuries given support to various European wars, most recently the struggle against fascism, based on Christian faith. There appeared to be a double standard at work, based on race, as to when the church would support an armed struggle. In his comments in the conference, Visser't Hooft drew on his own Calvinist theology, "worked out by John Knox and the Scottish confession of faith of 1560 according to which one of the good works which Christians are to undertake for the sake of their neighbours was the defence of the oppressed and the repression of tyranny."[46] This resistance might be violent, but "Christians should never resort to violence before having counted the heavy cost and before being quite certain that this was the one and only possibility of serving the cause of justice."[47] Mondlane's answer was clear, that all other legitimate forms of resistance to Portuguese oppression had been tried with the result being only even greater repression and injustice for the African population of Mozambique. As he had argued with his colleagues in the IPM-MS, the moment demanded a revolutionary response from the church, based on its understanding of God's will for justice for all people. The church could not stand aloof from the *real politik* of the context in southern Africa, tending only to its own needs, but was compelled by the gospel to declare itself on the side of the oppressed and to work by whatever means necessary to overcome this injustice, even if it meant standing on the side of those involved in the armed struggle. This resonates strongly with the South African *Kairos Document* of the 1980s which argued that the attempt on the part of the liberal, English speaking churches to play a role of peace maker and reconciler between the *apartheid* regime and

---

46. Visser't Hooft, *Memoirs*, 293.
47. Ibid.

the liberation movements prevented them from committing to the prophetic call to justice.[48]

It is helpful to return to the work of George Morier Genoud here, again writing from within the reformed theological tradition and with a profound experience of the life of the church in Mozambique:

> Witness is always a very difficult thing, even in stable countries like ours. But what to say about witness in countries at the boiling point, where the mentality is completely different? For example, the "simple" notion of social justice, or of human dignity . . . the translation of the Gospel in daily life must take into account the new givens and that will necessitate a theological development that is even more profound.
>
> It is there that our participation in the combat of the young Churches is necessary . . ."[49]

He goes on to approach the difficult question of violence:

> In the countries where African nationalism appears to the Whites as outside the law, and the law of the Whites appears to the Africans as completely arbitrary, because for them the Whites are usurpers . . . the theological problem of the legitimacy of the armed revolt becomes agonizing. . . . In the study of these problems the African Churches and the missions have the right to demand of European theology that it take it on very directly. . . . Because, if the missions must be the advocates of patience for the Africans (Christian or not), it is not for the convenience of a white social state which will again protect us, but only to save the future of these African peoples, who in using violence and revolt risk contorting their future in the long term.[50]

---

48. *The Kairos Document.*

49. Morier-Genoud, "Eglise et nationalisme," 13. "Le témoignage est toujours une chose très difficile, même dans les pays stable comme le notre. Mais que dire du témoignage dans des pays en pleine ébullition, où la mentalité est totalement différente? Par exemple, la notion si 'simple' de justice sociale, ou de dignité humaine . . . La traduction de l'Evangile dans la vie journalière devra tenir compte de données nouvelles et cela nécessitera un approfondissement théologique d'autant plus profond . . . C'est là que notre participation au combat des jeunes Eglises est nécessaire."

50. Ibid., 13–14. "Dans les pays où le nationalisme africain apparaît aux Blancs comme hors-la-loi, et la loi des Blancs apparaît aux Africains comme parfaitement arbitraire, parce que pour eux les Blancs sont des usurpateurs . . . le problème théologique de la légitimité de la révolte armée devient angoissant. . . . Dans l'étude de ces problèmes les Eglises africaines et les missions ont le droit de demander à la théologie européenne qu'elle les épaule très directement . . . Pour que, si les missions doivent à faire les avocats

Throughout his remaining life, and during the armed struggle in Mozambique, Mondlane would continue to be engaged with the WCC on this question. Precisely because of his deep integration in the life of the church, both in Mozambique and in the United States, he could not allow the church simply to forget this struggle on the margins of the global political agenda, as much of the world had done, nor could he allow it to dismiss its validity on the basis of the use of violence. If this indeed was a matter of confronting tyranny and doing justice then the church should understand itself to be called to be engaged in this struggle no matter if it was deemed necessary to use violence to achieve this goal.

## Consequences for Local Churches

This accompaniment on the part of the WCC and other ecumenical organizations would of course have serious consequences for the local Protestant churches in Mozambique. In December, 1964, after the FRELIMO military campaign had begun in the north, the PIDE conducted a number of sweeps and arrested more than 1,500 FRELIMO activists, effectively shutting down the internal resistance at that time.[51] Clearly among those arrested there would have been many with Protestant backgrounds. NESAM, the student organization begun by Mondlane and the most developed community of resistance within Mozambique, although all contacts with FRELIMO were covert, came under intense scrutiny by the PIDE. Teresa Cruz e Silva includes Luis Bernardo Honwana, Armando Guebuza (who would become Minister of the Interior and President in 2004), Pascoal and Adelina Mucumbi, Lina and Albino Magaia, Jorge and Cristina Tembe, and Josina and Esperança Muthemba among the new generation of student activists

---

de la patience auprès des Africains (chrétiens ou non), ce ne soit pas par complaisance pour un état social blanc qui nous protège encore, mais seulement pour sauver l'avenir de ces peuples africains, qui en utilisant la violence et la révolte risqueraient de fausser pour longtemps leur avenir."

51. Newitt, *History of Mozambique*, 523–24. Newitt also argues that this action eliminated the option of a *putsch* based in the capital as a military alternative. Cf. Manghezi, *Meu coração*, 260. Janet Mondlane indicates that members of NESAM were to create a fourth front for FRELIMO in Lourenço Marques but that the plan was foiled when the PIDE detained Mateus M'Boa and extracted information from him regarding the network of those involved.

Faith in FRELIMO 169

who had been raised within the IPM-MS.⁵² An information sheet in the PIDE archives reveals that Daryl Randall, Mondlane's friend and colleague from his time in South Africa and in the U.S., and nineteen American students visited Luis Bernardo Honwana and a cultural exhibit at the Centro Associativo dos Negros da Província in 1964. By this time, Randall was a Professor in African Studies at the American University in Washington. He had met with Holden Roberto in Leopoldville and was highly suspect by the PIDE.⁵³ Although there is no direct connection made between this meeting and the banning of NESAM in 1965, the link with Mondlane and FRELIMO must have been clear. Many of these students joined FRELIMO in Dar-es-Salaam after NESAM was banned.⁵⁴ Cruz e Silva indicates that another student organization the Grupo de Estudantes Evangélicos began to meet in 1964 and continued until many of its members were detained in 1967.⁵⁵ Although there was no direct challenge to the IPM-MS, it was clear that their continuing support for education for Africans through their system of schools and bursaries within the country and bursaries for study overseas continued to make them suspect by the Portuguese.⁵⁶

## WCC Conference on Church and Society

In 1966, Mondlane was invited to participate in the WCC World Conference on Church and Society held in Geneva, July 12–26. The theme of the conference was "Christians in the Technical and Social Revolutions of our Time." Mondlane spoke in the plenary session entitled "The Political and Economic Dynamics of the New Nations." In their introduction to the report on the conference, M. M. Thomas and Paul Abrecht write, "The plenary session on this topic . . . was an event that few present will soon forget. The theme, one of the most controversial of the Conference, was dealt with by a distinguished group of speakers providing a cross-section of Christian opinion on the issue."⁵⁷ Mondlane responded to two addresses, the first by Raul Prebisch, General Secretary

52. Cruz e Silva, *Protestant Churches*, 131–32.
53. Informação No 287-SC/CI(2) 12/9/64. TT PIDE/DGS SC SR 337/61 30513052, 369.
54. Manghezi, *Meu coração*, 261.
55. Cruz e Silva, *Protestant Churches*, 132–33. Information from Bento Sitóe.
56. Ibid., 131.
57. Thomas and Abrecht, *Official Report, World Conference on Church and Society*, 16.

of the United Nations Conference on Trade and Development and the second by Bola Ige, a lawyer and former General Secretary of the Student Christian Movement in Nigeria. Mondlane was joined in responding by Barbara Ward, an economist from England, a Roman Catholic, and a highly respected figure in the ecumenical movement. He stressed the need for Africans and others to remember what they were fighting for, and in some cases, what they had fought for. "We are first of all fighting to be ourselves, to determine our affairs according to our *own* needs . . . The time in which we had to *exclusively* blame colonialists ought to be past. There is time now to begin looking into the internal structures of our own nation, to see to our own selves. What are we? What are we capable of?"[58] He was critical of independent African countries which continued to seek financial favors in Europe and North America rather than planning their own economies and freeing themselves from dependence on one commodity and he used China as an example of charting its own course in the face of a U.S. blockade.

In conclusion, Mondlane writes,

> Now as we talk to each other as Christians I think that if we have a message we should begin to turn from saying to the white man, "Please continue to help us after independence." They love it, they were enjoying it, because it boosts their egos, they think they can always do that. No! Let's begin to build from within. We will be poor for a long time, maybe we will be poor for a long time, but we said it when we were telling the British, the French, when we were telling the Portuguese to get out, no matter what happens. And if we are going to be free we are not going to allow a few people who are corrupt, who are harlots, who want to live like I don't know what, in standards that are completely . . . outside of Africa.[59]

Mondlane was challenging not only western Christians, with their strong ties to the forces of colonialism and imperialism, but also African Christians in the emerging countries of the continent, to call on their own governments to create more just societies and to resist the temptation to seek personal enrichment. Once again, Mondlane was calling the church to be on the side of the marginalized, no matter if that marginal-

---

58. "Conference Address No. 46, World Conference on Church and Society, Geneva, 12–26 July 1966," unpublished manuscript, WCC PCR Box 300.

59. Ibid., 3.

ization was a product of colonialism or of neo-colonial African political and economic forces.

The World Conference on Church and Society represented part of a major shift in the engagement of the WCC with the world beyond the church. Hugh McCullum writes that the "tension between prophecy and reconciliation came to the fore at the ... conference. ... It challenged the churches to adopt a new and radical approach in the struggle to combat racism."[60] In the radical climate of the 1960s, and as the WCC's membership began to include more and more of the churches of the global south, the conference began to challenge the cooption of the church into the thinking and structures of the powerful western nations. The church could no longer be identified with the west, although the western churches still held the financial purse strings, and a new generation of leadership was emerging which reflected much more fully the wide diversity of people and communions that made up the WCC. W. A. Visser't Hooft, the first General Secretary of the WCC who was approaching retirement at the time of the Conference on Church and Society wrote,

> In 1960 a "teaching conference" was held in Strasbourg. ... But that conference became something very different from what the Federation leaders had hoped and expected. The addresses given by D. T. Niles, Lesslie Newbigin, Karl Barth and by me did not seem to give the students what they wanted. What had happened? David Edwards has put it this way: "There seemed to be too much speaking about the life of the church; what students wanted was action in the world. And there seemed to be too much mission; what students wanted was a welcome to this world." Six years later at the World Conference on Church and Society in Geneva, and then again at the Assembly in Uppsala, it became clear that this new orientation had come to stay.[61]

Of course with this shift within the WCC came serious criticism and fear, from those on the extreme right like Carl McIntire but also from those who were more moderate both politically and theologically, particularly in the West but not exclusively so, who felt that its Christian identity was being lost in its identification with the call for radical change in both

---

60. Hugh McCullum, "Racism and Ethnicity" in Briggs, Oduyoye, and Tsetsis, eds., *History of the Ecumenical Movement*, 351.

61. Visser't Hooft, *Memoirs*, 366.

church and society. Clearly, Mondlane was identified with this shift both by those who welcomed it and by those who feared it.

## Meeting with Zedequias Manganhela

While he was in Geneva for the World Conference, Mondlane arranged to meet Zedequias Manganhela, who was by then the President of the Synod Council of the IPM-Swiss Mission, through the offices of Charles Périer and Jean-Paul Widmer. Périer was clearly concerned for the safety of Manganhela but Mondlane was insistent and felt that the risk was not so great. Périer records that Mondlane said that "they will not commit the error of putting Manganhela in prison."[62] Mondlane wanted to clarify what was happening within Mozambique and particularly with the leadership of the IPM-MS after hearing many rumors from those arriving in Dar-es-Salaam from the south: "Those in the South of Moz. [sic] must know certain things. The young people who come to us from there say that the authority of Mang. [sic] is diminishing in the Church because of an overly great prudence and they are mistaken about the feelings that dictate the behaviour of Z.M. Naturally, I confront their point of view as with many other things. But here too there is a strong pressure from which can be born all sorts of serious misunderstandings. A meeting would help me to prevent these, to overcome them and avoid the tragic complications for tomorrow."[63]

The meeting took place on July 17 at Bassin after using complicated routes for the arrival of both so as not to alert the PIDE. Unfortunately there does not appear to be any record of what transpired. However, the significance of this meeting cannot be minimized for corroborating the link between the IPM-MS and the liberation movement in the person of Mondlane. Périer's notes also shed some light on the growing divi-

---

62. Notes from Charles Périer, "Entrevue Manganhela—Eduardo Mondlane, en l'absence de M. Ouwehand et M. Vittos, mercredi 13 juillet 1966," DM 793E, 8. "Ils ne commettront pas l'erreur de mettre M[anganhela] en prison." Cf. Cruz e Silva, *Protestant Churches*, 146–47.

63. Ibid. Périer: "Ceux du Sud du Moz. doivent savoir certaines choses. Les jeunes qui nous arrivent de là-bas disent que l'autorité de Mang. va diminuant dans l'Eglise à cause d'une trop grande prudence et ils se méprennent sur les sentiments qui dictent ce comportement à Z. M. Naturellement j'affronte leur point de vue comme pour beaucoup d'autres choses. Mais là aussi il y a une forte pression d'où peuvent naître toutes sortes de malentendus grave. Une entrevue m'aiderait à les prévenir, à les vaincre et à éviter de tragiques complications pour demain."

sion between those people, mostly young people, who left Mozambique to join FRELIMO in Dar-es-Salaam and those who remained and lived under the constant watch of the PIDE.

In Mondlane's discussions with Périer in 1966, he was also pushing for the Swiss Mission to provide more bursaries for Mozambican students to study in Switzerland; he had already corresponded with Frédéric Ouwehand concerning this matter before his arrival in Geneva without a positive response.[64] He recognized the risk this posed for the Swiss Mission's presence in Mozambique but felt that these bursaries could be given covertly through private organizations or Entraide Protestante Suisse (EPER), the newly formed development agency of the Swiss Federation of Protestant Churches, as was done in other countries. It is interesting that Mondlane says that the students do not understand why they are not sent to study in the "country of our parents."[65] Clearly, there was still a continuing relationship with the Swiss Mission and continuing insistence that it provide support for the movement. It seems that this pressure had results. In a letter to Pascoal Mocumbi in September 1968, M. Laufer asks when he might meet with Mondlane together with a representative of EPER to discuss bursaries.[66] There was also a great deal of correspondence between Janet Mondlane and Frédeéric Ouwehand at the Département Missionaire (DM) in this period concerning books and other support for the MI.

## Tensions within FRELIMO

The period between 1966 and 1968 witnessed continuing internal divisions within FRELIMO. A rival organization, the Comité Revolucionário de Moçambique (COREMO) had been established in Lusaka under the leadership of Adelino Gwambe and later Paulo Gumane after a final break with Mondlane in 1965. Although never a serious threat to FRELIMO as the primary focus of the liberation movement, it did act as a foil for future dissent both during Mondlane's leadership and after it.[67] One of the most serious challenges to Mondlane's leadership and

64. Letter from Mondlane to F. Ouwehand, June 14, 1966, DM 793E, 5; and letter from Pierre Vittoz to Mondlane, June 28, 1966, DM 793E, 7.

65. Letter from Mondlane to F. Ouwehand, June 14, 1966, DM 793E, 5, "pays de nos pères."

66. Letter from M. Laufer to Pascoal Mocumbi, September 16, 1968, DM 1848B, 2.

67. Cf. Costa Pinto, *Fim do Império*, 59–60; and Newitt, *History of Mozambique*,

the direction of FRELIMO in this period was related to the discontent of many students within the MI and those studying in the United States and the arrival of a Roman Catholic priest, Fr. Mateus Pinho Ngwengere. Initially Mondlane welcomed him when he arrived in Dar-es-Salaam in 1967 "as one of the most important Freedom Fighters that we managed to take outside."[68] Ngwengere had worked with a Belgian priest who had been expelled from Mozambique, Fr. Pollet, and was associated with the progressive Catholic Bishop de Resende; he was considered to represent the more radical face of the Catholic Church in Mozambique centered in the non-Portuguese mission communities and influenced by the more politically engaged and prophetic theology of the post Vatican II church.[69] Almost immediately after his arrival, he was included in a FRELIMO delegation sent to the United States to attend the General Assembly of the United Nations. In the U.S., he was able to have contact with many Mozambican students who were resisting a return to Tanzania where they would be integrated into the FRELIMO guerrilla forces. Ngwengere encouraged them in this resistance, arguing that the educated elite should not have to risk being killed in the armed struggle and on his return to Dar-es-Salaam he identified with students in the MI with similar ideas. Ngwengere argued that the movement was being controlled by "whites" and that Mondlane did not want anyone to have a superior education to his own. There were also links between the students and racialist elements within the Tanzanian government and police with similar concerns and which seemed to be gaining increasing influence with Nyerere. Conflicts within the MI escalated significantly and in March of 1968, the decision was taken to close it.[70]

A second challenge came from Lazaro Nkavandame and the traditional Makonde leadership which had been central to the membership of MANU. Much of the guerrilla war was being fought in Cabo Delgado, the traditional area of the Makonde, and had been successful

524.

68. Letter from Mondlane to George Hauser, September 12, 1967, quoted in Manghezi, *Meu coração*, 274, "como um dos mais importantes Combatentes da Liberdade que conseguimos trazer para o exterior."

69. Eric Morier-Genoud argues that it was Ngwengere's religious conviction that led him into conflict with the growing Marxist faction within FRELIMO and not primarily the racialist conflicts identified by Janet Mondlane and others (*Of God and Caesar*, 20–21).

70. The role of Ngwengere is well developed in Manghezi, *Meu coração*, 273–88.

## Faith in FRELIMO

in large part because of the support of the local chiefs.[71] Many Makonde's had a closer affinity to Tanzania than to an independent Mozambique and indeed there was also a vision of an independent Makonde state. There were also longstanding hostilities between the Makonde and the Macua and Yao ethno-linguistic groups. This conflict entered into the very heart of the FRELIMO leadership where the larger social revolution which was envisioned under the leadership of Mondlane came into conflict with the more traditional view of these leaders. In May, 1968, shortly after the closure of the MI, the offices of FRELIMO were attacked by dissidents with the Tanzanian police doing little to intervene. In this attack, Mateus Mathumba, a member of the Central Committee, was fatally injured.[72] These internal struggles were exacerbated by the significant military advances made by the Portuguese.

These conflicts were addressed by Mondlane in FRELIMO's Second Congress held in Niassa in July of 1968 which was seen to be a major triumph for Mondlane by most authors. The fact that the Congress was held within Mozambique was of great symbolic importance for the movement. Also, holding it away from Dar-es-Salaam lessened the influence of Nkavandame's supporters and potential hostile influences from within the Tanzanian government. The resolutions of the Second Congress affirmed Mondlane's position in all areas of the movement. The armed struggle was against the Portuguese government and the forces of imperialism and not against the Portuguese people;[73] it was not a racially based struggle. The armed struggle would also be a protracted one which would require the mobilization of the whole population.[74] Life in the liberated areas was to model the transformation of society in an independent Mozambique with emphasis being placed on the increase of agricultural production through scientific methods, basic education and health care available for all and the role of women enhanced.[75] The Second Congress also recognized that the struggle in Mozambique sought "the establishment of a social, democratic order" and was "part of

71. Newitt, *History of Mozambique*, 524.

72. For the conflict with Nkavandame, cf. Newitt, *History of Mozambique*, 524–27; Isaacman and Isaacman, *Mozambique*, 96–99; Munslow, *Origins*, 105–7, 134–35.

73. Resolution 6 on the armed struggle in Mondlane, *The Struggle for Mozambique*, 191.

74. Ibid., Resolution 3, 189–90.

75. Ibid., Resolutions on administration of the liberated zones, on national reconstruction and on social affairs, 191–95.

the world's movement for the emancipation of the peoples, which aims at the total liquidation of colonialism and imperialism, and at the construction of a new society free from exploitation of man by man [sic]."[76] Although the support of "progressive countries of the West" was recognized, it was the support of the "socialist countries of Europe and Asia" and of Cuba that was highlighted.[77]

## Fourth Assembly of the WCC and the Programme to Combat Racism

The WCC's 4th Assembly in Uppsala, Sweden in July of 1968 ran in parallel to FRELIMO's Second Congress and in many ways brought into reality Mondlane's hopes for the role that the Protestant churches might play in the liberation movement, both in Mozambique and throughout southern Africa. As has been noted above, the impetus to take action had been developed at the Conference on Church and Society in 1966 and this report was brought to the Assembly. Mondlane himself was invited to address the Assembly but had to decline because of the meeting of the Second Congress.[78] Martin Luther King was to have addressed the Assembly and to have given significant force to the call to take action against racial discrimination but he was assassinated in April. Under the leadership of the WCC's new General Secretary, Eugene Carson Blake, and a group of black executive staff, including ZK Matthews, it was decided to give the issue of race the highest profile possible throughout the Assembly. They were determined to push the Assembly to move beyond declarations to action. Hugh McCullum notes that for the first time, the Uppsala Assembly used and defined the terms "racism" and "white racism" and declared that racism "is a blatant denial of the Christian faith."[79] It also identified the explicit link between racism and poverty. Perhaps most importantly, the Assembly agreed that the WCC should "undertake a crash programme to guide the Council and the member churches in the urgent matter of racism."[80] This was the foundation of the soon to

---

76. Ibid., Resolution 1 on foreign policy, 195.

77. Ibid.

78. Maro, "The Last Rites for Dr. Eduardo C. Mondlane."

79. McCullum, "Racism and Ethnicity," in Briggs, Oduyoye, and Tsetsis, eds., *History of the Ecumenical Movement*, 352–53.

80. Goodall, ed., *The Uppsala Report 1968*, 242.

be inaugurated PCR with the details of its establishment to be left to the Central Committee.

Almost immediately after the Assembly, planning began for a consultation to be held in Notting Hill, London, in 1969, again under the vigorous leadership of Eugene Carson Blake. Although far from garnering unanimous support among member churches, the WCC had spoken on this crucial issue and it was important to act in the heated political and social climate of the time. George McGovern, prominent U.S. Democratic Senator and delegate to the Uppsala Assembly from the United Methodist Church, was asked to chair the consultation. It is significant that Mondlane was invited, together with Michael Ramsay, the Archbishop of Canterbury, to speak at a public meeting at Church House in Westminster during the consultation.[81] He was still sufficiently identified with the churches to be able to be seen as representative in such a high profile gathering, in spite of his decision to accept the need for an armed struggle against Portuguese colonialism and his distancing of himself from the churches in his attempt to build a broadly based political movement. While still playing a moderating role within FRELIMO, it could be said that Mondlane represented the radical edge of the changed position of the WCC to take a more overt stand in favor of those struggling for justice in the face of European colonialism and the various forms of white supremacy institutionalized in southern Africa. Of course this was to lead to charges of the WCC becoming a communist front[82] by many on the right politically and theologically. However, this change in position at a profound level represented a change in ecclesiology; the church could not continue to make pronouncements against racism but remain passive in the face of the racist oppression of so many of its members as well as those outside the church. Its own racism was evident, as Visser't Hooft had said, when armed resistance against fascism and other forms of political tyranny in Europe had been

---

81. McCullum, "Racism and Ethnicity," in Briggs, Oduyoye, and Tsetsis, eds., *History of the Ecumenical Movement*, 354.

82. Predictably, in South Africa, Prime Minister Vorster attacked the WCC and his brother, the Moderator of the NGK, said that the WCC was "not a church of God, but a church of the revolution." See Regehr, *Perceptions of Apartheid*, 207. However, the criticism of the WCC and its PCR was not limited to South Africa nor to the Dutch Reformed churches. Perhaps one of the best known critiques was in the populist *Reader's Digest* which in a series of articles beginning in October, 1971, accused the WCC of being a communist front.

given the blessing of the church while similar movements against colonialism and racist structures in other parts of the world were seen to be "un-Christian" if they engaged in armed resistance. The long identification of Christianity with European "civilization" was unmasked in this duplicity and it was essential that the WCC respond if it was to maintain any credibility among the African churches and among African peoples involved in the struggle. This is not to say that there was not opposition to the PCR from the churches in southern Africa, most notably from the South African Council of Churches (SACC)[83]. However, it represented a decisive step which was to provide the framework for the WCC's response to the struggles for liberation from racial oppression in southern Africa, and around the world, until the present.

## Assassination and impact on FRELIMO

The results of both FRELIMO's Second Congress and the 4th Assembly of the WCC appeared to vindicate Mondlane's position, both in the need for the movement to seek profound social transformation in its struggle for liberation and in his theological understanding of the role which the church should play in this struggle. However, he was not to see the fruit of this labor. Before he could attend the WCC consultation in London, Mondlane was assassinated by a letter bomb in Dar-es-Salaam on February 3, 1969. Although there is still significant debate about who exactly was responsible, it was without doubt related to the ongoing conflict within the movement, particularly with Nkavandame, and aided by the PIDE. It is interesting to note how the PIDE understood Mondlane's role, not only in Mozambique but in the larger struggle against Portuguese colonialism, "Under Mondlane's rule, FRELIMO was, without doubt, the most efficient movement of 'liberation' in southern Africa, obliging Portugal to deploy more than 50,000 soldiers to combat terrorism."[84] What is more telling perhaps is how they describe what happened to the movement after his removal: "In 8 months, the

---

83. See De Gruchy, *The Church Struggle in South Africa*, 123–34; cf. Regehr, *Perceptions of Apartheid*, 204-11. Regehr questions whether the black members of the English speaking churches which opposed the grants from the Special Fund of the PCR were as unanimous in their opposition as the official statements might suggest.

84. Processo No 295, Vol. 1 1964 a 1970, 86/70—Dinf2 18Fev.70. No. 7, TT PIDE/DGS L Gab 295 8032. "Sob as ordens de Mondlane, a FRELEMO era, sem dúvida, o mais eficaz movimento de "libertação" de África Austral obrigando PORTUGAL a deslocar para MOÇAMBIQUE mais de 50,000 militares para combater o terrorismo."

movement was transformed into a disorganized mob fighting among themselves, with the losers seeking the security of the Portuguese authorities. Still, this situation does have precedents. Presently there is not, in southern Africa, any party that has not fallen into divisions."[85]

With Mondlane removed, the various factions within the liberation movement would enter into a prolonged power struggle which would split the leadership and, for a time at least, weaken its military effectiveness. Eventually, the Marxist wing would gain hegemony and, although officially tolerant of religious belief and practice, would challenge the need for religious institutions. Its overarching framework of scientific socialism understood religion to be obscurantist and an impediment to the building of the new socialist society because of its divisive nature and its challenge to the truth of Marxist ideology. Throughout the liberation struggle, and during the time of the transitional government, tolerance and indeed cooperation, generally marked FRELIMO's dealings with religious institutions. However, after gaining power in 1975, this tolerance turned quickly to antagonism. Despite Mondlane's profound theological and political transformation, it is difficult to envision him supporting the kind of open hostility toward the churches and other religious institutions which was to occur. Although it has often been argued that the victory of the "progressive" forces in the leadership struggle following Mondlane's assassination consolidated Mondlane's own line articulated in the Second Congress,[86] it seems clear that there were also significant differences between the new leadership and Mondlane's position on many issues, including the place and role of religion in society. Eric Morier Genoud argues that beyond the struggles with Nkavandame fo-

---

85. Ibid., No. 8. "Em oito meses, o movimento transformou-se numa turba desorganizada que lutava entre si, com os vencidos a procurarem segurança nas autoridades portugueses. No entanto, essa situação já tem precedentes. Não há presentemente, na África Austral, um único partido que não se tenha dividido."

86. See John Saul's "Foreword" in the 1984 edition of Mondlane's *The Struggle for Mozambique*, iv-v. In describing the democratization of the movement before the Second Congress, Saul writes, "Yet it was precisely this shifting of the movement's centre of gravity from the narrow confines of an exile leadership to a broader base within the country which allowed progressive elements (Mondlane included) to build the support necessary to consolidate their position. . . . Moreover, it soon became clear that one group with the leadership—that which clustered around the then FRELIMO Vice-President Uriah Simango, Lazaro Kavandame and others—stood in opposition to precisely those emphases which were being celebrated in Mondlane's book." Cf. Isaacman and Isaacman, *Mozambique*, 84–100.

cused on Makonde traditional leadership and values, there was another dynamic at work which at least in part focused on the place of religion within the movement and the emerging new society and that this was represented by Ngwenjere and Simango. The victory of the Marxist faction did not mean simply a return to the views held by Mondlane, at least in relation to religion. "Contrary to what one could expect though, the resolution of the religious question did not mean that one went back to the situation prevalent in Frelimo before 1968, or else that things were to remain unchanged thereafter. Quite the reverse."[87] Perhaps Morier-Genoud overstates this position, especially in relation to Ngwenjere, but it is also clear that there was not an unambiguous continuation of Mondlane's position in the new leadership.

---

87. Morier-Genoud, *Of God and Caesar*, 21.

# 10

# Mondlane's Legacy of Faith

## Christian or Terrorist?

IN HIS *MEMOIRS*, W. A. Visser't Hooft wrote of Eduardo Mondlane, "[He] came to see us several times in Geneva. He participated in the World Conference on Church and Society in 1966. Three years later he was assassinated. I cannot think of him as a terrorist. He was a Christian who had had to make an impossibly difficult choice in what German theology called a *Grenzfall*—that is, a case on the borderland—and who had made that choice with full awareness of the sacrifice involved. I was glad that the World Council had shown enough imagination to make him feel that he belonged fully to the ecumenical family."[1]

When he was assassinated in 1969, many would not have described Mondlane, or his decisions, in the way that Visser't Hooft did; indeed for many within the church, the term terrorist would have seemed quite appropriate. For those who saw the white minority Portuguese regimes in the remaining African colonies, along with the regimes in South Africa and Rhodesia, as bastions of "western civilization" standing firm against the onslaught of communism in the region, Mondlane was anything but a Christian. For most who functioned within the paradigm which Bosch calls "Mission in the Wake of the Enlightenment," or the modern paradigm of Christian mission, predominant among Protestants from the eighteenth to the early twentieth century, western civilization and Christianity could not be separated. The role of Christian mission was to uphold the civilizing force of western colonialism among those

---

1. Visser't Hooft, *Memoirs*, 294.

within its influence which in turn would provide the context necessary for conversion.[2] Although the Protestant missions in Mozambique had from their beginnings found themselves in tension with the Portuguese colonial project, primarily because of the privileged place given to the Roman Catholic Church, they had, as has already been demonstrated, found it necessary to reach their own compromise with this project in order to carry out their work of evangelization and church development and did not challenge its fundamental assumptions.

Yet it is clear that at the time of his death, Mondlane was regarded by those in the global ecumenical movement, and indeed regarded himself, as a Christian and one who was at the forefront of the transformation in thinking concerning Christian mission. His funeral service was held in the Azania Front Lutheran Church in Dar-es-Salaam with Edward Hawley officiating and, significantly, assisted by Uria Simango, the Vice President of FRELIMO. Nicholas Maro, from the Christian Council of Tanzania wrote, "Dr. Mondlane was no crusading evangelist, but left no one who knew him in any doubt that he was a Christian. Consequently, for all the pomp . . . of a State funeral, the entire atmosphere was pervaded by the reality of an aura of a fallen Christian witness."[3] In Hawley's meditation, Mondlane's Christian conviction was emphasized, but also the radical way in which he lived out this conviction in the cause of the liberation of his people:

> Finally, behind all this was another, and still wider, view—a view he did not often have occasion to articulate, but which was at the root of the radiant life we knew—that this fallen world we know, in which deeds like this can happen, was ultimately in the hands of a just and loving God. For him, this conviction came to him by way of the Christian faith, and he frequently was called on to speak to great gatherings of the Christian Church. . . . He knew that this conviction could come to men [sic] of many faiths, Muslim, Hindu, Jewish, Buddhist, but for him it came through Christianity, as revealed in Jesus, the revolutionary carpenter of Nazareth, whom Christians call the Christ, who chose these words from the Jewish scripture to characterize his work: "To preach good news to the poor, proclaim release to the captives,

---

2. Bosch, *Transforming Mission*, chapter 9, "Mission in the Wake of the Enlightenment," esp. 302–13.

3. Maro, "The Last Rites for Dr. Eduardo C. Mondlane."

recovering of sight to the blind, and to set at liberty those who are oppressed."[4]

Hawley continued, addressing the difficult question of the use of violence given Mondlane's Christian beliefs:

> This strange yet compelling man, who called himself the Son of Man, and whom Christians call the Son of God, once said: "The kingdom of God comes by violence, and violent men take it by force." I do not wish to enter here into the long debates that have surrounded this passage, except to say that there have been many who, like Dr. Mondlane, filled with a burning love for the oppressed whom Jesus loved, and seeing justice long delayed and the cruel yoke harsh on the people, have been willing, against their natures, to become violent men, and to seek to seize the kingdom by force, trusting in a gracious God to rework the deeds they saw as necessary, into a larger pattern of justice and right. His was a faith inspired by love, inspired by truth, inspired by justice, inspired by one who, speaking of the false peace that acquiesces in injustice so commonly advocated by comfortable men [sic] today, said, "I have come not to bring peace but the sword." But beyond the sword was always the vision of the higher goals, of justice, righteousness, truth and love, and violence was but a regrettable but necessary means to these higher goals.[5]

For those involved in the ecumenical movement, Mondlane in life, and in death, held up a great challenge to become more actively engaged in the struggle for liberation in Mozambique and throughout southern Africa. In a tribute to Mondlane written by Hank Crane in 1969, this challenge is clearly articulated:

> Eduardo did not ask or expect too much from his friends in the churches. He did not expect us to come and join his guerilla forces. He did not even ask us for arms for the struggle; he knew where he could get those. The little money that was made available through the churches for Mozambique refugees, and for civilian projects such as the Mozambique Institute in Dar-es-Salaam, was little more than a token involvement on our part in a struggle that demands of us more than just token involvement. He asked for understanding of the issues that are at stake.

---

4. Edward Hawley, "Meditation at the Funeral Service for Dr. Eduardo C. Mondlane at Azania Front Lutheran Church, Dar es Salaam on Thursday, 6th February 1969 at 3:30 p.m." WCC/PCR File 5/2, Box 4223.3.11.

5. Ibid.

He pled patiently, and with amazing charity, for us to open our eyes and see how deeply our societies are involved in perpetuating injustices that scream to heaven to be redressed. His death leaves us still with the unanswered question: Are the churches willing to risk their institutional securities by getting involved in the struggle to unmask and eradicate the evil that effectively undermines their moral credibility among men [sic] of color in the world today? Are we as Christians ready to take on the incredibly difficult and thankless job of educating the churches as to what is at stake? The most fitting memorial that we could possibly create for Eduardo Mondlane would be well-organized lobbies of Christians dedicated to the goals of stopping the flow of NATO arms into Portugal's colonial war and to the political, economic and social quarantine of the present regime in power in Portugal, until such time as that regime is ready to negotiate a political settlement of the conflict based upon majority rule. This much we can do through the various institutions through which we express our political convictions as Christians. We cannot afford to do less.[6]

As noted above, the development of the WCC's PCR after the 4th Assembly in Uppsala did much to concretize the global ecumenical movement's desire to stand in solidarity with the liberation movements against Portuguese colonialism, both through grants for humanitarian purposes and in raising awareness of these situations among its member churches around the world. Clearly in taking this stance, the harsh reaction of the colonial regime which would impact negatively on the life of the Protestant churches within Mozambique was considered to be less important than the global solidarity of the churches and the ultimate liberation of the country. This was certainly consistent with Mondlane's increasingly pointed call for the local churches to speak and act more prophetically within the territory, despite the inevitable repression.

## Portuguese Resurgence and Increased Repression of the Churches

In 1969, General Kaulza de Arriaga was appointed as commander of land forces in Mozambique and in 1970 took over as commander-in-chief.[7] Arriaga believed that a decisive military victory was needed

---

6. Hank Crane, "Eduardo Chivambo Mondlane," October, 1969, WCC/PCR File 5/2, Box 4223.3.11.

7. Newitt, *History of Mozambique*, 530–31. Arriaga had served in political and dip-

and in May of 1970 launched operation "Gordian Knot" with a massive build up of troops and military equipment including helicopters. He was able to re-take large areas of Niassa and Cabo Delgado, pushing back FRELIMO forces into Tanzania. However, President Caetano, who had succeeded Salazar at his death in 1968, vetoed Arriaga's plans to attack FRELIMO bases in Tanzania. In addition to these military actions, new roads and towns were to be built and Portuguese settlement was to be increased in the north of the territory. Perhaps most spectacularly was the beginning of the construction of the Cabora Bassa dam on the Zambezi River in 1969 with the significant backing of western capital. This huge engineering project was designed to produce income for the Portuguese and to assert their legitimate occupation of the territory. Arriaga also built up special units of African troops, the Grupos Especiais and the Grupos Especiais Paraquedistas within the army and the Flechas within the Direcção Geral de Segurança (DGS) the new name for the PIDE.[8] These measures were all relatively successful and for a time reasserted Portugal's claim over the northern territory of Mozambique.

At the same time, the level of surveillance of the Protestant churches continued to increase. The banning of NESAM and the Grupo de Estudantes Evangélicos in the 1960s because of their connections with the nationalist movement has already been noted and the suspicion of the Protestant churches, especially the IPM-MS, had been longstanding. In June of 1972, the full weight of this suspicion was brought to bear in the arrest of hundreds of people thought to be involved in the resistance to Portuguese rule, including many from "religious associations".[9] The largest number of these religious prisoners was from the IPM, thirty-two in total, including four pastors, Zedequias Manganhela, Casimir Mati, Abrão Aldasse and Gabriel Macavi and three evangelists, José Sidumo, Mario Sitoye and Ernesto Muhlanga. The Portuguese were convinced

---

lomatic postings as well as military and was known to be opposed to any negotiation on the independence of the overseas territories.

8. Ibid., 532. Newitt notes that these groups were to play a significant role in the civil war in the post independence era.

9. Helgesson, *Church, State and People*, 368 ff. The exact numbers differ in various sources. Helgesson quotes the *Johannesburg Star* that 1,800 people were arrested but suggests the number was closer to 1,000. Helgesson also notes, from a confidential document written by Marcel Vonnez, the Legal Representative of the Swiss Mission in Mozambique, that these prisoners included Zionists, Full Gospel, Adventists, Pentecostals, Wesleyans, and Congregationalists as well as Presbyterians.

that the IPM was an internal front for FRELIMO and that, in addition to those who left the country to join its ranks, it also provided financial support and maintained communications with the movement through the DM in Lausanne, the WCC and other international ecumenical and denominational bodies. In this regard, Manganhela was clearly identified as the primary link because of his longstanding friendship with Mondlane and his frequent international travel. As noted previously, Manganhela had participated in the meeting with Mondlane at Ricatla in 1961 and had met with him in Switzerland in 1966 and perhaps at other times. He was also suspect because of his frequent trips to the north of Mozambique after the Synod of 1968 which had prioritized mission work there under the leadership of Felix Khosa.[10] The final stage in granting full autonomy to the IPM in 1970 also led to heightened suspicion on the part of the Portuguese who accused the church of being a Provisional Government of Mozambique, with Manganhela replacing Mondlane as President,[11] building on the long held Portuguese fear that an autonomous church was code for an autonomous nation.

Mondlane's success in helping to bring global ecumenical support to the liberation movements in southern Africa was, therefore, to have serious implications for the Protestant churches in Mozambique, particularly the IPM. Every attempt had been made by Manganhela to remain "prudent," the word most often used in describing his relation with FRELIMO, and this prudence had in turn been mirrored by the DM, seeking not to jeopardize the lives of church people in Mozambique. However, the growing international church solidarity with FRELIMO, particularly through the PCR of the WCC, meant that Manganhela could no longer remain exempt from the interrogations of the police. In a report written by the *Chefe de Brigada* to António Fernandes Vaz, the Director of the DGS in Lourenço Marques explaining why the arrests of people in the IPM had been made, it is recorded,

> The repression put into effect against the people who were in the circle linked to the Swiss Mission, caused some apprehension in other quarters connected with the "World Council of Churches," an organization which defends "FRELIMO," leading to the arrival in Lourenço Marques of two Swiss, by the name of GEORGE ANDRIE and WILLIAM DE'RHAM [sic] who were allowed a

10. Cruz e Silva, *Protestant Churches*, 141.
11. Ibid., 371. Helgesson is again quoting from Vonnez's report.

visit, in the Recuperation Centre, with the most highly placed detainees from the Mission in question, a Mass being celebrated at the same time. This visit also included Dr. PINA CABRAL, BISHOP OF THE LIBOMBOS, who knowing latterly of the visit of the two Swiss, asked permission to accompany them, which was granted.[12]

It appears that this report was used by Vaz in writing his report to the Presidente do Conselho, Caetano, and copied to the Governor General, justifying the number of prisoners held and the length of time taken for the interrogation. He wrote, "We are in possession of very serious facts which involve one whole Protestant Church, reaching its highest placed members based in Geneva."[13] The link with the international ecumenical movement is clear and to some extent at least, the IPM, and particularly Manganhela, were paying the price for this increased solidarity.

### The Imprisonment and Death of Zedequias Manganhela

The visit to the prisoners held in the prison in Machava is corroborated by Georges Andrié and Marcel Vonnez.[14] In an interview, Andrié recounted that it was through the agency of Pina Cabral, the Anglican Bishop and a friend of President Caetano,[15] that they were allowed to make the visit and to celebrate communion. Manganhela and the other prisoners refused to worship in the chapel because it had been built

---

12. Report from the Chefe de Brigada to António Fernandes Vaz, 3/11/72. TT PIDE/DGS SC C1(2) 19639 7844, 43–45. "A repressão levada a efeito nas pessoas dos elementos ligados à Missão Suíça, causou certas apreensões em outros meios ligados ao 'Conselho Mundial das Igrejas,' organização protectora da 'FRELIMO,' motivando a vinda a Lourenço Marques de dois suíços, de nomes, GEORGE ANDRIE e WILLIAM DE'RHAM [sic] a quem foi permitida a visita, no Centro de Recuperação, aos detidos mais em evidência da dita Missão, sendo na mesma altura celebrada missa. A este visita assistiu ainda o Senhor Dr. PINA CABRAL, BISPO DOS LIBOMBOS, que conhecedor do fim da visita dos dois suíços, solicitou permissão para os acompanhar, no que foi atendido."

13. Report from the Director of DGS to the *Presidente do Conselho* and copied to the *Governador Geral*, December 12, 1972. TT PIDE/DGS SC CI(2) 6629 7450, 11, "estarmos em presença de factos muito graves que envolvem toda uma Igreja Protestante, atingindo os seus mais altos membros baseados em Geneve."

14. Marcel-Raymond Vonnez, "Souvenirs des Années 1971–1972."

15. Alf Helgesson quotes the Anglican missionary John Paul describing the arrival of Pina Cabral in 1969, "Almost overnight, the Anglican Church achieved respectability in the eyes of the Portuguese . . ." (*Church, State and People*, 367).

by the labor of political prisoners. Rather, they took communion in a large open shed. Andrié commented on the changed appearance of Manganhela and that he was very submissive to the Portuguese police, because of torture he surmised. None of the Protestant pastors was allowed to celebrate the sacrament, only the Anglican bishop. The prison guards took communion with them and Andrié recalls that Manganhela said to one of them at the end of the eucharist that he should understand that through this act they were brothers.[16]

The prisoners were held in detention without charge for four months. Only in October did the interrogations begin and it soon became clear that the police were most interested in extracting information about Manganhela and his relationship with FRELIMO. People were tortured until they "confessed"; this information along with what had been gathered from informers for years was used to build up the case against Manganhela. By December 9, the DGS had produced a "confession" of fifty-five pages, supposedly written in Manganhela's own hand and responding to a series of questions. It is impossible to authenticate any of this document; even if the responses were written by Manganhela, it is most probable that they were extracted from him by means of torture. In the questions and responses though, it is still possible to discern the information for which the DGS was searching. The questions centre around Manganhela's meetings with Mondlane in Mozambique in 1961, in Switzerland in 1966 and a possible second meeting in 1968. They wanted to know what the role was which Mondlane wanted Manganhela to play, particularly in recruiting youth to join FRELIMO, in raising funds for FRELIMO within Mozambique, and in raising awareness of the cause of liberation through church gatherings and networks.[17] However the information was gained, it is clear that Manganhela did everything possible to protect people not already implicated in the charges or whose names would not be a matter of record in church documents. It does indicate though, that funds were raised for FRELIMO and sent to the DM and then passed on to FRELIMO through the WCC. Again, it is impossible to know of the accuracy of this confession and this may have been simply a way to divert attention from the local church. However,

16. From an interview with Georges Andrié in Lausanne, April 3, 2003.

17. "Primeira Parte—Depoimentos prestados pelo arguido Zedequias Manganhela, até ao dia 9 do corente mês e escritos pelo seu próprio punho"—December 1972, TT PIDE/DGS SC CI(2) 6629 7450, 34–89.

## Mondlane's Legacy of Faith

clearly the WCC and the DM had a significant place in the picture that is being painted and, again, their actions have implications for the local church.[18] Although in the end he does ask forgiveness from his *"patria"*, Portugal, he never, as Cruz e Silva also asserts,[19] denied his connection with Mondlane nor his sympathy for the cause of independence.

A second document was purportedly written by Manganhela on December 9 and 10, just before he was alleged to have committed suicide in his cell. In this document is also included a suicide note. It contains some further information about Manganhela's meeting with Mondlane in Geneva in 1966 but then repeats information about how money is collected in the church and ends rather abruptly.[20] There is no evidence outside the police record to support the assertion that Manganhela committed suicide; rather it is most likely that he was killed by the police during interrogation or that he died of cardiac failure.[21] A German prisoner, Hans-Theodor Thomsen, held in a prison cell near Manganhela's later gave the following testimony to the International Commission of Jurists: "I and my Spanish prison mate listened to the last words of Manganhela. Manganhela said: 'If you want to kill me, do it! I have nothing to declare and nothing to confess.' After that we only heard the noise of two strokes

---

18. It is interesting to read an account of the case that was built against the prisoners in a report from Rev. Schneider of the Swiss Mission in Transvaal on a trip to Mozambique, February 3–23, 1973, "The church is alleged to have collected funds in Mozambique for transmission to the Frelimo via Switzerland. Journeys abroad or visitors from abroad serve that purpose. A connection is made between the church's ecumenical relations (links with Swiss churches, membership of the World Alliance of Reformed Churches) and the W.C.C. grants to liberation movements, alias terrorists. The autonomy of the church, and the gradual withdrawal of white control over its activities are viewed with great suspicion. There are other Protestant churches in Mozambique with connections abroad (Republic of S.A., America, Scandinavia, etc …) but none of them has been attacked as broadly as ours, and their leaders questioned about church activities as such, as far as I know." WCC General Secretariat (GS) Box 42.3.005 File 4.

19. Cruz e Silva, *Protestant Churches*, 146–47. Here she is drawing on G. Honwana, "Um Episódio de Justiça Colonial."

20. "Segunda parte—Depoimentos prestados pelo arguido Zedequias Manganhela, na sua própria cela, nos dias 9 e 10 do corrente mês, escritas pelo seu próprio punho." December 1972. PIDE/DGS SC CI(2) 6629 7450, 90–94.

21. "The Security Police (D.G.S.) in Mozambique," International Commission of Jurists, Geneva, Switzerland. No date. WCC PCR Box 301, 1974.

followed by a total silence! The next morning we were informed that Manganhela was found hanged in his prison cell."[22]

Janet Mondlane, on hearing of Manganhela's death in Dar-es-Salaam wrote to Baldwin Sjollema, the Director of the PCR in Geneva, "No matter what the 'evidence', he committed suicide to the same degree that Eduardo committed suicide! I know that he was an innocent man . . ."[23] Marcel Vonnez, the legal representative of the Swiss Mission in Mozambique at the time wrote, "For having accompanied him and often travelled with him, I knew him intimately, in particular his 'scared' side in relation to violence, that would never have allowed him to commit suicide. On the basis of this conviction, I do not give any credence to the possibility of a suicide, as the local police wanted us to believe."[24] Thousands of people came to Manganhela's funeral and stood in silence but it was cut short by the police and the coffin was not allowed to be open.[25]

## Local and International Reaction

The detention and death of Manganhela, and the evangelist José Sidumo, brought into clear focus the discussion among the leaders of the IPM, the DM, the WCC and the World Alliance of Reformed Churches (WARC) concerning the strategy that should be used in the face of Portuguese intransigence. Even before Manganhela's detention, the DM had been in discussion with the IPM concerning the withdrawal of Swiss personnel based on a suggestion from the WCC. The rationale was that the presence of the missionaries was authorized by the colonial regime and therefore added to its credibility. The discussion was held in secret in Chicumbane in order to avoid the agents of the DGS but

---

22. As quoted in Cruz e Silva, *Protestant Churches*, 147.

23. Letter from Janet Mondlane to Baldwin Sjollema, December 13, 1972. WCC PCR Box 4223.2.11.1, Special Fund File 1 & 2.

24. Vonnez, "Souvenirs des Années," 4. "Pour l'avoir côtoyé et souvent voyage avec lui, je le connaissais de l'intérieur, en particulier son côté 'effrayé' face à la violence, qui ne lui aurait jamais permis de se suicider. Sur la base de cette conviction, je n'ai laissé aucune place à la possibilité d'un suicide, comme la police locale voulait nous le faire croire."

25. Helgesson, *Church, State and People*, 370. Cf. Biber, *Cent Ans*, 132; and Honwana, *Memórias*. However cf. Vonnez, "Souvenirs des Années," 4. Vonnez says that he saw the body at the funeral with his face intact but with only one hand placed on his chest.

Georges Andrié suspected that they knew of it.[26] Andrié's recollection of the IPM's response is significant: "[They] told us that from their point of view . . . there were many more positive reasons to continue the collaboration rather than to stop it. And after all, we were always considered by colonial authorities as *persona . . . non grata!*"[27] It seems though that the WCC was pressuring the DM to take a much more public position against the Portuguese. In his letter to Janet Mondlane, in response to hers concerning Manganhela's death, Sjollema wrote, "I believe that [the Swiss Mission] now start understanding that they should have spoken out much earlier. There is growing uneasiness amongst Swiss about the silence they have kept on these and other matters and reactions are starting to come, which is important, but rather late!"[28]

The detention of the Presbyterian prisoners and the death of Manganhela and Sidumo led both the DM and the WCC to advocate for them at the highest levels and, on the part of the DM, to begin to sacrifice some of the "prudence" which they had practiced in favor of confrontation with the Portuguese authorities. At the time of the arrests, Clément Barbey, Assistant General Secretary at the WCC wrote to Cardinal Jean Willebrands seeking the intervention of the Vatican.[29] He also wrote to John How, the Secretary General of the Anglican Consultative Council thanking him for the support of Bishop Cabral and also seeking the assistance of Archbishop Taylor of the Church of the Province of South Africa.[30] Pina Cabral also met with Visser't Hooft in Geneva and then with Caetano in Lisbon concerning the prisoners.[31] It also seems to have led to a much broader discussion of the possible

26. Georges Andrié, quoted in Cruz e Silva, *Protestant Churches*, 143.

27. Ibid., 150. Cruz e Silva documents a secret meeting of the DM in 1971 in which they discussed the right to independence of people in southern Africa. In relation to Mozambique, their position maintained the usual prudence: "They discussed the kind of public political position to be assumed by the DM so as to avoid the possible increase of repression against the IPM or any further prejudice to Mozambicans or Swiss missionaries working within the Mozambican Church."

28. Letter from Baldwin Sjollema to Janet Mondlane, December 19, 1972, WCC PCR Box 4223.2.11.1, Special Fund File 1 & 2.

29. Confidential letter from Clément Barbey to Cardinal Jean Willebrands, June 28, 1972, WCC GS Box 42.3.005 File 4.

30. Letter from John Howe to Clément Barbey, July 10, 1972, WCC GS Box 42.3.005 File 4.

31. Confidential memo from C. Barbey to P. Potter, November 11, 1972, WCC GS Box 42.3.005 File 4.

role of the WCC, through contacts with the DM, as an intermediary between the Portuguese government and the liberation movements.[32]

After the deaths of Manganhela and Sidumo, the DM and other ecumenical and human rights organizations brought pressure to bear on the Portuguese authorities. An inquiry was held presided over by Judge Valadas Preto, the President of the Court of Appeal at Lourenço Marques. Manganhela's body was exhumed and a post-mortem conducted. Vonnez accompanied Manganhela's widow, Leonor Hunguana, to view the body and noted that one of his hands had been placed in a plastic glove. He presumed it was because his fingernails had been pulled out during torture.[33] Although the post-mortem confirmed death by suicide, the judge did find that there had been systematic torture of the prisoners during interrogation. The report was suppressed and the judge removed from his position although he was reinstated after significant protest was raised within the legal community in Lourenço Marques.[34] The DM, with the support of the IPM, organized an international enquiry into the deaths of Manganhela and Sidumo with the participation of the International Committee of the Red Cross (ICRC) and the International Committee of Jurists (ICJ). In addition, in August of 1973, the President of the International Commission of Jurists denounced the situation before Committee 24 of the UN.[35] With the help of the Igreja Evangélica Presbiteriana de Portugal, they were able to gain access to Portuguese authorities. A delegation from the DM was received by the Governor General of Mozambique[36] and on February 7, 1974, three representatives of the DM, G. Guinand, the Chair of the Council, G. Morier-Genoud, General Secretary and G. Andrié, Secretary Responsible for Relations with the IPM, met with Marcello Caetano. They vigorously denounced the arrests and deaths in prison of the Mozambican Presbyterians and the accusations made against them before the head of the Portuguese government, but with little sympathy from Caetano.[37]

32. Ibid.

33. Vonnez, "Souvenirs des Années."

34. "The Security Police (D.G.S.) in Mozambique," Report of the International Commission of Jurists, Geneva, Switzerland, Undated but after May, 1973, WCC PCR Box 301 File 1974.

35. Cruz e Silva, "Zedequias Manganhela," 45.

36. Ibid., 44–45.

37. Letter from Georges Guinand and Georges Andrié to Philip Potter, March 13,

## A Changed Understanding of the Role of the Churches

It is clear that despite continuing concerns about the safety and work of those involved in the IPM, both Mozambican and Swiss, the understanding of the role of the church in the struggle for liberation in Mozambique of the DM had shifted markedly. Cruz e Silva comments,

> It is probably the case for most Swiss pastors and leaders working in Mozambique, that condemning colonial policies and practices did not at first result in the easy acceptance that Mondlane was the leader of a movement aimed at liberation through armed struggle, while the Church's mission was for peace. Nevertheless, with the changing events in Mozambique, they became sympathetic to the movement, understanding the necessity to make war in order to have peace. Among them, I must emphasize two names: Charles Périer and André-Daniel Clerc. . . . For the pastors of a new generation, those beginning in the 1960's, it seems likely that it was much easier to accept what was happening in the country and to understand the necessary adjustments of the Church with regard to Portuguese policies. What is very clear is that the Presbyterian Church refused to take the same side as the dominant power, and like its followers it also became a victim of the system.[38]

Marcel Vonnez describes the DM's new posture as a "choix politique" when it was decided to report the arrest of Manganhela and the other prisoners in a very public manner. Recounting his speaking to African pastors after the arrests had been made he wrote, "I show that I am with them, ready to make a political gesture and to see them when they are decimated by the police. The expressions changed. We now know that the Swiss not only talk about independence but that they are also aware of the political consequences."[39] This shift however not only had implications for the life of the church in Mozambique and the role which the DM would play in solidarity with them, it also led to a much closer identification with FRELIMO as the agent of liberation in the country.

---

1974, WCC GS Box 42.3.005 File 4.

38. Cruz e Silva, *Protestant Churches*, 149.

39. Vonnez, "Souvenirs des Années." "Je montre que je suis avec eux, prêt à faire un geste politique et pour les voir quand ils sont décimés par la police. Les regards ont changé. On sait maintenant que les Suisses n'ont pas seulement parlé d'indépendance mais sont aussi [original text unclear] des conséquences politiques."

This was even more pronounced with the WCC for whom FRELIMO became the principle interlocutor in formulating its policies and actions in relation to Mozambique. Mondlane's personal history with the WCC meant that there was a great deal of confidence in the movement he had founded and despite his death and the prolonged leadership struggle in FRELIMO the WCC continued to recognize it as its obvious partner, particularly through the PCR. Clearly, because of the precarious situation of the Protestant churches in Mozambique under Portuguese rule, the solidarity of the ecumenical movement needed to be expressed through other means. However, it is interesting to note that in the correspondence extant between Baldwin Sjollema of the PCR and Marcelino dos Santos and Janet Mondlane, before independence, there is almost no mention of the local church. This does not mean that the Mozambican churches were not considered in the transformed society which FRELIMO envisioned and which it sought to build in its bases in Tanzania and in the territory it controlled in northern Mozambique but their role was not discussed. In this regard the ideological shift in the FRELIMO leadership after Mondlane's death must be considered.

## FRELIMO Leadership after Mondlane and Relationship with the WCC

Many anticipated that Uria Simango would become the next President of FRELIMO after Mondlane's assassination. Immediately after his death, a Council of Presidency was established which included Simango, Samora Machel, the military commander, and Marcelino dos Santos. However, in November, 1969, Simango was expelled from the party after publishing a manifesto against opponents within FRELIMO and joined other dissidents in COREMO in Zambia. Samora Machel became President of FRELIMO in May 1970. Although COREMO argued that its differences with FRELIMO were not ideological, it was clear that they did reject the more radical Marxist position followed under the leadership of dos Santos and Machel. COREMO argued that their disagreement with FRELIMO was primarily over the role of ex-patriots within the party and the dependence on money raised outside Mozambique, particularly in the United States.[40]

---

40. "Conversation with the Representative of COREMO." Undated, probably 1972, WCC PCR Box 301 File COREMO

In February, 1971, a request for support came from COREMO to the Division of Inter-Church Aid of the WCC for their work with Mozambican refugees in Zambia.[41] It was endorsed by the Christian Council of Zambia[42] and was considered in the various departments of Unit II of the WCC. The request was denied and Sjollema gave the following rationale, "Our line is that although we fully recognize the human needs in liberated Mozambique, it would be best to coordinate our support through FRELIMO, as the generally recognized and effective movement. This is in a way a political decision, but we do not think we can or should avoid this."[43] Part of the reasoning for withholding support from COREMO was that it was not recognized by the Liberation Committee of the OAU. Another request was received from COREMO in 1974 with a similar response from the WCC. It is interesting to note in this request that COREMO raises the issue of WCC support for more than one liberation organization in Angola and Rhodesia and wonders why different standards seem to be used for Mozambique.[44]

It does appear that the WCC was determined to maintain its support to FRELIMO and not to consider the possibility of support to other movements or organizations, particularly COREMO. Once again, it would appear that the legacy of Mondlane's relationship was very strong and that the WCC, particularly those in the PCR, identified with the liberation movement which he had founded. The commitment to political and social transformation in FRELIMO resonated with the WCC's emerging understanding of the "*missio Dei*" as stated, for example, in the "Report on World Economic and Social Development" approved at the 4th Assembly: "Our hope is in him who makes all things new. He judges our structures of thought and action and renders them obsolete. If our false security in the old and our fear of revolutionary change tempt us to defend the *status quo* or to patch it up with half-hearted measures, we may all perish. The death of the old may cause pain to some, but failure to build up a new world community may bring death to all. In their faith

---

41. Letter from Absolom T. Bahule to H. Hellberg, February 18, 1971, WCC PCR Box 301, Correspondence 1971,72.

42. Letter from K.C. Mwenda to K. Ankrah, June 13, 1972. WCC PCR Box 301, Correspondence 1971,72.

43. Memo from B. Sjollema to K. Andrah, September 15, 1972. WCC PCR Box 301, Correspondence 1971,72.

44. Letter from Paulo José Gumane to the Africa Department, WCC, February 15, 1974, WCC PCR Box 301, 1974.

in the coming Kingdom of God and in their search for his righteousness, Christians are urged to participate in the struggle of millions of people for greater social justice and for world development."[45] Certainly this resonance could also be felt in other liberation movements but Mondlane's *imprimatur* on FRELIMO seemed to ensure that it would manifest this new world community in the Mozambican context in a way that merited the full support of the WCC.

The danger in this position, which would become more obvious after independence, was that the WCC appeared to be expressing its solidarity not only with those involved in the struggle against Portuguese colonialism but with a particular project and organization which saw itself as the exclusive bearer of liberation and which, through its ideology, was expressing an ever more critical view of the role of the church in an independent Mozambique. Eric Morier-Genoud interprets FRELIMO's increasing antipathy toward religious organizations as an example of Mbembe's theory of the "theologian state." It was the movement, and not the churches, which would "define for social agents the way they have to see themselves, interpret themselves and interpret the world."[46] In the discussion concerning a possible grant to COREMO, an interesting caveat in regard to the close identification of the WCC with FRELIMO is raised by Kedwo Ankrah:

> The first question "whom do we help" is also crucial. My understanding has been that WCC, i.e. any of its units or sub-units, in supporting any organization not related directly to member churches in any locality, will take into consideration the government and non-governmental organizations operating and existing in the area. At the same time, these local organizations will *not* determine for WCC what it should or should not do. Of course, WCC will consider seriously the advice and comments of these organizations. This hitherto has been the position of PCR regarding its assistance to the liberation movements in Africa. PCR is not bound by OAU views on the liberation movements. On the other hand, it takes seriously the comments of the OAU. This position allows PCR freedom in maintaining its integrity, and that of OAU vis-à-vis support and control of liberation movements.[47]

---

45. Goodall, ed., *The Uppsala Report*, 45.

46. Morier-Genoud, *God and Caesar*, 20.

47. Memo from Kedwo Ankrah to Helmut Reusche, April 8, 1974, WCC PCR Box 301, 1974.

## The Carnation Revolution

The end of Portuguese colonialism in Mozambique came somewhat unexpectedly with the so-called "Carnation Revolution" in Portugal which began on April 25, 1974. The revolt was led by young officers of the Movimento das Forças Armadas (MFA) and overthrew the government of Marcello Caetano.[48] Despite modest reforms in colonial policy under Caetano's leadership, it was clear that the whole imperial structure was no longer operating to Portugal's advantage. The country's orientation was becoming more and more focused on integration into western Europe, both politically and economically. Portugal joined the EFTA in 1960 and relaxed foreign investment restrictions in 1961, restrictions which had been at the heart of Portuguese colonial policy of the Estado Novo. In Mozambique, this meant that by 1973, South Africa, not Portugal, had become the territory's major trading partner and source of new capital.[49] The cost of fighting the wars in the colonies, both financial and human, was becoming intolerable especially as many in the military realized that these wars were not winnable.[50] The Portuguese army had grown from 60,000 in 1960 to over 200,000 in the early 1970s and male compulsory military service had been extended to four years in 1967.[51] Discontent among young officers in the so-called "Captain's Movement" coupled with the calculated political maneuvers of General António de Spínola and the publication of his book *Portugal e o Futuro* in February 1974 brought about the bloodless coup in April with Spínola acceding to the presidency of the Junta de Salvação Nacional.

In Mozambique, as in the other overseas territories, the coup was not expected. However, in its aftermath Portuguese troops retreated to their bases and FRELIMO was able to expand rapidly into the central and coastal parts of the country. The new Portuguese government would not initially guarantee independence for the colonies; Spínola

---

48. For a full discussion of the military coup in Portugal and its impact on the colonial territories including Mozambique, see Chabal et al., *A History of Postcolonial Lusophone Africa*; MacQueen, *The Decolonization of Portuguese Africa*; and Costa Pinto, *O Fim do Império Português*.

49. Newitt, *History of Mozambique*, 537.

50. Ibid. However, Newitt argues that the cost of the war actually was responsible for an economic boom in the metropole with the modernization of both the military and industry and an increase in foreign investment.

51. MacQueen, *Decolonization*, 76–77.

hoped to create a kind of lusophone commonwealth with a gradual process of decolonization. Nevertheless, a peace agreement was signed on September 7 in Lusaka. This initiated a cease fire and put in place a transitional government which was to last for nine months under the leadership of Joaquim Chissano. Machel remained outside the transitional government.

### The Role of the Churches under FRELIMO

Even before the transitional government was formed, in August 1974, a small delegation from the IPM traveled to Dar-es-Salaam to meet with representatives of FRELIMO. In a report written by the IPM's new General Secretary, Isaias Funzamo, a very energetic new program of work was envisaged for the church. He wrote, "FRELIMO counts heavily on the support which the Churches, and in particular the Presbyterian Church, can offer it in its struggle for the construction of the country."[52] He speaks of expanding training programs and facilities in health and education in order to meet the challenges before them. However, he also indicates that this challenge comes in the midst of a worsening financial crisis in the country and that the continued and indeed increased financial support of the Swiss churches would be important. In another report written by Funzamo at this time and entitled, "Informações e Análise da Actual Situação Política em Moçambique" and addressed to "Nossos Estimados Missionários"[53] he attempted to define more clearly the role of the church in this time of transition: "The Church feels called to exercise its function as an instrument of Peace and Reconciliation through information and explanations which it can give in the current confused political situation. It feels that its task is to enliven the despairing with a message of Hope and of the love of God for men [sic] and for the neighbor. . . . Our greatest present concern is to seek to be a prophetic Church, and to attempt from now to create bases of Social and religious

---

52. "Orientations." Annexe au PV du Bureau-Secrétariat du 17 septembre 74, WCC PCR Box 301, 1974. "Le FRELIMO compte beaucoup sur l'appui que les Eglises, et en particulier l'Eglise presbytérienne, peuvent lui offrir dans sa lutte pour la construction du pays".

53. "Information and Analysis of the Current Situation in Mozambique" addressed to "Our esteemed Missionaries."

## Mondlane's Legacy of Faith

development that will allow a peaceful co-existence between the several races and tribes which make up the Mozambican People."[54]

Following the coup in Lisbon, the WCC began discussions as to what the relationship to the churches in the former colonial territories should be.[55] In September Isiais Funzamo and Casimiro Matié travelled to Switzerland where they met with Simão Chamango and had conversations with the DM and others. On September 24 they met with representatives of the DM together with three representatives of the Sacred Heart Fathers from Holland, two of whom were missionaries in Mozambique. It was a significant meeting of Protestants and Catholics albeit in Switzerland and without Mozambican Catholics present. The deep-seated anger toward the Roman Catholic Church is clear in the comments of the Mozambicans and the concern over division and dependence, both major themes of FRELIMO's critique of the church, was very much in evidence. Matié commented on the meeting with FRELIMO in Dar-es-Salaam: "FRELIMO wants to leave the Churches free to do their job, but foresees difficulties. It is afraid that the work of the church will again constitute a privileged group, while it desires that the whole population would unite and celebrate as one in the reconstruction of the country."[56] Funzamo reflected, "The African Church is independent. Other churches are missions with European origins. The Catholic Church must give a public sign of repentance and conversion."[57]

54. Isaias Funzamo, "Informações e análise da actual situação política em Moçambique", August 10, 74. WCC GS Box 42.3.005 File 5. "A Igreja se sente chamada para exercer a sua função de instrumento da Paz e de Reconciliação através da informação e esclarecimentos que possa dar na actual confusa situação política. Sente como sua tarefa animar os desesparados com mensagem de Esperança e de amore de Deus aos Homens e para com o próximo. . . . A nossa grande preocupação actualmente é procurarmos ser uma Igreja profética, e tentamos desde já criar bases de desenvolvimento Social e religioso que permitirá uma convivência pacífica entre as várias raças e tribos que constituem of Povo moçambicano."

55. Memo from Jean Fischer to C.I. Itty, May 24, 74, WCC GS Box 42.3.005 File 5.

56. "Breve relatório do encontro em Lausanne, no dia 24 de Setembro de 1974," Notes from meeting among representatives of the DM, IPM and the Holy Heart Fathers, September 24, 1974. Archives of CIDAC, Base de Dados Anti-Colonial, BAC 580. "A FRELIMO quer deixar liberdade às Igrejas para as suas tarefas, mas prevê dificuldades. Tem receio que na obra eclesiastica se va constituir novamente um grupo priviligiado, ao passo que deseja que o povo inteiro se una e celebre como uma unidade na reconstrução do país."

57. Ibid. "A Igreja africana é independente. As outras Igrejas são missões de origem europeia. . . . É necessário que a Igreja Católica dê um sinal público de arrependimento e de conversão."

They were also very critical of any possibility that expatriate missionaries could represent the Mozambican people. Their experience of the Roman Catholic Church had been of the compromised Portuguese church and it seems it was difficult for them to imagine a more progressive form of Catholicism.

## The Beginnings of Repression and Nationalizations

F. Randriamamonjy and José Chipenda visited Mozambique in late 1974 and discussed the relation of the WCC with the local churches and with the FRELIMO government. In correspondence from Marcel Vonnez, who had been the Swiss Mission's official representative in Mozambique but by then was working in Beira, to WCC staff, it appears that there was a significant difference of opinion over the role of the churches in the social development of the country in the new context. Vonnez argued that because of the desperate need in the country the churches had to respond and not leave all initiatives to the government and to the "people." In theological terms he writes, "There is already great confusion now in the reflection of the churches, it seems to me. The proper activity of the Church is to speak, worship, meetings, prayer, teaching, etc. The rest is the business of the 'secular', of the government, of others. But from where do we get this notion, this division of the Word and of the practical?"[58] In another letter to WCC staff written in June of 1975, Vonnez began to raise an alarm concerning what Machel was saying about religious organizations, including the Protestant churches, as he travelled throughout the country before independence. He cites a speech of Machel's quoted in the *Noticias da Beira* of May 18, "I know that here in the south religion is very strong. But us, we fought the war without the support of religion. Understand? Neither the Protestants, nor the Muslims and even less so the Catholics. We fought the war without them. Listen well to this: here there are Catholics, there are Protestants and there are Muslims, but we have won the war without them, we won over them all. This is the truth.

---

58. Letter from Marcel Vonnez, April 24, 1975, WCC PCR Box 301, 1975. "Il y a une assez grande confusion actuellement dans la réflexion des églises, me semble-t-il. L'activité propre a l'Eglise c'est de parler, les cultes, les réunions, la prière, l'enseignement etc. Le reste c'est l'affaire des 'laïcs', du gouvernement, des autres. Mais où donc tire-t-on cette notion, cette division de la Parole et de la pratique?"

... No Church that exists has ever done anything for the victory of the Mozambican people...."[59]

Another early warning of the general break down of the rule of law in the country and, more particularly in regard to this study, the harassment and suppression of the church by FRELIMO is contained in a report on a visit to Mozambique by Barend van Niekerk, Professor in the Faculty of Law at the University of Natal, on behalf of Amnesty International (AI) and the ICJ in June, 1975 and shared with staff at the WCC. Van Niekerk had made a previous visit to Mozambique in 1973 on behalf of AI and ICJ to investigate the detention of two Spanish priests and also to investigate the death of Manganhela. His report paints a very sombre picture of the situation of political prisoners, and the development of re-education camps and of "popular" tribunals in the absence of a functioning judicial system. Perhaps more disturbing was the encouragement of this "popular" justice in the government controlled press. His contacts with the church were primarily Roman Catholic but his comments are still instructive:

> ... Mr. Samora Machel made several highly critical references to the Church indicating very clearly that the new regime regarded the Church as an intolerable alternative object of the people's allegiance.... There can be no doubt that staring Mozambique in the face today is a bleak period in which the Church will be forced entirely and unequivocally to do the bidding of the State.... The likely result will probably be that there will be a progressive disengagement from Mozambique by the Church which could in the short-run have a disastrous effect on education, hospital and clinical services and even, considering the ubiquitous presence of the watchdog influence of the Church, on the rule of law.[60]

Mozambique became independent on June 25 1975 with Samora Machel as its first President. The critique of the churches was repeated

---

59. Letter from Marcel Vonnez, June 20, 1975, WCC PCR Box 301, 1975. "Je sais qu'ici au sud la religion est assez forte. Mais nous, nous avons fait la guerre sans l'appui de la religion. Compris? Ni les Protestants, ni les musulmans et encore bien moins les catholiques. Nous avons fait la guerre sans eux. Ecoutes bien ceci: ici il y a des catholiques, il y a des Protestants et il y a des musulmans, mais nous avons gagné la guerre sans eux, mais nous avons gagné contre eux tous. Voilà ce qui est vrai... Aucune Eglise, qu'elle soit n'a jamais rien fait pour la victoire du peuple mozambicain..."

60. Barend van Niekerk, "Confidential Report on Visit to Mozambique June 1975." WCC PCR Box 301, 1975.

and expanded in Machel's crucial speech at Machava Stadium on July 24, before up to one hundred thousand people:

> We know that you are divided. The Catholic Church has its headquarters at the Vatican. There are Catholics here, it is true or not? When we ask, the first thing that is said is, "I am Catholic." Myself, when someone asks me, I say, "I am Mozambican" first off. . . . Therefore, as a Mozambican I only obey FRELIMO. FRELIMO is father and mother to me. . . . Others are Presbyterians, connected to Switzerland. They think about Switzerland rather than thinking about Mozambique. . . . Why is it that they don't make these churches into Mozambican churches! . . . Others are Methodists. They have their head in America, far away, there in America and their body in Mozambique. . . . These countries were linked with Portuguese colonialism. They helped Portuguese colonialism to massacre the Mozambican People and to build jails throughout the world, throughout our country. Why didn't the Swiss come, why didn't the Americans come, why didn't the Romans come to free you? Some are going to use religion to impede the development of our country . . . .[61]

Following this speech, all schools, hospitals, funeral services and medical services were nationalized and foreign currency bank accounts were frozen. Although the Protestant churches had expected that education and health would eventually come under the control of government, and indeed believed that these were properly the responsibility of the state, they did not expect that this would happen so soon, in such an abrupt manner, or in the climate of mistrust which the government was building.

---

61. Machel, *Revolução*, 28–29. "Sabemos que vocês estão divididos. A Igreja Católica tem a sua sede no Vaticano. Estão aqui católicos, é ou não é? Quando perguntamos, a primeira coisa que se diz é 'Eu sou católico.' Eu, quando alguém me pergunta, digo 'Eu sou moçambicano' em primeiro lugar! . . . Portanto, como moçambicano, só obedeço à FRELIMO. A FRELIMO é pai e mãe para mim. . . . Outros são presbiterianos, ligados à Suiça. Pensam na Suiça, em vez de pensarem em Moçambique. . . . Porque é que não fazem dessas Igrejas, Igrejas Moçambicanos? . . . Outros, são metodistas. Têm a cabeça na América, longe, lá na América e o corpo em Moçambique. . . . Esses países estavam ligados ao colonialismo português. Ajudavam o colonialismo português a massacrar o Povo Moçambicano, a criar cadeias em toda a parte do Mundo, em toda a parte do nosso país. . . . Porque é que não vinham os suíços, porque é que não vinham os americanos, porque é que não vinham os romanos para vos libertar? Alguns vão utilizar a religião para impedir o desenvolvimento do nosso país . . ."

It must be recognized that this denunciation of the churches does follow clearly from Mondlane's critique of the compromise which the Protestant churches had made with the Portuguese colonial project. The silence of the Protestant churches and missions, and the various churches which had founded these missions from different parts of the world, did continue to give a certain legitimacy to the colonial regime as has been demonstrated. However, to equate the identification of the Roman Catholic Church with the Portuguese state through the *Concordat* with this compromise is to deny the long history of resistance to colonialism and support of liberation of many within the Protestant churches, both Mozambican and expatriate. This is especially true given the experience of the IPM and other Protestant churches only three years earlier with the detention, torture and death of so many of their number including Manganhela. Indeed, it also did not recognize the much more diverse face of the Roman Catholic Church in the latter colonial period with the pro-independence position and work of the White Fathers and the Burgos Fathers resulting in their expulsion as well as the courageous witness of the Bishop of Nampula, Dom Manuel Vieira Pinto. In its attempt to define its exclusive role as the builder of the new revolutionary society, FRELIMO was alienating its allies, and potential allies, in the churches, particularly those who had been the victims of Portuguese colonialism because of their prophetic faith commitment and who had stood in solidarity with the struggle for liberation. Although the concern here is with the place of the church, FRELIMO's increasingly vehement demand that it be the unique vehicle of transformation in Mozambique affected other sectors of society and alienated many other allies who had been a part of the struggle for liberation and who would have been supportive of a radically different post-colonial society.[62]

## The Response of the WCC

Michael Testa was employed by the CICARWS of the WCC as a Consultant on Mozambique and visited the country between July 25 and August 17, 1975, immediately following the nationalizations. In December, 1974, CICARWS had agreed to make the exception of channelling aid through the new governments in the former Portuguese territories, which was

---

62. Cf. Barend van Niekerk, "Confidential Report on Visit to Mozambique June 1975." WCC PCR Box 301, 1975.

contrary to the policy of the WCC. In his report, Testa supports this decision and is very positive in his assessment of the new FRELIMO government: "One is impressed by the dedication, the competence, the idealism, and the unsparing devotion to duty evidenced by those with responsibility for the planning and execution of government."[63] He also at least partially acknowledges Machel's critique of the Protestant churches: "It is certainly true that the Portuguese colonial policy did hamper unity among the churches and did place restrictions on the indigenization of Protestant church leadership, but it is also true that most missions and churches accepted too readily this rationale to justify narrow sectarianism and paternalistic dominance. For instance, although never officially recognized, the Christian Council of Mozambique was organized in 1948 but, until recently, most churches withheld participation in the Council or failed to give it adequate support."[64]

Testa also gives the following opinion of how the local churches should find their role in the new society:

> At a time when the political and social pattern of the whole nation is being transformed, and when race, class and ethnic barriers erected in the past are being razed, and the economic structures that supported the "exploitation of man by man" [sic] are being dismantled, the compartmentalized churches can no longer remain as independent witnessing and serving communities on the thin margin of national life. The inherited divisions and separateness among Protestants, too often based on Western theological nuances, an alien polity and historical factors, must be surrendered in order that the Gospel of Jesus Christ may become incarnated in the life of the People of God as they actively participate in the task of bringing a new dignity and a more human quality of life in a nation hopefully striving to redress the injustices, the humiliations and the exploitation of half a millennium.
>
> The churches may make a beginning by sloughing off the "compound" mentality and ecclesial divisiveness, streamlining the implanted cumbersome church polity, modifying borrowed forms and liturgies, moving "outside the camp" into the main stream of the new society. The alternative is to become ineffec-

---

63. Michael Testa, "Report on Mozambique: CICARWS Consultant Appraisal of Visit, July 27-August 17, 1975," WCC PCR Box 301, 1975.

64. Ibid.

tual, irrelevant, obsolete, consigned to the sterile periphery of the life of the nation.[65]

Testa does recognize many of the concerns with the government which were impacting on the local churches, especially in his letter introducing his report.[66] However his report in general reads like an apology for the FRELIMO project and for the WCC's ongoing support for what had been transformed from a liberation movement into a government. He makes no comment about the way in which the nationalizations were carried out. In relation to the concerns raised by a local church leader that "what was not anticipated was to find ourselves again hedged in and slandered by the new government and, as churches, our participation in the 'new society' rejected,"[67] he writes, "It is understandable that, in confronting monumental social and economic problems requiring urgent solutions, drastic measures are called for and that these must be applied indiscriminately. In the process individual human rights and basic liberties are seriously restricted and, in some cases, sacrificed. The freedoms of expression, of religion, of dissent and political action have been either narrowly limited or abolished. Conformity to a predetermined ideological pattern and programme is the order of the day."[68] Clearly, the primary interlocutor for the WCC would continue to be FRELIMO with the local churches expected to play their proper role in relation to the grand experiment in social transformation initiated by the government. The longstanding relationship between FRELIMO and the WCC developed largely through Mondlane was to continue in the face of all criticism, even in the face of increasing repression of the churches and the more general curtailment of fundamental human rights. The prophetic role of the church in relation to the new government is never mentioned.

## Growing Repression and the Dilemma of the Churches

A further breach between the government and the churches occurred with the publication of "The People's Struggle Organized against the Banners of Imperialism—A Communication from the National Political

65. Ibid.
66. Letter from Michael Testa to CICARWS re. Report on Mozambique, September 18, 1975, WCC PCR Box 301, 1975.
67. Ibid.
68. Ibid.

Commissariat of FRELIMO" under the name of The National Political Commissar, Armando Guebuza and published in the daily *Notícias* on October 17, 1975. It is a direct attack on several churches, mostly independent and evangelical churches, and the Jehovah's Witnesses and includes the Church of the Nazarene which was a member of the Christian Council. The churches are accused of obscurantism, of collaboration with the colonial regime, of fostering disunity and of sending money to their offices in other countries. There is also a more general critique of all the churches, "All religious sects in close collaboration attempted to throw doubt on Frelimo's ability to govern. We do not know from whence this evidence comes, but this is important—during the armed struggle, none of them joined in the fight against colonialism, nor even publicly opposed the oppression of the people."[69] Although, again, the legitimate critique of the Protestant churches can be heard in this[70] the lack of distinction among the various churches and religious organizations and the absence of recognition of the support of many Protestants and Catholics for the liberation struggle does not do justice to the role of the church. Many church members and some foreign missionaries, including the Superintendant of the Church of the Nazarene, Armond Doll, and several pastors of the Seventh Day Adventists, were arrested and held without charge for months.

The news of the nationalizations and the arrests of church leaders reached the DM and the WCC from a variety of sources. The public response was to deny that there was a general persecution of Christians and members of other religions by the FRELIMO government[71] and in-

---

69. Quoted in "Text of address given by the Rev. Ted Smith, Superintendent of Methodist Missionary Work in Mozambique to the Annual Conference of the Methodist Church of Southern Africa on October 21, 1975," WCC PCR Box 301, 1975.

70. Ibid. Smith writes, "In Mozambique the Church has lost its credibility with most of the leaders and a large majority of the population, first of all because of the identification of the Catholic Church with the State, with the oppressors, and secondly because of the silence of the Protestant Churches. We did not collaborate with PIDE; but neither did we protest when wrong and injustice were flaunted before our eyes, because it was far too dangerous to do so. It was dangerous personally, and we had to safeguard the few privileges which we still held, so that we could go on preaching, go on baptizing, go on erecting buildings, raising denominational banners, counting statistics. Men [sic] were saved in that period, do not misunderstand me. For a few men [sic] God became real, but for many more our God became irrelevant."

71. Press Release from DM, "Pas de persecutions au Mozambique," September 16, 1975, WCC PCR Box 301, 1975.

## Mondlane's Legacy of Faith

deed this was generally the response of the churches in Mozambique. However concerns began to be raised and a more nuanced interpretation of the situation in the country in regard to the churches began to emerge. In a report to Philip Potter, the General Secretary of the WCC after a visit to Mozambique and participation in a meeting of the Christian Council, Jurgen Hilke wrote,

> Looking from within the country, Frelimo in many respects judges the churches, in a secular frame of reference, of course, on the grounds of past performance. Looking from within the Christian community, *PCR was a witness made also implicitly on behalf of those who were unable to join into it under Portuguese oppression.* [emphasis mine] This is true as far as the explanations of the situation at that time bring you. From then on, the unambiguous stance taken by the WCC inadvertently becomes a yardstick, a point of reference in asking: why did we, Christians in Mozambique, not do more? Why have we not stood up more firmly and vigorously?
>
> I hesitate to mention this at all, because it touches upon such a complex set of factors, emotions, and sensitivities that it is almost impossible to verify, at least as far as facts and figures are concerned. Yet, I am convinced that this ambiguity is a real one and is important to keep in mind because it hides a whole range of theological issues which in themselves are important to the WCC and churches that emerge from similar situations.[72]

Indeed, it was this ambiguity which would be the greatest challenge for the Protestant churches following independence. They had been challenged by Mondlane and others to take a more public and prophetic stance in the face of Portuguese colonialism. In fact the decisions of the WCC and other international church bodies to publicly condemn Portugal and to openly support the liberation movements through the PCR meant that the local churches would inevitably pay a price. Yet when the end of the colonial era came, this contribution was not recognized. Rather than being welcomed as partners in the struggle against oppression and partners in building the new society, they found themselves identified with the forces of reaction. Although the new constitution guaranteed freedom of religion[73] the new government clearly identified

---

72. Memo from Jurgen Hilke to Philip Potter re. Visit to Mozambique, September 12, 1975. WCC PCR Box 301, 1975.

73. *Constituição da República Popular de Moçambique.* Article 19 guaranteed the

religious belief as being divisive and damaging to the unity of the country. Although the government did not officially persecute the churches and in fact often engaged the church leaders in discussion,[74] its rhetoric and lack of censure of the excesses of the local Grupos dinamizadores which often harassed church members, put the churches constantly on the defensive. On the other side, the decision of the WCC to continue its support to the FRELIMO government complicated its relationship with the local churches especially when they were in conflict with the government. Ironically, the prophetic voice which Mondlane had advocated so strongly for the Protestant churches was subdued in relation to the new government. The challenge to the Protestant churches was to engage with the government in the rebuilding of the nation while at the same time not identifying itself so closely with this project that its prophetic witness would be lost.

### Living Out a Changed Paradigm of Mission in a Changed Context

Despite their location on the margins, these small Protestant communities and particularly the IPM, had been at the cutting edge of a shift in paradigm in relation to the mission of the church which was impacting the global ecumenical movement. Although the challenge to a revolutionary change in their theological self understanding came from various quarters, the life and thought of Eduardo Mondlane was key to this transformation. They had been challenged to be the church with others, to see the larger needs of the men and women with whom they lived rather than being concerned only with their own survival, growth, and development. They had been challenged to risk taking a prophetic stand in the cause of justice and to be willing to suffer the violent response of a tyrannical state. They had been challenged to engage in the quest for human liberation manifested in the here and now rather than only preaching the hope of heaven. They had been challenged to look beyond their own "missions" to the *missio Dei*, and to discern where this would lead them in their own context. What was perhaps surprising, and perhaps would have been surprising for Mondlane himself, was that this process of discernment did not end at the moment of political independence.

---

separation between church and state, Article 26 prohibits discrimination on the basis of religion, and Article 33 guarantees the freedom to believe or not to believe in a religion.

74. Morier-Genoud, *God and Caesar*, 30–31.

Like FRELIMO, the churches could say, "A luta continua"; the prophetic witness of the church needed to be ongoing. Its solidarity with the new government and its project of social transformation needed to be critical solidarity. In the incredibly difficult years of war and devastation which would follow, the churches again would have to find their prophetic voice in order to be the catalysts in building peace and reconciliation in the country together with those in the Roman Catholic Church, in other faith communities and with those of no faith. Mondlane's deepest desire to make the faith of the church "practical" and engaged in the life of the world would be made manifest not only in the church's important contribution to the liberation of the country but also in risking itself to work for justice and for peace in an independent Mozambique.

# Bibliography

Alder, J. C. "Scientific Socialism: Some Lessons from Mozambique." *Southern African Freedom Review* 3 (1990) 21–24.
Alves de Sousa, José Augusto. *Os Jesuítas em Moçambique 1541–1991: No Cinquentenário do Quarto Período da nossa Missão*. Braga: Livraria A.I., 1991.
Azevedo, Mario. *Historical Dictionary of Mozambique*. Metuchen, NJ: Scarecrow, 1991.
Berthoud, Paul. *Considerations sur la Constitution des Eglises Indigènes dans la Mission Romande*. Neuchatel: Delachaux et Niestlé, 1912.
Biber, Charles. *Cent Ans au Mozambique: Le parcours d'une minorité*. Lausanne: Editions du Soc, 1992.
Blaser, Klauspeter, et al. "The Ambivalence of Ethnic Identity: A Response to T. S. Maluleke." *Missionalia* 22/3 November (1994) 193–200.
Bosch, David J. *Transforming Mission: Paradigm Shifts in Theology of Mission*. Maryknoll, NY: Orbis, 1991.
Briggs, John, Mercy Oduyoye, and Georges Tsetsis, eds. *A History of the Ecumenical Movement, Volume 3, 1968–2000*. Geneva: World Council of Churches, 2004.
Butselaar, Jan van. *Africanos, Missionários e Colonialistas: As origens da Igreja Presbiteriana (Missão Suiça), 1880–1896*. Translated by Franciso da Cruz. Lausanne: Département Missionnaire des Eglises Protestantes de la Suisse Romande, 1987.
———. "The Ambiguity of (Crosscultural) Mission: Swiss Missionaries and Tsonga Christians in the Context of South Africa." *Missionalia* 24/1 April (1996) 63–77.
———. "The Gospel and Culture in Nineteenth-Century Mozambique." *Missiology: An International Review* 16 (1998) 46–54.
Cavert, Samuel McCrea. *The American Churches in the Ecumenical Movement, 1900–1968*. New York: Association, 1968.
Chabal, Patrick, et al. *A History of Postcolonial Lusophone Africa*. Bloomington: Indiana University Press, 2002.
Chamango, Simão. "L'Articulation de l'Évangile a la Realité Africaine: Considerations systematiques et pratiques." Mémoire de licence de dogmatique, Universté de Lausanne, Faculté de théologie, 1975.
———. "A Chegada do Evangelho em Moçambique." Unpublished manuscript. Ricatla: 1982.
———. "Church, Theology and Society in Postwar Mozambique." Translated by A. L. Milton. Explanatory notes from Robert Faris. *Toronto Journal of Theology* 18/1 (Spring 2002) 181–91.
———. "The Role of Christianity in Development, Peace and Reconstruction." Translated by Robert Faris. Unpublished manuscript. N.d.
Christie, Iain. *Samora: Uma biografia*. Maputo: Editora Ndjira, 1996.

Clerc, André-Daniel, *Chitlango: Filho de Chefe*. Translated by Maria de Lurdes Torcato and Ana Maria Branquinho. Maputo: Cadernos Tempo, 1990.

*Colloque sur les religions, Abidjan, Avril 1961*. Paris: Présence Africaine, 1962.

*Constituição da República Popular de Moçambique, Lei da Nacionalidade e Constituição do Primeiro Governo*. Maputo: Imrpensa Nacional de Moçambique, 1975.

Costa Pinto, António. *O Fim do Império Português: A Cena Internacional, a guerra Colonial, e a Descolonização 1961–1975*. Lisbon: Livros Horizonte, 2001.

Costea, Peter. "Church-State Relations in Marxist-Leninist Regimes of the Third World." *Journal of Church and State* 32 (1990) 281–308.

Cox, Harvey. *The Church amid Revolution: A Selection of Essays Prepared for the World Council of Churches Geneva Conference on Church and Society*. New York: Association Press, 1967.

Cruz e Silva, Teresa. "Igrejas Protestantes no sul de Moçambique e Nacionalismo: O Caso da Missão Suíça (1940–1974)." *Estudos Moçambicanos* 12 (1992) 19–39.

———. "A Missão Suíça e a Formação da Juventude: a experiência de Eduardo Mondlane (1930–1961)." *Estudos Moçambicanos* 16 (1999) 67–104.

———. *Protestant Churches and the Formation of Political Consciousness in Southern Mozambique (1930–1974)*. Basel: P. Schlettwein, 2001.

———. "Protestant Churches and the Formation of Political Consciousness of Southern Mozambique (1930–1974)". PhD diss., University of Bradford, 1996.

———. "Zedequias Manganhela: Notas para uma Releitura das Relações Estado-Igrejas Protestantes na Década de 70." *Estudos Moçambicanos* 13 (1993) 27–49.

Davidson, Basil. *The Black Man's Burden: Africa and the Curse of the Nation State*. London: James Curry, 1992.

Carvalho, Emílio J. M. de. *A Igreja Africana no Centro da sua História: Subsídios para a História da Igreja nos Países de Língua Oficial Portuguesa em África*. Lisbon: Núcleo, 1995.

De Gruchy, John W. *Christianity and Democracy: A Theology for a Just World Order*. Claremont, South Africa: David Philip, 1995.

———. *The Church Struggle in South Africa*. 25th anniversary edition. London: SCM, 2004.

———. *Liberating Reformed Theology: A South African Contribution to an Ecumenical Debate*. Grand Rapids: Eerdmans, 1991.

Dodge, Ralph. *The Pagan Church: The Protestant Failure in America*. Philadelphia: Lippincott, 1968.

*Eduardo Mondlane*. London: Panaf, 1972.

Ennes, António. *A Guerra de África em 1895: Cartas Inéditas e um estudo de Paiva Conceiro*. Lisbon: Prefácio, 2002.

Fatton, Paul. *Du Clan à l'Église: 75 ans de Mission au Sud de l'Afrique*. Lausanne: Mission Suisse dans l'Afrique du Sud, 1950.

Freeman-Grenville, G. S. P. *The New Atlas of African History*. London: Macmillan, 1991.

Friedland, Elaine A. "A Comparative Study of the Development of Revolutionary Nationalist Movements in Southern Africa—FRELIMO (Mozambique) and the African National Congress of South Africa." PhD diss., The City University of New York, 1980.

Gifford, Paul. *The New Crusaders: Christianity and the New Right in Southern Africa*. London: Pluto, 1991.

Glazer, Nathan. "Out of Africa." *The New Republic Online*. February 7, 2005. http://www.newrepublic.com/article/out-africa-0.
Goodall, Norman, ed. *The Uppsala Report 1968: Official Report of the Fourth Assembly of the World Council of Churches, Uppsala, July 4–20, 1968*. Geneva: World Council of Churches, 1968.
Grandjean, A. *La Mission Romande: Ses racines dans le sol Suisse romand. Son épanouissement dans la race thonga*. Lausanne: Georges Bridel, 1917.
Groves, C. P. *The Planting of Christianity in Africa*. Vols. 1–4. London: Lutterworth, 1948.
Hallencreutz, Carl Fredrik, and Mai Palmberg, eds. *Religion and Politics in Southern Africa*. Uppsala: Scandinavian Institute for African Studies, 1991.
Harries, Patrick. *L'entreprise missionnaire et la politique de l'identité en Suisse*. Lausanne: DM-Echange et Mission, 1999.
———. "The Roots of Ethnicity: Discourse and the Politics of Language Construction in South-East Africa." *African Affairs* 87/349 (1988) 25–52.
———. "The Theory and Practice of Race: The Swiss Mission in the Late Nineteenth and Early Twentieth Centuries." *Le Fait Missionnaire* 9 (June 2000) 41–54.
———. *Work, Culture, and Identity: Migrant Laborers in Mozambique and South Africa, c. 1860–1910*. Johannesburg: Witwatersrand University Press, 1994.
Hartford Seminary Foundation. *Missionary Statemanship in Africa: A Present-Day Demand upon the Christian Movement. Proceedings of the Study Conference May 28–31, 1953*. Hartford, CT: Hartford Seminary Foundation, 1953.
Hastings, Adrian. *African Christianity: An Essay in Interpretation*. London: G. Chapman, 1976.
———. *The Church in Africa, 1450–1950*. Oxford: Clarendon, 1992.
———. *A History of African Christianity, 1950–1975*. Cambridge: Cambridge University Press, 1979.
———. *Wiriyamu: My Lai in Mozambique*. London: Search, 1974
Helgesson, Alf. *Church, State and People in Mozambique: An Historical Study with Special Emphasis on Methodist Developments in the Inhambane Region*. Uppsala: Uppsala University Press, 1994.
Henderson, Lawrence. *A Igreja em Angola*. Translated by Margarida Martiniano Palma. Lisbon: Editorial Além-Mar, 1990.
Henriksen, Thomas H. *Revolution and Counterrevolution: Mozambique's War of Independence, 1964–1974*. Westport, CT: Greenwood, 1983.
Hjelm, Norman A. "Evanston After Fifty Years." World Council of Churches, September 14, 2004. http://www.oikoumene.org/en/press-centre/news/evanston-after-fifty-years.
Honwana, Raúl Bernardo. *Memórias*. Rio Tinto: Edições ASA, 1989.
Houtart, François. "O meu Encontro com Eduardo Mondlane." *Estudos Moçambicanos* 16 (1999) 53–59.
Houtart, François, and André Rousseau. *The Church and Revolution: From the French Revolution of 1789 to the Paris Riots of 1968; From Cuba to Southern Africa; From Vietnam to Latin America*. Translated by Violet Nevile. Maryknoll, NY: Orbis, 1971.
Hume, Cameron. *Ending Mozambique's War: The Role of Mediation and Good Offices*. Washington, DC: United States Institute of Peace, 1994.
IDOC. *Dossier Mozambique*. Rome: IDOC, 1973.
International Missionary Council. *The Church in Changing Africa: Report of the All-Africa Church Conference held at Ibadan, Nigeria, January 10-19, 1958*. International Missionary Council, 1958.

Isaacman, Allen, and Barbara Isaacman. *Mozambique: From Colonialism to Revolution, 1900–1982*. Boulder, CO: Westview, 1983.
Junod, Henri A. *The Life of a South African Tribe*. Vols. 1–2. London: MacMillan, 1927.
*The Kairos Document—Challenge to the Church : A Theological Comment on the Political Crisis in South Africa*. Braamfontein: The Kairos Theologians, 1985.
Keys, Clara. *We Pioneered in Portuguese East Africa: A Methodist Missionary's Memoirs of Planting Christian Civilization in Mozambique*. New York: Exposition, 1959.
Kitagawa, Daisuke. *L'Afrique en Devenir: Temoignage et Engagements chrétiens*. Kitwe: Conférence Pan-africaine des Églises, 1962.
Kitchen, Hellen. "Conversation with Eduardo Mondlane." *Africa Report* (November 1967) 32.
Machel, Samora. *Mozambique: Sowing the Seeds of Revolution*. Harare: Zimbabwe Publishing House, 1981.
———. *Revolução: Tranformação profunda das estruturas, transformação profunda da nossa vida*. Maputo: Edição da Imprensa Nacional, 1975.
———. *The Tasks Ahead: Selected Speeches of Samora Machel*. Edited by Afro American Information Service. New York: Afro American Information Service, 1975.
MacQueen, Norrie. *The Decolonization of Portuguese Africa: Metropolitan Revolution and the Dissolution of Empire*. London: Longman, 1997.
Magaia, A. "Religiões, Estado Colonial e Estado Popular." *Tempo* 637 (1982) 20–23.
Maluleke, Tinyiko Sam. "Mission, Ethnicity and Homeland—The Case of the EPCSA." *Missionalia* 21/3 (1993) 236–52.
———. "North-South Partnerships—The Evangelical Presbyterian Church in South Africa and the Département Missionnaire in Lausanne." *International Review of Mission* 83/328 (1994) 93–100.
———. "Some Legacies of 19th Century Mission: The Swiss Mission in South Africa." *Missionalia* 23/1 (1995) 9–29.
———. "The Valdezia Mission Station, Then and Now: A Missiological Appraisal." *Missionalia* 31/1 (2003) 156–76.
Manghezi, Nadja. *O Meu Coração está nas Mãos de um Negro: Uma História da Vida de Janet Mondlane*. Translated by Machado da Graça. Maputo: Centro de Estudos Africanos, UEM e Livraria Universitária, UEM, 1999.
Marcum, John A. *Portugal and Africa: The Politics of Indifference (A Case Study in American Foreign Policy)*. Syracuse, NY: Syracuse University Press, 1972.
Mário, M. "Destaca Papel de Igreja na Libertação do Pais." *Tempo* (June 1987) 8.
Maro, Nicholas J. "The Last Rites for Dr. Eduardo C. Mondlane." February 7, 1969. Unpublished manuscript, Archives of the World Council of Churches, Programme to Combat Racism, File 5/2, Box 4223.3.11.
Marques, A. H. de Oliveira. *Breve História de Portugal*. Lisbon: Editorial Presença, 1995.
Martin, Stephen. "Faith Negotiating Loyalties: An Exploration of South African Christianity through a Reading of the Theology of H. Richard Niebuhr." PhD diss., University of Cape Town, 1999.
Matthews, Z. K. *Freedom for My People: The Autobiography of Z. K. Matthews, Southern Africa 1901 to 1968*. Cape Town: D. Philip, 1981.
Mbiti, John. *African Religions and Philosophy*. London: Heinemann, 1969.
McKenzie, Cynthia. *The People of Mozambique and the Church*. Johannesburg: Dept. of Mission, Church of the Province of Southern Africa, 1988.
"Moçambique—Uma Igreja Profética." *Reflexão Cristã* 61 (July/September 1988).

Mondlane, Eduardo. "La lutte pour l'Indépendance au Mozambique." *Présence Africaine* 48/4 (1963) 10–26.

———. "Role Conflict, Reference Group and Race." PhD diss., Northwestern University, Chicago, 1959.

———. *The Struggle for Mozambique*. 2nd ed. London: Zed, 1983.

Mondlane, Janet. "O Sonho de Eduardo Mondlane para o Povo de Moçambique." *Estudos Moçambicanos* 16 (1999) 11–18.

Moreira, Eduardo. *Open Letter to the Bishop of Angola and the Congo*. London: World Dominion Press, 1935.

Morier-Genoud, Eric. *Of God and Caesar: The Relation between Christian Churches and the State in Post-Colonial Mozambique*. Lausanne: Le Fait Missionnaire, 1996.

Morier-Genoud, Georges, "Eglise et nationalisme." Unpublished manuscript of lecture presented at Bossey, Switzerland, December 3, 1957.

Mudenge, S. I. G. *Christian Education at the Mutapa Court: A Portuguese Strategy to Influence Events in the empire of Munhumutapa*. Harare: Zimbabwe Publishing House, 1986.

Munslow, Barry. *Mozambique: The Revolution and its Origins*. London: Longman, 1983.

Nelson, Harold D., ed. *Mozambique: A Country Study*. Washington, DC: United States Government as represented by the Secretary of the Army, 1984.

Newitt, Malyn. *A History of Mozambique*. London: C. Hurst, 1995.

Ngoenha, Severino Elias. *Por uma dimensaõ Moçambicana da Consciência Histórica*. Porto: Edições Salesianas, 1992.

Nichols, James Hastings. *Evanston: An Interpretation*. New York: Harper, 1954.

Noronha, Eduardo de. *A Rebellião dos Indígenas em Lourenço Marques*. Lisbon, 1894.

Núñez, Benjamin. *Dictionary of Portuguese African Civilization*. Vols. 1–2. London: Hans Zell, 1996.

Ottway, Marina. "Mozambique: From Symbolic Socialism to Symbolic Reform." *Journal of Modern African Studies* 26 (1988) 213–17.

Paul, J. *Mozambique: Memoirs of a Revolution*. London: Penguin, 1975.

Pélissier, René. *Africana: bibliographies sur l'Afrique luso-hispanophone 1800–1980*.

———. *História de Moçambique: formação e oposição, 1854–1918*. Lisbon: Editorial Estampa, 1994.

———. *Le Naufrage des caravelles: études sur la fin de l'Empire portugais, 1961–1975*. Montamets: Éditions Pélissier, 1980.

Penvenne, Jeanne-Marie. "A History of African Labour in Lourenço Marques: Mozambique 1877–1950." PhD diss., Boston University, 1982.

———. *Trabalhadores de Lourenço Marques (1870–1974)*. Maputo: Arquivo Histórico de Moçambique, 1993.

Regehr, Ernie. *Perceptions of Apartheid: The Churches and Political Change in South Africa*. Scottsdale, PA: Herald, 1979.

Reis, J., and A. Muiuane, eds. *Datas e Documentos da História da FRELIMO*. Maputo: Edição da Imprensa Nacional, 1975.

*Républica de Moçambique Constituicão*. 1990.

Rossouw, G. J., and Eugenio Macamo Jr. "Church-State Relationship in Mozambique." *Journal of Church and State* 35/3 (1993) 537–57.

Saayman, Willem A. *A Man with a Shadow: The Life and Times of Professor ZK Matthews*. Pretoria: Unisa, 1996.

Saul, John S., ed. *A Difficult Road: The Transition to Socialism in Mozambique*. New York: Monthly Review, 1985.

Schneidman, Witney W. *Engaging Africa: Washington and the Fall of Portugal's Colonial Empire*. Lanham, MD: University Press of America, 2004.
Schubert, Benedict. *A Guerra e as Igrejas: Angola 1961–1991*. Basel: P. Schlettwein, 2000.
Second Assembly of the World Council of Churches. *The Christian Hope and the Task of the Church: Six Ecumenical Surveys and the Report of the Assembly prepared by the Advisory Commission on the Main Theme*. New York: Harper, 1954.
Sengulane, Dinis Salomão. *Vitória sem Vencidos*. Maputo: Conselho Cristão de Moçambique, 1994.
Serapião, Luís. "The Preaching of Portuguese Colonialism and the Protest of the White Fathers." *Issue: A Quarterly Journal of Opinion* (Spring 1972) 35.
Serapião, Luis, and Mohammed El-Khawas. *Mozambique in the Twentieth Century*. Washington, DC: University Press of America, 1979.
Serra, Carlos. "Exclusão Social e Paradigma de Mondlane." *Estudos Moçambicanos* 16 (1999) 119–25.
Shore, Herbert. "Resistance and Revolution in the Life of Eduardo Mondlane." In, *The Struggle for Mozambique*, by Eduardo Mondlane, xiii–xxxi. London: Zed, 1983.
Simango, Uriah. "Mozambique My Country." *African Communist* 25 (1966) 51–57.
Sitoe, Bento. "La Mission vue par l'actuelle génération noire: le cas de l'Église presbytérienne du Mozambique". *Le Fait Missionnaire* 9 (2000) 101–8.
Smith, Edwin W. *Aggrey of Africa: A Study on Black and White*. London: SCM, 1929.
Sopa, António. "Eduardo Mondlane (1920–1969): Lista Bibliográfica." *Estudos Moçambicanos* 16 (1999) 127–67.
Stanley, Brian, ed. *Missions, Nationalism, and the End of Empire*. Grand Rapids: Eerdmans, 2003.
Stillman, Calvin W., ed. *Africa in the Modern World*. Chicago: University of Chicago Press, 1955.
Sumbane, Natala. *Le Christ au pays des mintsondzo*. Lausanne: Mission Suisse dans L'Afrique du Sud, 1948.
Sundkler, Bengt. *A History of the Church in Africa*. Cambridge: Cambridge University Press, 2000.
Taylor, J. V. *Christianity and Politics in Africa*. London: Penguin, 1957.
Thomas, M. M., and Paul Abrecht. *Official Report, World Conference on Church and Society: Christians in the Technical and Social Revolutions of our Time*. Geneva: World Council of Churches, 1967.
Tobias, Phillip V. "A Little known Chapter in the Life of Eduardo Mondlane." *Genève Afrique* 16/1 (1977) 119–24.
Vieira Pinto, D. Manuel. *A Igreja e o Tempo*. Lisbon: Ulmeiro, 1979.
Vines, Alex. *RENAMO: Terrorism in Mozambique*. London: James Curry, 1991.
Visser't Hooft, W. A, ed. *The Evanston Report: The Second Assembly of the World Council of Churches 1954*. London: SCM, 1955.
———. *Memoirs*. London: SCM, 1973.
Vonnez, Marcel-Raymond. "Souvenirs des Années 1971–1972." Unpublished manuscript addressed to Georges Morier-Genoud, October 20, 2001.
*War and Peace in Southern Africa: Namibia and Mozambique in the Frontline*. Harare: EDICESA, 1989.
Zita, A. "West Not More Christian." *New Nation* 12 (1989).

# Archives Consulted

When I have cited material from archives in the text, including published material, I have provided descriptive information concerning each item and the location of each item in the collection. Most of this research was carried out in 2003.

Basler Afrika Bibliographien, Basel, Switzerland

The primary focus of the archival collection is Namibia but there is some material available on Mozambique and other countries in southern Africa.

Centro de Documentação de CIDAC, Lisbon, Portugal.

This collection contains material related to lusophone Africa, particularly concerning issues of development. There is considerable material concerning organizations related to the liberation struggles, including the churches.

Département Missionnaire des Eglises protestantes de la Suisse Romande, Lausanne, Switzerland.

There is extensive material in this collection concerning the Swiss Mission in both South Africa and Mozambique and the churches which succeeded the mission in both countries. I primarily consulted material related to Eduardo Mondlane from the index cards.

Instituto dos Arquivos Nacionais/Torre do Tombo, Arquivo da PIDE/DGS, Lisbon, Portugal.

These are the archives of the Portuguese Ministry of Culture and include the arquives of the former Polícia Internacional e de Defesa do Estado and the Direcão Geral de Segurança. I consulted files related to Eduardo Mondlane, Janet Johnson, Operação Vendavel, Zedequias Manganhela, Ralph Dodge, and the World Council of Churches. As noted in the text, most of the records of the PIDE/DGS in Mozambique were destroyed at the time of the transitional government and independence.

World Council of Churches, Geneva, Switzerland.

From the extensive collection of the WCC, I consulted material related to Mozambique from the files of the General Secretariat, the Programme to Combat Racism and the Commission on Inter-Church Aid, Refugee and World Service.

www.ingramcontent.com/pod-product-compliance
Lightning Source LLC
Chambersburg PA
CBHW051641230426
43669CB00013B/2394